D0906146

HIGH TREASON

High Treason

by

Vladimir Sakharov
and
Umberto Tosi

G. P. Putnam's Sons
New York

Library of Congress Cataloging in Publication Data

Sakharov, Vladimir.
  High treason.

  1. Russia (1923- U.S.S.R.) Komitet
gosudarstvennoĭ bezopasnosti. 2. United States.
Central Intelligence Agency. 3. Sakharov, Vladimir.
4. Intelligence officers—Biography. 5. Elite
(Social sciences)—Russia. I. Tosi, Umberto, joint
author. II. Title.
HV8225.S24 1980   327'.12'0924 [B]   79-21227
ISBN 0-399-12451-9

PRINTED IN THE UNITED STATES OF AMERICA

To Marlene and Michael
with love

The three aims of the tyrant are, one, the humiliation of his subjects; he knows that a mean-spirited man will not conspire against anybody; two, the creation of mistrust among them; for a tyrant is not overthrown until men begin to have confidence in one another—and this is the reason why tyrants are at war with the good; they are under the idea that their power is endangered by them, not only because they will not be ruled despotically, but also because they are too loyal to one another and to other men, and do not inform against one another or against other men—three, the tyrant desires that all his subjects shall be incapable of action, for no one attempts what is impossible, and they will not attempt to overthrow a tyranny if they are powerless.

Aristotle, Politics, Book V, Chapter 11

PART ONE

Back in the U.S.S.R.

1: Survivors

The secret police came for my grandfather in 1936, but he wasn't home. When they came for me in 1971, I wasn't home either, but circumstances were much different then. For one thing, the police state apparatus had become more sophisticated in those thirty-five years. For another thing, my grandfather, like the legions of other less fortunate souls who were arrested, executed, or deported to camps for political crimes, had done nothing against the state. He was in fact an old soldier of the Revolution who had always done his duty. I, on the other hand, had given them good reason to try to arrest me—I had committed high treason.

My grandfather was a Bolshevik who took part in the October Revolution. Before becoming a commissar he had been a member of the much-feared Cheka from 1918 to 1921 when Lenin was consolidating power. His squadron fought against counter-revolutionary forces in the Ukraine and southern Russia. Cheka was the "All-Russian Extraordinary Commission for Combating Counter-revolution and Sabotage." Some of Cheka's units, such as my grandfather's, were involved in conventional war operations. But many others had the mission of carrying out Lenin's sweeping order on Red terror through widespread executions and lightning attacks that succeeded in terrorizing the populace and establishing the Communist Party as the supreme power in the Soviet Union. The Cheka evolved into the secret police under various names—NKVD, MVD, MGB, and today's KGB (Committee for State Security). The Chekists were heroes of the Revolution. Their informants are now everywhere, in apartment buildings, in offices; detested perhaps, but considered a legitimate part of the scene, in the same way that a deer in the forest may fear and avoid the wolf but accept him as part of the environment.

I never heard my grandfather express any bitterness, if he felt it, about the incident in 1936. At the time, he was lucky enough to be away in the Ural Mountains on army business. Stalin had ordered another purge and old Bolsheviks were a special target. My grandmother Maria, who was at home awaiting her husband's return, became apprehensive when she heard that two of Alexei's best friends had been picked up by the secret police. The wife of one of these friends visited her the next night. Grieving and fearful, she told Maria about the arrest of her spouse and warned her that she'd learned that Alexei would be next. It was a courageous thing for the woman to do because she herself could have been seized for giving such a warning. Maria immediately packed a few belongings and caught the next train for the Urals to intercept her husband. He knew there was a purge taking place, but was astonished that Stalin was about to put away one of his staunchest supporters. They decided to lie low. Instead of going back to Moscow, my grandfather invented for himself an official inspection tour of army recruitment stations in Ural villages that allowed them to stay away for three months. By that time, the purge was over and they were able to return home safely.

This may sound bizarre today, but back then the secret police were sloppy about their records, especially during the purges. They were interested only in numbers. When an order came down, they would round up enough people to satisfy their superiors and that would be it. The main object was to keep the population cowed; so if they missed one arrest, they would simply grab someone else.

My grandfather was a survivor. So were most of my family, on both sides. They were first and foremost Great Russians, and the ability to live with oppression, even turn it to advantage, was in their blood. Being a Russian didn't necessarily make one a dedicated

Soviet Communist. Though Russians do predominate in politics and fill many of the higher positions in the party, they are at the same time dominated by that apparatus, whose top leaders have not been Russians—Josef Stalin was a Georgian, and Nikita Khrushchev and Leonid Brezhnev, Ukrainians. And although we were prosperous, most Russians, outside of the small minority of officials in Moscow to which we belonged, lived and still live at a subsistence level, particularly those outside the Moscow area, in the underdeveloped northern part of Russia. These Russians indeed see themselves as being worse off than other national minorities in the Soviet Union. My family was strongly nationalistic about its Russian heritage to the point of being chauvinistic in many regards. Their attitude toward the plight of other Soviet ethnic groups—Kazakhs, Armenians, Jews, Georgians, Azerbaidzhanians, Latvians, Ukrainians—or about Eastern Europeans, was that these people had it even better than most Russians, so what were they complaining about.

As Russians we were an endangered species, my family would say; and indeed, the higher birth rate of most other Soviet nationalities has produced a trend which will soon put Russians in the minority in the Soviet Union. Yet as Russians we were indomitable, not only against outside invaders, but in the face of the repression of our own system from within.

The key to this survival is the family. In the Soviet Union it is the richness of one's personal relationships—the closeness of family, the quality of marriage, the love for one's children, the enjoyment of friends—that makes the rest tolerable.

The Sakharovs were a particularly successful family. This was true both in the closeness of their ties and in the attainment of influence and material wealth in the exclusive ranks of the inner governmental bureaucracy. We were members of what Milovan Djilas, the Yugoslav Communist political thinker and social critic, called the New Class, which in effect is the Soviet Union's aristocracy.

On my father's side, this privileged status had predated the Revolution for generations. My paternal grandfather, Peter Sakharov, was a very wealthy sugar and silk manufacturer, who survived the Revolution in chameleon-like fashion by turning over his large factories voluntarily to the Bolsheviks and helping the new government manage those plants thereafter. He was thus able to assure the continued ascendancy of his family. The party was glad for

13

his help and he was rewarded with a large house outside Moscow and a comfortable living. However, he was no longer a millionaire. He was no zealous Communist, but he was a Russian patriot. When the Nazis invaded in World War II, he volunteered for military service even though his advanced age would have kept him from being conscripted. He was made an officer and was killed in action in 1941. This, too, added to the prestige of the family.

My father, Nikolai Sakharov, was luckier, having been assigned as deputy "director of control" of a manufacturing plant in Bisk, Siberia during the war. This was during the period when Soviet industry was moved east *en masse* to escape the invading German army. He moved up from that assignment to a position with the Ministry of Foreign Affairs (MFA).

In 1946, a year after I was born, my father was assigned to a diplomatic post in Rome. It was a welcome opportunity to escape the terrible shortages of food and housing in postwar Moscow. He was allowed to bring my mother and me, which made the assignment even more attractive. He worked as a diplomatic liaison on security matters for the Soviet Embassy. This involved arranging for security and administration services for embassy relations with Allied forces.

We stayed in Italy three years, living in the embassy compound in Rome. My parents hired an Italian maid and I spent most of my time with her; so much, in fact, that I learned to speak Italian instead of Russian as my first language. By the time we returned to Moscow, I was an Italian-speaking four-year-old who had to be taught Russian.

We returned when my father's diplomatic tour was over, and moved into an apartment in Moscow—two blocks away from the old Ministry of Foreign Affairs Building and the headquarters of the KGB—on Stretensky Boulevard. The apartment was on the third floor of a handsome, Italian-style building erected in 1902. Before the revolution it belonged to the Rossiya Insurance Agency, which also owned the building that houses KGB headquarters. Our apartment was on the third floor overlooking a tree-shaded square that was a favorite place for Moscow lovers to rendezvous in comparative privacy. We lived there from 1949 until 1963, when we moved to a larger flat, a cooperative on Tchaikovsky Street near the United States Embassy. Although our Stretensky Boulevard apartment had only two rooms, it was spacious considering the acute housing shortage, and was luxuriously decorated with modern Finnish and

Polish furniture. My mother hired a maid, having been used to this in Italy. Few Russian families had domestic servants, even in our circles, but it was not unheard of to have someone living in to help with the children, especially for two busy parents like my own. The maid and I slept on folding beds in the living room. She was a kindly old lady who would tell me Russian folk tales that I had never heard or read anywhere else, and she introduced me to many of the old values of Russian culture through her stories.

The size of the apartment did not prevent my parents from having many parties to which family and friends were invited, about once a week. In addition there were special dinners for holidays, or when my father would return from a long trip. My parents seemed intent on enjoying gracious living and good company to the utmost. My mother and father were a perfect example of the successful, chic, attractive couple whose cosmopolitan lifestyle and fashionable tastes would have fit in just as well in Paris, London, or New York. They were well liked by a wide circle of influential friends and associates. They dressed fashionably in contrast to the dowdy attire of most Moscovites. My mother was blonde and strikingly attractive. She was literate, well educated, and seemed always in command of her situation. She was also very practical and, above all, energetic. She loved to travel, and went to resorts often. She ran the household, while my father seemed to be more like an honored guest. She had her own career, working as an X-ray technician and a cosmetologist, but never gave up her household responsibilities. Consequently, she always was on the go and she influenced me to be the same, prodding me never to waste time. "Why are you sitting around?" she would nag me if she caught me in an idle moment. "Why don't you read something, or go play soccer, or skate?" The generosity with which she welcomed anyone who'd come to our apartment—very often guests showed up unannounced—always astounded me. Food and drink would immediately appear on the table and the visitor would be made to feel as if he'd walked in on a surprise party in his honor. My father was fun-loving and down-to-earth, less of a social climber than my mother. He loved the camaraderie of what he called "real people"—unpretentious and spontaneous. He bore a striking resemblance to Johnny Carson and even exhibited gestures similar to those of the comedian. This caused me to do a double-take the first time I saw *The Tonight Show*. We owed our lavish standard of living to

15

my father's special position in the Ministry of Foreign Affairs and, more importantly, his relationship with the KGB. Such privilege and influence don't come by good fortune, nor by dint of hard work or talent alone. One had to play ball with the secret police to get anywhere.

I was sheltered from the particulars of KGB intrigue as a child, and told by my parents to learn, be diligent, exercise, and be of good character. By the time I was nineteen, being groomed for a diplomatic career and wooed by the KGB myself, my father finally let me in on more of the details of his own involvement. One evening, after a couple of drinks, my father, advising me on my career, confessed to me, "Volodya, I could come home tomorrow wearing a KGB colonel's uniform, because that's my rank. You know that we have been better off than the rest."

"I've thought about it," I said. "For some reason my schoolmates have always treated me as if I were the son of a KGB bigshot."

"You're right about that," he said. "I've worked in the KGB since 1941. That job in Bisk was . . . I was director of control, not only of production control, but people control. You know, wartime. They needed someone qualified there, too, you know. Not everyone went to the front. Plus, Uncle Naboychenko was serving in England in intelligence at the time. So he recommended me." The uncle to whom he referred, Vladimir Naboychenko, was brother-in-law to my father's mother. During the war he served as one of the KGB deputy residents in London, alongside Sergei Kudryavtsev, an old Soviet master of espionage.

"In any event," father continued, "I stayed out of the draft. I listened very carefully. Then, in 1945 Uncle Vladimir came back and suggested that I be transferred to the MFA and be sent to Italy. Then you were born; conditions were terrible after the war, so Italy sounded appealing. The only opening they had was for diplomatic communication officer in the Soviet Embassy in Rome, so we went there. NKVD, as the KGB was called at the time, let me go there provided I retain my affiliation with them. So I did ever since, while I've been promoted through the KGB ranks also." I wasn't shocked by the revelation. I had already surmised my father's KGB connection for some time. Nor was I disapproving. Being a KGB man had a certain glamour attached to it for many in my generation at the time.

My father's MFA job made the KGB connection unavoidable in

16

any case, given the way Soviet international operations are run. He was a diplomatic courier of the highest rank, what was nicknamed a "dip." There were only 120 of these couriers working for the MFA at the time and he was one of the most trusted and well-connected. As such he traveled nine months out of the year delivering documents, coded messages, and other top secret items from Moscow to Soviet embassies and consulates around the world.

The KGB naturally availed itself of the immunity of his diplomatic pouch from time to time; although he was tight-lipped about this, I did manage to learn about a few missions. Once, for example, he used the pouch to smuggle an electronic surveillance device, powered by a radioactive cell, into Canada. Another time he was caught in some political upheaval in Turkey while carrying highly sensitive directives from the KGB to its agents. He barely escaped detection by triggering a self-destruct device that was packaged with those directives for just such an emergency. His identification card had a red line crossing it, a symbol of high security clearance and a license to go anywhere; he could go through customs without checks and board planes *gratis;* he could enter movie theaters without tickets, go into the Kremlin, shop in special KGB stores in Moscow which offered imported goods unavailable to the average Russian. When he was home, he worked in the Ministry of Foreign Affairs Building, just down the street from the KGB Building. Because of the proximity of the two building, MFA diplomats would refer to KGB men as "neighbors." I would see very earnest "neighbors," some in uniform, going through the brass-rimmed doors into a dark hall of the massive gray edifice, symbol of the might of the Soviet security apparatus and site of the underground Lubyanka Prison, where many have been taken, never to be seen again. These "neighbors" always had a haughty demeanor, exuding a chilly contempt for passers-by.

When the new MFA Building was erected on Smolenskaya Square in 1956, my father was transferred there. The structure was designed in the typically grandiose style of the Stalin era. It looks rather like a Mormon temple, with a large twenty-eight–story tower in the middle, dominating two elaborately structured wings. The entranceway for limousines is framed by huge bronze doors which lead in to a marble hall. Only employees and those specifically authorized on a checklist as guests are allowed to pass by uniformed guards at the entrance. As one passes the guards he can immediately go to the left and diagonally across the hall toward the entrance into the Ministry of Foreign Trade, which also has a separate entrance on a side. But in order to get into the central tower—the MFA tower—one must pass another security check by going through the guarded barrier which separates the hall from the tower elevators. The whole structure projects the image of stability and power. Made of white stone, brass, marble, and gypsum, with carpets and parquet floors, it oppresses an individual or builds him up, depending on how he's treated by his colleagues.

My father's office was on the twenty-second floor of the tower, where only those with top security clearance were allowed. This area is so restricted that the floor is not marked on the elevator. One has to go to the twenty-third floor and take stairs to the twenty-second, whereupon another security check is conducted. My father's office didn't look like a working office, because actually no work was done there. Since sixty percent of the MFA personnel work for the KGB, their home office duties are often done in the KGB building. This is where my father would go to make his report after each trip. The remainder of his working hours while in Moscow would be spent studying languages, reading books—mostly Western literature— exercising at the nearby Dynamo stadium (which is sponsored by the KGB) and going to the shooting range for target practice with his Makarov pistol, which every "dip" must carry on his trips.

My father led the life of a well-groomed playboy. His job was lucrative and carried with it much more prestige than that of an ordinary diplomat or KGB *sotrudnik*. (*Sotrudnik* is a word meaning an employee, but it also has a peculiar connotation: "Someone who works for the state and enjoys the privileges and trust of the party.") Yet, for all its advantages, it was free of the liabilities of other high-ranking bureaucratic positions. He had no responsibility for political decisions, productions, or directives, no bureaus to operate, no teams to lead. He did not have to worry about conniving, ambitious underlings, nor capricious, sadistic bosses. He was simply a trusted messenger. As such he was able to rub elbows with the mighty without suffering their paranoia.

There were some unnerving moments, nevertheless. One night in 1952, two hours after he had arrived home from London, my father suddenly was called back to the MFA where the chief of his department awaited him. It was shortly after midnight and my father had to chew on some raw tea leaves to eliminate the alcohol on his breath—the usual consequence of a welcoming party that had been in progress back at the apartment.

The department chief took my father and his partner (they always go in pairs) in his limousine to the Kremlin. A patrol met the limousine and an NKVD general escorted the *troika* to Stalin's work office. The reception area was not large, mostly wood-panelled, like a movie producer's Hollywood screening room without the screen. They waited one minute, and were invited in through a double door into Stalin's office. My father said later that he didn't dare lift his eyes and look at Stalin, because as soon as he did Stalin's eyes drilled holes where my father's eyes were supposed to be. Stalin, as always, wore a semi-military suit, and appeared much smaller and fatter than the way he was pictured on screen and on posters. Stalin looked sick and old, too. This was a year before his death.

He said, "Good day, comrades," as though he couldn't tell night from day. "We invited you here to carry out an important job." He nodded towards Molotov, four meters to his left. It was rumored that Stalin couldn't tolerate anyone standing to his right. Molotov, almost hidden in the darkness, only his glasses reflecting the light of the lamp in the middle of the table, lifted an envelope and handed it over to the department chief. Molotov could have been taken for a family doctor under different circumstances. "This is an important document which must be in Peking tomorrow, or rather, today." He looked at his watch. "I trust you selected the best people for the job and they will be taken to the plane immediately." The department chief introduced my father and his partner by name, describing them as the best and most trusted *sotrudniks* in the department. Stalin waved good day while Molotov remained silent. The whole scene took only a minute or two. The plane out of Vnukovo Airport, piloted by a military crew, flew to Peking. Mao Tse Tung had the document the same day.

My father met Molotov on several occasions later. In fact, Molotov often insisted that Comrade Sakharov be available to deliver documents whenever necessary. Since then, my father became one of the most reputable and respected "dips" in the MFA. However, after Molotov's demise, my father preferred not to even mention that special relationship, but it continued in the form of our family friendship with Lev Skryabin, Molotov's nephew. Skryabin was

Molotov's original name; "Molotov" (or "hammer" in English) was a nickname which he assumed during the 1917 Revolution.

So it was that only sixteen years after my grandfather nearly became one of Stalin's victims, my father was personally carrying out an errand for the dictator himself. Only sixteen years after that, I too would be called to serve the KGB, but only to turn and bite the hand that had been feeding us so well.

2: Stuchat *in Russian Means to Knock*

Today my grandfather would not have escaped so easily. The KGB permeates the society more than the old NKVD; it has computers and a far more sophisticated electronic communication system at its disposal. The KGB no longer needs mass arrests to keep everyone in line. It's all neatly individualized. KGB informants are plugged in at every level of society, numbering in the hundreds of thousands. There are continual, regular reports on everyone. If a person is showing signs of nonconformity or rebelliousness, it will be noted. Sometimes informants will make up things even when the person does nothing. In any event, the person can be called in to his superiors and warned. If the misbehavior continues and the miscreant is unlucky enough to be detected, it could mean the loss of a job, or a demotion, or being sent to work on the farms, or off to some godforsaken outpost in Siberia—or worse, for political "crimes" he could be deported to a labor camp, or placed in an insane asylum, or executed.

Few resent this. The system isn't imposed from outside. We grew up as part of it and were trained to take our place in it. In elementary school, children are spoon fed propaganda about the glories of the Revolution and exaggerated tales about the exploits of the Soviet heroes. This is followed in later grades by thorough indoctrination in

the official Marxist-Leninist catechism. Soviet patriotism is emphasized, with little said about the United States, other than referring to
it as enemy number one.

Every child is taught that obedience to authority is a virtue, and
that personal loyalty to anyone or anything other than the state is a
vice. From the beginning, the individual means nothing; betraying
one's schoolmates is encouraged. My first grade class in Moscow was
typical of all first grades in the Soviet Union. There were about thirty
children. The class was organized along military lines and it was
impressed upon us that we were part of the system. We were required
to wear gray cadet uniforms with brass buttons. We marched in and
out of the classroom and otherwise were expected to behave in a
disciplined fashion. We were told that we now were *Oktyabryata*
(Octoberites), or children of the Socialist Revolution of October
1917. As *Oktyabryata,* we were expected to live up to high standards in
order to be worthy of eventually becoming Young Pioneers like our
older brothers and sisters.

Like all other Soviet grammar school kids, we had a class leader,
one student selected by the instructor for exemplary behavior. In the
United States such a child would be called a teacher's pet and be
teased for it. Our class leaders, however, were backed by all of the
teachers and parents and, although the other children might grouse
behind his back, most were too respectful of authority to confront
him. The class was divided into three "links" consisting of ten
children apiece. Each link had a leader, who was elected by his group
on a rotating basis. The link leaders were under the command of the
class leader.

Every morning the link leader would go before the class and
denounce failings he or she had observed by link members. "Sasha
didn't finish his homework. Nina has dirty fingernails. Boris picked
his nose. Sakharov, again you are wearing non-uniform trousers."
Everyone had a chance at being a snitch. It put each of us into a
bind. The children didn't like snitching on the whole, although some
took a perverse pleasure in it. At the same time, the teacher and the
class leader expected the link leaders to be critical. One learned to
play the game. I hated my turn as link leader. I avoided what I felt
was tattling and therefore didn't do a very good job. To get by, I had
to fake it with halfhearted, made-up criticisms.

During my elementary school years I always took pride in myself as being special. I took pains to add some extra touch to my drab uniform. I'd wear my British-made shoes, or Italian socks, or Danish shirt. There was no end to the supply of fine clothes my father kept bringing back for me. Once in a while, I'd come to school in one of my foreign-made suits, or pants and Italian sweater, telling the teacher that my uniform was being cleaned. I knew that I was one in a million Soviet children who had spent any time abroad, who had imported luxuries, whose father traveled, whose family ranked among the privileged. The other children admired and envied what was to them resplendent attire.

Occasionally this envy was manifested in hostile acts. Once, for example, I went to a birthday party for one of my fellow first graders. I wore a British-tailored suit my father had bought me. The kids laughed at me and one of them threw a jar of ink on me. We fought. So much for the suit.

I became a tough kid, and was frequently in fights. I didn't worry much about being accepted by my peers. Vsevolod Bobrov, who was captain of the Soviet Army hockey team, was one of my early heroes. He was a frequent visitor in our home. He and my father would talk, drink vodka, and listen to records by the hour. They loved "Vaya con Dios" by Peter, Paul and Mary; on the other side was "Johnny You're the Boy for Me." He never seemed to hear enough of this record. He talked to me often about hockey and, to emulate him, I took up the game. My father encouraged me by returning from one of his trips with a pair of professional-quality CCM Canadian hockey skates for me. At the time, any kind of skates were unobtainable at any price. I joined a junior hockey club, but when I showed up with my new skates, everyone ridiculed me. I got used to such things. I always had Canadian-, Swedish-, or French-made skates. Once when I was twelve, one kid deliberately stepped on my skates with his own in order to cut the shoetops. I quit the hockey club because of the hard time the kids were giving me and formed my own team of kids who lived in the neighborhood. We put water on the playground between our buildings and let it freeze to make our own ice rink. We practiced hard and eventually won a regional city championship.

This type of freewheeling individuality, however, was the exception during my growing up. Most of my existence as a child was too circumscribed to allow for such blatant displays of independence. My rebellion usually had to take more subtle forms. By the time I was ten

23

years old I found I could avoid being suffocated by the conformity of the system only by disobeying in my own quiet way and taking care not to be caught. When I occasionally would get caught, I didn't feel remorse; I simply learned to be more careful.

When we reached the third grade, we graduated as *Oktyabryata* and automatically were inaugurated into the Young Pioneers. The teacher made a speech about our new responsibilities to carry forth the banner of the Revolution and we were given red ties which we were told to wear with honor at all times.

I felt silly wearing the tie and took it off whenever I wasn't in class. A girl in the class told the teacher about this and I was called on the carpet. "What kind of a Pioneer are you?" the teacher berated me. "If I hear of you not wearing your tie once more, we are going to discuss your unworthy behavior in front of the whole class." Rather than scaring me into wearing the tie, however, the result of this lecture was that I resolved to be more careful not to let any snitches catch me again. I developed a tactic of wearing the tie while I was in and around the school, but tucking it under my shirt when I was playing outside. Whenever I came near the school or saw someone who might be a snitch, I could easily flip my tie out like a good boy. This all would have meant little more than petty disobedience, except that such experiences enabled me to discover, practice, and perfect strategies for coping with the system on my own terms, strategies I came to use in situations later where much more than a red tie was at stake.

Other children at the same time were establishing lifelong habits, too, especially the class leaders and other snitches. They were in training to become informants, to grow up to be the *stukachi. Stuchat* in Russian means to knock. It also means to inform on someone with malicious intent; in colloquial terms, to snitch. A *stukach* is a person who snitches regularly—voluntarily or in the line of duty—a person who makes a career out of informing. It is the underground pejorative term for an informer.

There were two ways of earning advancement throughout the schooling process. One way was to work hard, earn good grades and volunteer to perform helpful activities. This was the way I consistently took; not that I was self-righteous, I just naturally fell into this kind of pattern. One of the things I would do all the time, for example, was volunteer to tutor other children. This was a regular opportunity, since the schools relied heavily upon the peer tutoring system.

The second way to get ahead was to be a snitch. I remember one boy in particular who already was a career snitch in the second grade. His name was Valery and he had a group of followers. I had my own group of friends and we became rivals. On several occasions he snitched on me, making up stories, and I only managed to stay out of trouble because of my extra credits for good work. One day I caught him outside the school and we had a big fight. The next day, the teacher called both of us in front of the class and demanded we shake hands and be friends for the sake of maintaining a "healthy socialist school *kollektif* (student body)." I was the first to extend my hand to the sonofabitch, keeping in mind I was going to get him sooner or later. After school the teacher asked me to stay. "Why do you bother with him?" she said, "he is from a poor, uncultured family. Shame on you." "But he lies about me," I answered. "I know," the teacher said, "he won't be the last." "But why?" I asked. She smiled sadly. Later in life, Valery's image would come to mind, when I would encounter *stukachi* in more serious situations.

School snitches grow into professional informers who supply grist for the KGB dossiers. They are people with whom you work, go to school—your neighbors. They are easy to spot. The incompetent who keeps getting promotions, for example, or the too ambitious assistant, or the minor official everyone seems to fear and who seems able to get away with anything, drinks a lot, has fine clothes, owns a nice car. The one who weathers a purge unscathed. The KGB needs them, for it could not exercise the control it does without them—and they need the KGB. It is a self-perpetuating system that rewards and encourages parasites. It gives power to those with the least integrity, at the expense of those who do the real work.

Through his reports, the *stukach* has the power to influence the KGB to cut off someone's freedom or mobility, or he can secure employment, promotion, or other rewards for himself. He can ruin a life quickly with a series of well-placed reports. The *stukach* has a quota, like a cop giving traffic tickets. His duty is to watch people and report on them to the local KGB staffers. If he doesn't come up with enough reports, it means he isn't working hard enough. The staffers too must show results to their superiors in order to justify their jobs.

A *stukach* must take advantage of what he finds. Thus if he hears a

young engineer or factory worker or clerk suggest how production could be increased or conditions improved by changing some procedures, the *stukach* would be inclined to interpret this suggestion as "criticism" of the boss. Now a dossier can be built up. They look more carefully at the man's lifestyle. Perhaps he likes parties, or listens to the BBC. They will write a report saying, "although this collective is ideologically sound, there are within it vulnerable, non-Soviet elements who deserve closer attention." That means more work for the whole KGB department, and more work means more promotions, and the system keeps on rolling.

All this was far above me as a child. But I did develop an instinctive contempt for authority. I knew what a snitch was and didn't like it; nor did I much care for the teachers and their snitches. Nevertheless, I did want to be part of the group in some ways and suffered some discomfort at being different from other kids. At first I tried to convince my parents to make me less visible and buy me cheap Soviet-made clothes and toys. Their usual answer was that I was being ungrateful to voice such sentiments. After all, they had lived through an era of real deprivation during the 1930s and 1940s, and could not understand my wanting anything less than the best. "Your father is working hard for what you have and you should appreciate it," my mother would tell me. This in turn made me feel guilty for even thinking that I should reject my parents' largess. If other kids envied me and gave me trouble, I resolved, I'd fight back. I'd be proud of what I had. I would show them that I was different because I was better, and prove that I was no sissy.

Occasionally this got me into trouble. Once, for example, I was angered by something a girl sitting next to me in class said, so I pulled out one of my baby teeth that was loose and threw the tooth onto her desk. She fainted and I was suspended from school.

Still, I was happy to be in a regular school. At first I had been entered in the Moscow Conservatory for exceptional children because of my early musical talent. I had begun taking piano lessons at age five, and by six I gained entry to the school through an audition in which I had to play a Tchaikovsky piece and sing a Russian folk song. There was a lot of competition and being admitted was considered an honor. But once I started school, I found that the conservatory required that I practice the piano six to eight hours a day, plus two hours for my regular studies. My mother objected to the disproportionate time given to music, but it was my father's anti-Semitic leanings that got me out of the school after only two months.

Like many Russians of his class and generation, my father had a negative attitude toward the Jews, and for the most part toward other non-Russian ethnic groups, such as Ukrainians, Georgians, and Tartars. The cliché about some of his best friends being Jews was true. But he also was a chauvinistic Russian and, above all, a man with a shrewd sense of which way the political winds blew. The history of anti-Semitism in Russia had closed certain areas of endeavor to Jews. Officially, these barriers had been removed many years before my birth, but many areas—such as the arts and sciences—remained more open than others. The age-old prejudices, though officially denied, operated then as they do now to exclude Jews from any real political power, although it did allow for their relative prosperity. No one was more conscious of this than my father. I was first and foremost his young hope being groomed to take my place in high bureaucratic circles. It would not do for me to be too closely identified with the Jews, and the conservatory was predominantly Jewish. In fact, I was the only non-Jew in my class of twenty-five children. So my father, upon finding out the details, had me transferred to a regular school. I continued my piano lessons and practiced privately after school.

There was nothing remarkable about this in terms of the way I grew up. It was a childhood full of contradictions to which I adapted by learning that nothing was as it seemed and the way to survive was to be able to play many roles convincingly. My experiences in the aftermath of Stalin's death were characteristic of this. I was eight years old at the time. I remember people talking as if the world had ended. I cried. Everyone else cried, except my maternal grandmother. She smiled and said she was glad the bastard was finished at last. My mother said nothing. My grandmother visited with us in Moscow the day after Stalin's death to talk my mother out of going to Stalin's funeral. "You'll see. Pretty soon people'll know how many people the Georgian idiot has murdered. Don't like to talk badly about the dead, but in this case, the poor sonofabitch deserves it," she said, puffing on her Belomor as always. "I don't understand what you're talking about!" my mother almost cried. "You'll see," my grandmother replied, and she was right.

The years that followed were unstable politically, but as before, my father's position was unaffected. He had no designs on anyone's job, no ambitions other than to continue performing his tasks. By being on the fringes of power rather than in its mainstream, we garnered all its privileges without being exposed to its dangers.

It had been different for the father of a friend of mine, Lavrenti Ludvigov. His father had been a number one deputy to Lavrenti Beria—in fact, he named his son after his boss. Beria had been Stalin's last secret police chief and one of the most dreaded men in the Soviet Union. Little Lavrenti, however, grew through early childhood with little awareness of the bloody politics around him. Like myself, he enjoyed the gracious living befitting the son of a high official. To hear him tell it, the executions, arrests, deportations, and phony trials of the Stalinist period were nothing but a cleanup job of undesirable elements, finishing the job started by Lenin.

But under Khrushchev, Lavrenti's father was arrested and executed in 1954. After the father's execution, the large and luxurious Ludvigov flat was divided into smaller apartments. One of the new tenants was a man we all knew to be a KGB agent. Little was said about him, but Lavrenti knew that he and his mother were being watched, just as a KGB precaution. Lavrenti and I remained good friends up until we were about twenty. After that we saw less of each other. He had two marks against his making it in the kind of career for which I was destined. One was his Stalinist father, the other was that he was Armenian. We would be going to different schools, moving in different circles.

With Khrushchev's ascendancy in 1956, there was some hope expressed amongst the Moscovites in our circle that a new era of relative prosperity could be at hand. His promises to increase agricultural production and to shift toward making goods more available to Soviet citizens was the basis of his appeal. The brief period of political liberalization characterized by the rise of poets like Yevtushenko, Voznesensky, and Okudzhava during the late 1950s and early 1960s that was so widely touted in the West as evidence of a change in the Kremlin's ways was only so much window dressing. We knew that Khrushchev, just like Brezhnev now, was in great need of trade with the United States and other Western countries in order to supply consumer goods to the Soviet Union and thus allow the country's industrial growth to continue to be harnessed toward increasing its military might.

Khrushchev's espousal of peaceful coexistence had an added advantage for us in that more contact with the United States meant more trips there for my father, which meant more recordings, clothes, appliances, and other luxuries for all of us.

When Khrushchev was at the United Nations General Assembly in 1959, father delivered messages personally to him by diplomatic pouch from the Central Committee. One day Khrushchev invited him to stay for a while at his suite in a hotel and enjoy some vodka. They hit it off marvelously. Father loved peasants—"real people." Often he would go on fishing trips in the country and hike around unshaven, unkempt, wearing old clothes, sharing vodka and stories with the locals. He would tell my mother what a down-to-earth peasant he was at heart and she would remind him that the truth was that he came from aristocracy.

His peasant act went over better with Khrushchev. Before long the two were telling jokes, talking about fishing, and drinking more and more vodka. Khrushchev inquired solicitously about my father's family and how he liked his job. By the time my father left, Khrushchev was quite drunk, giving him bear hugs and telling him he was a great pal. This didn't mean anything more than an evening's entertainment for Khrushchev, however; it was rather like being called upon to amuse the Tsar, and my father was wise enough not to construe it to mean more.

Like most Russians, we liked Khrushchev, but thought of him as rather a clown and a boor, whose foul manners and uneducated Ukrainian manner of speech made us wince. Everyone would make fun of the way he talked on television, just as Russians now sneer at Brezhnev's crude, Ukrainian-accented Russian.

3: Pirozhki and Parker Pens

Northeast of Moscow, factories and apartment buildings of the suburbs eventually gave way to fields and finally to a thick forest of firs, birches, and aspens which flanked the highway like ghosts in the predawn gloom, all silvery in caps of freshly fallen snow. We reached the checkpoint at the entrance to the restricted zone, a wide area around some of Moscow's reservoirs which the government keeps off-limits to most citizens. My grandfather showed his permit to the guard and we were waved onward. Nikita, my grandfather's chauffeur, started our M.K. sedan again and we continued. The winter sun rose, breaking through the clouds and lighting the white and green landscape. It was a sight I had been eagerly anticipating for days.

Nikita, my grandfather and I rode through this sparkling wilderness for another hour without encountering another vehicle. We were about one hundred miles out of Moscow. Thirty miles farther down this same road was a labor camp. It had been built by German prisoners of war, but since the late 1940s it had been crowded with Soviet political prisoners and regular criminals.

Prison camps, however, were the furthest things from our minds. In fact, I did not even know of the camp's existence at the time. We

30

were on a much more pleasant errand. This was the last day of the year and we were off to get a tree, an annual ritual during my childhood. Russian families put up and decorate Christmas trees in their homes every New Year's day. The trees are left standing for ten days during the holiday celebrations, not much different from Christmas festivities elsewhere, except that they were secularized. While other kids had to be satisfied with trees their parents purchased in the marketplace, however, I was privileged to choose my own right out of the forest.

My grandfather would obtain a special permit from the local forestries department office to select and cut a tree. The night before our trip to the woods, my grandmother would prepare a basket of delicious snacks for us to take—*pirozhki,* potato pancakes, deviled eggs, beef sandwiches. I'd barely be able to sleep all night and at six the next morning, Nikita would ring the doorbell and we'd be on our way.

As we drove on through the woods, my grandfather sang old Russian songs. He had a rich voice and sang with great relish. His repertoire was seemingly limitless. Out the window I would catch sight of deer and snow rabbits. Finally we stopped beside a clearing in the woods. Nikita opened the trunk and got out the big basket of food, an axe, and a pair of long knives for chopping branches. He went to some bushes in snow above his knees and cut some firewood. Meanwhile, my grandfather set up a folding table near the car. It was a crisp five degrees below zero Celsius (about nine degrees Fahrenheit). When Nikita returned, we started a bonfire. My grandfather opened a bottle of Georgian brandy, poured the two of them some and said, "Let's drink to the health of our closest and let's remember those who are not with us." Nikita raised his glass and nodded, "Yes, Comrade Colonel, peace be with them."

Food never tasted better. After we had eaten, the three of us put on skis and made our way into the forest. It was said the best trees grow in the depth of the forest, especially the *yolka,* a fir most prized as a Christmas tree. Besides, it was more of an adventure to explore the woods. After an hour's search we found the one we wanted in a small opening. After the fir was chopped down and loaded atop the car, the snow began to fall faster and my grandfather said it was time to head home. That evening, New Year's Eve, the family put up a *yolka* in the living room and decorated it. For a young boy such times created

31

feelings of contentment, acceptance, and love that were to serve as ballast in years to come.

Like most Russians I developed a strong attachment to the land; my identity was bound up in those endless fields and forests no matter how urbane a life I would lead. The land has a special meaning for Russians; it possesses them and they possess it. The notion of private ownership is alien, but collective ownership is very much felt. A Russian can stand in the middle of a large field with a dark green forest off in the distance and say, "It's mine, my country." It doesn't belong to anyone personally.

The land also gives Russians their sense of freedom—Russians love the outdoors and those who live in the cities get out to the countryside whenever they can. From this, Russians derive at least an illusion of freedom, a feeling of open spaces. The virtual absence of private property—with a few exceptions—is viewed not as deprivation but as a boon. Since few people owned property even in Tsarist days, property rights meant only special privilege to most Russians, who now cherish what they feel is the privilege to wander through their land. Every weekend, for example, Moscovites fill the woods beyond the suburbs of Zhukovka, Peredilkino, Pirogovo, Mozhaisk, Zagorsk, or Checkovskaya. They wander off the main highways and follow dirt roads that go deep into the forests, reaching spots where perhaps a hundred years ago some local landlord traveled in a two-wheel horse cart. In summer they go to rivers, lakes, and beaches. In winter whole families take *elektrichka* trains to the woods for cross-country skiing.

The emotional attachment to the countryside, however, goes deeper. The Russian countryside overwhelms you—vast fields and lush forests in which one could wander forever. It is not so much to be seen as to be felt. Amid this imposing vastness, it is the minutiae of personal experience that finally overwhelms you. Scents of birches, aspens, pines, and grasses draw you deeper and deeper into the forest. A forest road suddenly ends in a sunlit opening that welcomes you to a dark forest lake. The silences ring in your ears until you cease to be an individual and dissolve into the scene.

These were the feelings I experienced so often while hunting mushrooms in those forests as a boy in late summer. Mushroom hunting is a national mania. More than a pastime, it is a sport requiring skill, cunning and knowledge. In middle Russia mushroom

32

hunting means good times and excitement. It is a big event when a child is taken along on his first mushroom hunt. The lore is handed down through the generations. The young learn the many types of mushrooms and how to tell the edible from the poisonous ones, so that cases of poisoning are unheard of despite the widespread popularity of gathering wild mushrooms. There are many kinds of mushrooms picked, and like other Russian children I learned which ones to hunt during each season or after what types of rain, and in what types of terrain each could be found. Each of these kinds of "forest meat" is brought home and prepared in different ways. Some are for soup, others for sauces or stews; some are made into pies or fried with potatoes; some are sautéed, others boiled, still others pickled. These pickled varieties are considered the greatest delicacy when consumed with ice-cold vodka—one sampling of this alone makes the mushroom hunt worthwhile.

The sport comes in hiking to just the right spots. One studies the terrain, reads, or listens to intelligence reports from friends and neighbors. With experience, I developed a sense of knowing just what trees, grass, and soil were most likely to be harboring prizes. Then it would take deception and cunning to protect my finds. Once mushrooms are discovered in a spot, there most likely will be more in the same place the following week. So I would hide my spot and walk right past it when I was with a group, then double back later when the group would thin out. As we spread out through the forest we would call out each other's names occasionally so that no one would get lost. Echoes would bounce off the trees and multiply through the branches and tall grass.

Afterwards we would talk about our hunt, sometimes waxing poetic—poems about mushroom hunting have indeed been written—referring to the fungi in fanciful terms, as if they were persons. "There he is hiding under that little fir tree, and the moss is so deep that only a bit of his brown hat shows. So I approach the tree, get on my knees, carefully lift a branch. And, oh, I see a whole family—the father, the mother, and three babies. So I picked them and feel around the moss some more and find three more tiny babies! So of course I cover these up, so no one would notice. I'll go back there next week."

My grandfather's commissariat of Narofominsk—a large area near Moscow—included these forests. Through it flowed the small Nara

River, a picturesque forest tributary which flowed into the Oka, one of Russia's major rivers, often mentioned in folklore. Now it is polluted, but when I was a boy my grandfather and father often took me there to fish. I still remember catching my first fish when I was four. We had walked a mile into the forest to our fishing spot; I carried the new pole my father had given me. It was a bright summer morning and the shadows of the trees vibrated in the passing waters. I got a bite almost immediately upon casting and to my amazement a fish came out of the water as I pulled on the pole. I dropped the gear and ran away. "Look, Vladimir, come back here," they said, "it's only a baby bass." I cautiously went back, not daring to touch that fish. It sparkled silver and gold in the sun. "Congratulations on your first catch. Now put it in your bucket," my grandfather said. I wanted to save it and show it to everyone, so I filled the bucket with water and brought it back with me to my mother and grandmother. At dinner, my grandfather raised a glass of Georgian wine and toasted, "Here's to our young man, the fisherman."

I spent about half my youth at the home of my mother's parents (Alexei and Maria). This was because my father was away on assignment so much of the time, and my mother, too, who loved to travel to resorts. Then my grandfather was transferred to Kaliningrad, an aerospace center twenty miles north of Moscow. The cradle of the Soviet aerospace industry, Kaliningrad enjoyed many privileges as the so-called "satellite city" of Moscow. The stores were better supplied with food and consumer goods. People on the streets looked better dressed than other suburban Muscovites. Streets seemed to be more neatly paved. My grandparents' apartment was on the third floor of a five-story white brick building that had been built by German prisoners of war in 1952 and was one of the first apartment buildings in the area. By Russian standards it was spacious, with four large rooms—a family room where I slept when I visited, a reception room, a bedroom, and a large kitchen.

My grandparents had decorated it simply but elegantly. The redwood floors were covered with Persian rugs in the family room and bedroom; the walls of the bedroom were hung with Persian rugs, too. The furniture was expensive, but of simple style and sparse because my grandfather detested clutter.

My grandfather's office in the Kaliningrad military headquarters not far away bore the same imprint as the apartment, and was airy and elegantly furnished—sixty feet by thirty feet with a large desk and a matching conference table on each side of the room. His duties were numerous and, at times, quite vague. He would meet one day with the chief engineer of the space complex to discuss civil defense matters and then, the next thing, send a patrol to dig up a young army deserter. I figured his main duty as military commissar—or *voyenkom*—was to manage and supervise whatever was going on in and around Kaliningrad on the military side. And a lot was going on there in the fifties. The space center was spreading into the nearby forests with new scientific research facilities, new rocket plant wings, new chemical and biological laboratories. The strictest security seemed to be around chemical and biological laboratories. Someone told me then that they were refining all that German know-how obtained as the result of the war.

The city itself was off limits. Patrols could stop anyone after dark and question him. But that was accepted as a necessity, an ordinary element of life. Along with stealing alcohol from the plant the engineers and scientists somehow managed to launch Sputnik, the first space satellite ever. I happened to be in Kaliningrad at the moment and saw people celebrating. They said on the occasion that drunkenness became legalized for one week. The work at the plant and the research center came to a halt for two reasons—one, there was no alcohol to wipe fine parts and machinery; another, who could hold the wild Russian character at such a moment of glory? Our neighbor, an engineer at the center, told us a joke. "You know, the Chinese just sent one up there, too. All six hundred million got together and pulled a giant rubber band and shot a portrait of Mao through a catapult. And the Americans say they might consider going up there if Wall Street collects enough profits. The French decided to stay on the ground, since the availability of women in the cosmos is very doubtful." Sputnik had further bolstered the people's belief in the superiority and unlimited might of the Soviet system.

During the summer we spent a lot of time at my grandparents' *dacha* near the Pirogovo Reservoir, a wooded area forty-three kilometers from Moscow. A *dacha* is a vacation house. It can be a humble cabin or luxurious resort home of the kind used by Central Committee members. We were among the fortunate few to own one. Most are provided by the government for vacations. The practice is so common that *dacha* is also used as a verb, meaning to go on

35

vacation. My grandfather paid 1,400 rubles in 1958 to have the *dacha* built on a lot provided for him by the Kaliningrad space center. It was in a resort compound mostly used by Soviet space scientists, engineers, and party officials, including S.N. Korolev, a top rocket scientist and considered the father of the Soviet aerospace industry. There were about fifty *dachas* in the community, surrounded by a high wood and concrete fence and guarded by watchmen at all times. Beyond the fence, the forests and the reservoirs of Pirogovo and Klyazma stretched out as far as the eye could see.

The *dacha* itself was of wood, consisting of a kitchen and two rooms that were used for many purposes, depending on the number of guests we had. The W.C. (as we called them in Moscow) was thirty yards back of the house—I built it myself. The large garden had apple and cherry trees, raspberry bushes and rows of vegetables.

These bucolic surroundings enriched an idyllic boyhood, in which my parents saw to it that I developed social graces, athletic prowess and, above all, had plenty of expensive toys. When I was thirteen, for example, I had a crush on a girl my age whose parents' *dacha* was across the reservoir from ours. She was a figure skater, bright, strong and lively, but unfortunately for me, she was going with a big albino boxer who was eighteen. Later that summer when the boxer was away, I asked my parents to buy me a speedboat and they did so. This one, my first, had an experimental Soviet-made motor, and was very fast. Later, I was to switch to American-made motors. Near the end of the summer, I took the girl for a spin on the lake. She was duly impressed and enjoyed herself enough to want to go with me again. But it was the last day of summer and time to leave the resort, so I wasn't able to follow up the romance. I lost track of her, but ran into her four years later in Moscow. She looked fat and ugly; I mentioned later to my father how homely she had become and, in his ever paternal way, he told me, "Son, I thought she was no good for you when you fell for her, but I never told you so since I wanted you to experience what falling in love with an illusion is all about. Now you know." I'm not so aware that I absorbed the lesson all that well, in light of what happened to me later. I did learn, however, that it was better to have a motorboat than not.

The richness of my boyhood went beyond material things. I grew up steeped in uniquely Russian cultural traditions that shaped my consciousness and, ironically, set up conflict with the Soviet system, especially the KGB. I thought too much of myself and knew too much of the world to accept repression. This is not to say that, on the surface at least, I did not pay allegiance to the Marxist-Leninist principles taught to me just like everyone else. But my awareness of heritage and the mentally stimulating environment in which I matured produced in me one fatal flaw as far as being a good Communist was concerned. That is, by the time I was a young man I was able to think for myself.

My grandmother Maria was most responsible for this. When I would spout some bit of party propaganda, she would tell me not to take everything at face value. "Sit, listen, and make your own conclusions, go by your heart and by what you see and not by what people tell you, not by what you hear all the time," she would say. She considered illiteracy and ignorance to be the worst evils that have afflicted the Russian people over the centuries. Illiteracy had been eradicated, but the people still are kept in ignorance by the Communist Party and its KGB that decide what they shall read, see, and hear. She saw Soviet politics, furthermore, as eroding the national identity of Great Russians. "If we cannot preserve our identity, I do not want to build communism for those damn Moldavians, Armenians, Jews, Georgians, and Ukrainians," she would say. "Fuck the Communists; fuck the party; we are Russians number one."

She was, like the rest of my family, a strong Russian nationalist, as I have explained, but this didn't make me so much a traditional Russian myself. The contradiction between what my grandmother would say and the official line led me to be a skeptic. I developed a more sophisticated outlook on the world than my elders. But underneath it all was the foundation of tradition, a strong sense of family, of being conscious that I was an individual and a Russian— and of what being a Russian really meant.

Our family adhered to many traditions that were de-emphasized or said to be eliminated by party propaganda, and these rituals contributed greatly to an extremely happy youth. These were celebrations that reaffirmed family closeness and its ties with our culture. Christmas and New Year would have been unthinkable without our *yolka,* not so much out of religiosity, but for the spirit of enjoyment and closeness the ritual engendered. We would follow traditions associated with the Russian Orthodox Church; for example, fasting before Easter, because it was considered a Russian tradition.

At Easter both sides of the family would gather at my parents' place in Moscow. We would color eggs and prepare *paskha*, special Easter cake, and a dessert of sweetened curds, butter, and raisins that takes several days to make. For Easter dinner my mother would cook *bliny*, or Russian pancakes. We would have red and black caviar, and *balyk*, a smoked filet of sturgeons, along with other delicacies. Everyone would drink a toast and my mother would walk in with a plate piled high with the pancakes. A special egg and butter mixture would be poured on top of the pancakes, then the caviar and *balyk* added. These special pancakes also were made at Christmas time.

The *bliny* were baked, not fried, by the dozen to be served in a huge plate in the middle of the table. Each of us would put one *blin* at a time on his or her plate, butter it and add some of the meat or fish, wrap it up and eat it. Red caviar wrapped in a *blin* was best. My mother was a great cook, for all of her other social and career activities. Guests took great delight in her creations. She made not only Russian dishes; having spent three years in Italy, she had mastered Italian cuisine as well. Several times a year, we'd feast on a whole stuffed suckling pig or a stuffed goose. The holiday meals were occasions for downing much good wine and vodka and singing songs. After dinner the stereo would be turned on and everyone would "boogie-woogie" or tango or cha-cha or calypso.

We also celebrated other religious holidays. July 20, the day of Elijah, usually was the occasion for a party at the *dacha*, if we were not at a Black Sea resort. We celebrated saints' days, too, with special festivities commemorating saints whose names were borne by members of the family. St. Peter's Day, for my paternal grandfather, for example, and St. Vladimir's Day for me.

My mother taught me to read when I was four and I took to it avidly, devouring literary classics that my grandfather, Alexei, continually provided me. The first books I remember were *The Three Musketeers* and *The Count of Monte Cristo*, which probably helped me develop a penchant for romanticism and derring-do that I had to keep under control later in life. I stuck pretty much to English, French, and Russian classics at first—Swift, Voltaire, Balzac, Flaubert, and of course, Tolstoy. Having read *Madame Bovary* by the time I was ten and *War and Peace* at eleven created in me a rich repository of fantasy, ideas, and impressions of the world that I could not readily share with children my own age nor, indeed, with many elders outside our literate circle of family and friends.

When I wasn't in school, or playing sports, or at a family event, I spent most of my time reading. Along with the literature, I tried to read some popular books by modern Soviet writers. Most of them were of the government-inspired variety, unfortunately, and were dull. They pictured KGB agents in their fights against foreign spies and subversives, glorifying the KGB as guardian of the peaceful lives of Soviet citizens. The KGB heroes were always brilliant, brave, and disciplined. Their opponents were always venal and stupid, ready to sell their souls for a dime. Another genre of novels depicted the brave exploits of Russian soldiers against the Germans during World War II and were permeated with hatred for the Germans. These books presented Russians as superior to the other nationalities—Poles, Czechs, French, Americans. I was ready to accept all this propaganda as true, but I found it so predictable and boring as to lay it aside for more interesting literature—*Madame Bovary*, for example, which I read over ten times, more out of prurient interest than literary inclinations, I suppose, but certainly a more illuminating experience than the official clap-trap.

We always had a high quality record player and plenty of American popular music recordings my father would buy on his frequent trips abroad. The record collection was always a hit with our guests. I grew up listening to American music. You might say I first was influenced to become a U.S. sympathizer by Vaughn Monroe, whose recording of "There, I've Said it Again" was the first American music I remember hearing, and an oft-played favorite with my parents. We had most of the U.S. artists popular at the time, with a leaning toward jazz stylists, including records by Benny Goodman, Perry Como, and Frank Sinatra. These influenced me to become a jazz musician later.

My parents had a television set. It was an RCA with a 19-inch screen which my father had brought back from the United States. This was in 1953 and what few TV sets there were in Moscow then had screens four or six inches wide. We had a technician from the KGB office come to our apartment to modify the set so that it could receive signals from the Moscow station. There was only one channel at the time and it broadcast a few hours a day, usually live hockey or soccer games, plus a couple of mostly Russian old films. One movie shown often was *Sun Valley Serenade,* with Glenn Miller and Sonja Henie. I was greatly impressed with and fully believed its sentimentalized depiction of American culture. Best of all, I liked the swing music, which I'd already heard on the recordings we had at home. The movie had been sent to the Soviet Union during World War II lend-lease and was still being shown in Russian theaters and on television through the 1960s. I wouldn't be surprised if they are still showing it.

There were few people with whom I could communicate freely. I had little in common with my schoolmates, and although I could play hockey or soccer with them, I certainly couldn't discuss French literature nor American jazz. Teachers were Pecksniffian party-line pedants, for whom I had to play a role. One of my closest friends, therefore, all through primary school, was our eighty-year-old neighbor in Moscow, the Countess Germaine Gruenfeld. She was a *grande dame* left over from the Tsarist days, who had somehow survived revolutions and wars with her sensibilities intact. The original Count of Gruenfeld had come to Russia from Western Europe in pre-Napoleonic times and, until the Revolution, the family had held a large estate just outside Moscow. Remnants of the old luxuries not taken from her by the Bolsheviks remained in her apartment. A couple of master-crafted French sofas, a Renaissance commode, a dinner table, regal-looking chairs, centuries-old knick-knacks, and some old paintings by unknown artists were all that surrounded the countess. She had a grand piano on which she played and taught me to play marvelous French and Russian romantic pieces which I had never heard before. She spoke French fluently and translated books for me. I would spend hours listening to her talk about France, the old days in Moscow, the Comédie Française, French etiquette, absorbing the romanticism of bygone days that she seemed to exude. She was crippled with arthritis and walked with the aid of an ancient cane which stood against her chair, but her wit was sharp and she seemed to bring alive the richness of the past which filled so many of the books I read at the time.

Soviet society emphasizes what is new and how the party is building the future, but Russia is an ancient land, the Russians an historic people, and the undercurrents of the past were vividly and unavoidably part of my experience. This came not only from the fine old buildings, churches, museums, and other historic landmarks, but in private life, too. My father's mother, for example, kept many religious ikons in her house. I remember being fascinated with them as a child. She kept one in every corner of every room. In school I had been taught to look at religion as an imperialist tool to suppress the working people. So, one day while visiting her house I went over to one of the ikons and began spitting on it. My grandmother came up behind me, put her hand on my head and said, "Don't do that. He sees it and it hurts Him to see you do things like that."

"Who's He?" I asked.

"Jesus."

"Who's Jesus?"

"He's our God and He takes good care of us, of you, me, your mother and father."

"But I thought He was a capitalist, like Morgan, you know," I said. "They suck people's blood."

"No, that's not true," she said. "He lives in the sky and loves us." I didn't believe that, but my belief in what they taught me in school about religion was altered. I didn't spit on ikons nor throw rocks at church windows anymore.

My paternal grandmother, whose name also was Maria, was the only religious believer of the family. She was very devout and even insisted that I be baptized. I did not share her piety, and she didn't try to force it on me, but it did influence me, nevertheless. Not long before she died of lung cancer in 1962, I visited her with my mother and father. We knew that she was terminally ill. She told me, "You cannot know everything in this world. There are things no human being can understand. You do not have to accept God, but just accept that there is something that is stronger than you, something that is much misunderstood by all your peers and by all these Communists. Therefore, I will go in peace. I know that I will not die. There is no such thing as death." She said that the laws of physics show that nothing disappears; things only change from one state to another. "So you should know that death is simply another transformation. There is no such thing as death as we try to understand it because it is beyond our experience and we cannot know it beforehand." I was only seven years old at the time, but the memory is vivid.

Aside from the standard anti-church doctrine taught in school, this

41

was my only exposure to religion, and though I never had a desire for more training nor for the religious life, the message of my grandmother stuck with me. Her words have come to mind often. I don't consider myself a particularly courageous person, but those thoughts did give me comfort. They convinced me that if I should be killed, I need not fear it. This was contrary to what was expressed to me by many dyed-in-the-wool Communists, who seemed to fear death to a great degree. Many seemed obsessed with that fear, and in fact, it permeates all of Soviet society.

My upbringing engendered in me a strong sense of family and tradition, which made me self-confident, even smug, but did not make me an idealist nor an intellectual. One characteristic that was very un-Russian also was engendered in me. This was that I was very strong-willed and hated to compromise, although the circumstances of my later life made playing many roles a matter of survival. I always had to hold down my anger in order to placate my superiors. I never accepted authority as necessary, the way most Russians do, and once I decided I wanted something, I stubbornly pursued it. Obedience wasn't in my repertoire, only the pretense of it. My parents had a strong influence on me, but even they couldn't always control me, even in a society where parents' authority is much stronger than that in the West. When I was nine, for example, my parents would not let me have a sword. I wanted to learn to fence like the Three Musketeers. I talked a neighbor, Nadya, the mother of one of my playmates, into getting us both swords, so that he and I could thrust and parry away at each other without my parents' knowledge. Nadya was a tough woman whom I admired. She was an attractive former actress and musician. She was hard-bitten but very alive. Her son Vova and I used to shoot at cats with BB guns from their apartment window. Nadya's most frequent admonition to Vova and me was, "Don't trust anybody. People will screw you up." But how was I to avoid it? She didn't say.

Even as a boy, I knew what I wanted. I would be like my father, free to travel. I would roam even further, make more money, buy luxury goods, sleep with beautiful women all over the world, become so successful that no one would interfere with my pursuit of the good life. For this, I had to become a diplomat. The thought of doing anything else never occurred to me. Even as a young boy I felt I was a citizen of the world. To be a good Communist in the best sense—or in a naïve sense—meant sharing. We were a collective society, they taught us in school. Being unselfish was held to be one of the greatest virtues of a good Soviet citizen. I was glad to oblige. My mother told me, "Don't be selfish. You have to live with people. Share what you have and leave a little for yourself." Being generous at heart, I would give away many of the toys, Parker pens, and other foreign-made things my father had provided for me. I made many instant friendships in school this way, but found they didn't last long.

My father, on the other hand, made a point of educating me to the realities of Soviet life. Once, my father had given me a model garage filled with toy American cars. I played with them for days, but little by little, I gave all the cars away to my playmates. When he found this out, my father said, "Well, how do you feel now?" (Father was fond of the Socratic method.)

"Glad, because my friends have cars," I said, "but unhappy because you bought me the cars and I gave them away."

"See now," he said, "you have a problem. You would like to please me and you would like to please your friends. Whom would you rather please?"

"You, father," I answered.

"Good," he said, "Remember your family comes first. Then come your friends. And the rest of your needs will always be taken care of by me until you grow up; and then, by yourself, when you will be working for the government."

It all seemed so simple.

PART TWO

An American in Moscow

4: All That Jazz

For Americans the most memorable event of the 1958 United States exhibit in Moscow was then Vice President Richard Nixon's "kitchen debate" with Khrushchev over the respective merits of the U.S. and Soviet ideological systems. Moscovites, on the other hand, couldn't have cared less about ideological debate. Neither were they very interested in Nixon. It was the exhibit itself that fascinated them— the clothes, appliances, cars, machinery. The crowds poured into Sokolniki Park on the outskirts of Moscow where the exhibition was held. Everyone wanted a chance to taste the exotic forbidden fruit from the trees of the rotting Western culture.

This had little allure for me, however, since I knew about all that American stuff. I was surrounded by U.S.-made goods and was familiar with American society. My father, returning from trips to New York and Washington, had told me all about it. Americans were very rich, drove big cars, lived on beautiful tree-lined streets in big houses or luxurious penthouse apartments. People played jazz, and dressed in fancy clothes; they spent a lot of time in pursuit of pleasures, going to the theater, dancing, partying, traveling, skiing, sailing.

I didn't think I'd see anything new at the exhibition. As a twelve-

47

year-old I would much rather have stayed home and played soccer with my neighborhood pals, but my mother and Aunt Tanya, a half sister of my father's, insisted upon dragging me with them. I hated my aunt on top of it. She was a modish social climber whom I knew was always around for the foreign-made goodies my father doled out to her. She was dying to feast her eyes on the exhibition, just like all the crass *Vanki* and *Vaski* (Johns and Jacks) going out there. I hated crowds and even at that age I already was status conscious enough to want to avoid anything accessible to the peasants.

We took the subway and got out at the Sokolniki exit. The exhibit was in a huge park where summer festivals usually were held. We walked up one of the lovely tree-shaded lanes to get there. In winter I used to ice skate all up and down these lanes. In later years, I made use of the hideaways among the park's many trees and bushes which offered young lovers some relative privacy in crowded Moscow.

We had to wait an hour in line and pay a small fee to get inside. We milled about looking at the various thematic exhibits which were housed in makeshift structures, one for fashions, one for scientific exhibits, one for household appliances, and so on. Moscow house-wives crowded around the appliances, letting out oohs and aahs, as if viewing gear from an alien spacecraft. Everyone wondered what American housewives must do in their spare time, since obviously they didn't have to clean and cook.

I deduced the answer to that question from the fashion exhibit. They bought clothes, of course, and walked around in them looking beautiful. "And now the latest in American fashion," said a voice out of a loudspeaker. Russian women, in their dowdy attire, crowded close to a platform for a closer look.

"Look, poor girls, how skinny they look," one of the ladies said as the first two U.S. models appeared on stage. For the first time, I became interested. The models looked quite appealing to me. In fact, I thought, if that is the way American women look, I'm ready to go there right now.

I was beginning to like this already, but that was nothing compared to my reaction to the next exhibit we saw. I was dazzled by the sight of American cars. They were like nothing else I had seen, sleek fantasy machines in reds, blues, and greens, simply dripping with chrome, accented with sweeping lines of tailfins that said power and speed. I must have spent an hour or two going over every detail of these cars until my aunt and mother finally dragged me away. I talked to one of the American guides who spoke some Russian. He was standing by an Oldsmobile and told me he had a car like it at home. He told me he was a student and I didn't believe him. It was impossible for a student to have a car like that.

I began to fantasize about driving a fancy car. I picked the Cadillac El Dorado Brougham. I could see myself driving it down Madison Avenue. Sitting beside me would be one of those beautiful models. I'd own a second car too, for driving at night—the Pontiac Bonneville with tinted glass, automatic transmission, a four-door model to accommodate my friends.

I asked the guide how he could afford his Oldsmobile. He said he got it on credit. I was puzzled. I thought credit meant good behavior, but if so, an Oldsmobile was some prize even for exemplary deportment. After the cars, another guide offered me some Pepsi Cola. It tasted like medicine to me. I concluded it made you thirsty so that you would buy more—a typical capitalist ploy. One day, though, I would have one of those El Dorados, I thought to myself. Before leaving I collected all the brochures on the cars. I kept them for years, looking at them and thinking about those shiny machines long after the rest of the exhibition had been forgotten.

America became a utopia for me during my teenage years. It was the American style and culture that enraptured me. It represented the carefree, unfettered, glamorous, privileged kind of life I wanted. Like my life at home, the American fantasy was a buttress against the claustrophobia of Soviet conformity.

The acquisition of Western finery and *savoir faire* had always been considered marks of status in Russia. Just as French acculturation was favored in Tsarist times, when I grew up my intimate knowledge of American things set me a notch above everyone in my social set. I had to keep that knowledge to myself because teachers, Communist youth officers, and the other *stukachi* only interpreted it as a sign of being subversive. For them I played the role of patriotic Communist youth. But among my friends my ability to get and share U.S.-made items—phonograph records for example—and especially my talent for playing jazz, made me someone special.

The music was even more important to my inner life. It sustained and nurtured my secret identity. At first I listened to my parents' collection of Sinatra, Nat King Cole, Vaughn Monroe, Glenn Miller and Artie Shaw. Later my tastes expanded to other jazz artists and I amassed a collection that included Dave Brubeck, Erroll Garner, Anita O'Day, Duke Ellington, Art Tatum, Frank D'rone, Miles Davis, Thelonius Monk, Sonny Rollins, Gerry Mulligan, Oscar Peterson, Dizzy Gillespie, Charlie Parker, and the Brazilians Joao Gilberto, Antonio Carlos Jobim, and Sergio Mendes.

There would have been nothing remarkable about this collection in the United States, even in Poland or Czechoslovakia today. But in the Soviet Union during the sixties, having these records made me something of a celebrity. As a teenager I always took recordings to parties—and usually I'd supply imported Scotch or bourbon or rye as well. Most of my friends really didn't understand American music. (Those who did know jazz, however, knew it thoroughly, having practically memorized numerous contraband Western books on the history of jazz.) The rest simply enjoyed the rhythm and feeling of the music.

I heard the classics constantly as well. My parents played recordings and we often went to the ballet, opera, and concerts. I was inundated with Bach, Beethoven, Brahms, Verdi, Tchaikovsky, and Shostakovich. I like the music now but resented it then because I heard it so often and because it was approved by the government. And it was hard to avoid the patriotic songs about Stalin's rye pickers, Khrushchev's steelworkers, and Lenin's revolutionaries which blared incessantly from loudspeakers and radios.

American music was a very important part of my life. Often when I recall a specific event from my youth, I still associate it with a recording I was listening to at the time. The songs talked about love, blues, jealousy, desire, feeling. They had real meaning for me as opposed to Communist party popular music that instructed you on the virtues of building a dairy factory, or increasing cattle productivity.

After my brief stint at the Moscow Conservatory, I took piano lessons at home. One of the best teachers from the conservatory came to our apartment three times a week for two hours. My musical schooling was exclusively classical, but when the teacher left I would play jazz, having picked it up by ear. By the time I was a teenager, I could mimic many of the jazz keyboard artists like Erroll Garner.

Although jazz was considered anti-Soviet and subversive, my parents didn't mind it as long as I didn't neglect my other studies.

50

The music was entertaining and chic, and not dangerous so long as we didn't flaunt our tastes.

Moscow officialdom had a schizophrenic policy toward Western music that was arbitrary and irrational. Jazz, for instance, had been banned since 1936, when Stalin decided it was a tool for capitalist exploitation. By the sixties, however, rock and roll was allowed. The party favored the European artists, and under this aegis the Beatles were approved because they were working-class British youth. But this tolerance toward rock didn't last very long. As soon as Khrushchev was removed, the party tightened its ideological screws, but the influence of rock remained and Soviet music was brightened up. It meant that instead of singing a polka about daring geologists in Siberia, they were allowed to sing about daring geologists in a modified rock style.

Meanwhile the censorship of jazz remained. The fact that jazz could also be classified as having a working class derivation was an inconsistency that didn't bother the party. The disfavor with which jazz was regarded heightened its appeal for me. The popularity of rock, on the other hand, immediately lessened its charm in my eyes.

My vision of America was pure fantasy. I pictured men who looked like Clark Gable and John Wayne, and women who looked like Marilyn Monroe and Ava Gardner, who all lived lives of romantic adventure. In my mind America bustled with night life and glittered with skyscrapers. In the countryside I envisioned snowcapped mountains and crystal lakes, and people racing down open highways in their magnificent cars. I knew that there was a more sober side of American life, but I discounted its importance.

Many of the images were from the American movies I saw with my father at special screenings at the Ministry of Foreign Affairs. Even the gangsters seemed glamorous. *The Joker Is Wild,* in which Frank Sinatra portrayed a singer victimized by mobsters, was a favorite that I saw several times. "All the Way," which Sinatra sang in the film, fully expressed my adolescent desire to live life to the limit.

I yearned for a life of adventure and I knew the only way I could realize that life was to have a career that would provide it. There was never any question about my working for the MFA, and by the time I was fourteen my future was absolutely set in that direction. Besides, as a member of the New Elite, it was expected that I would follow in my father's footsteps. I had to start early, however, and fourteen was none too soon. Unlike my father who got into the diplomatic corps via wartime KGB duty, I would have to follow the conventional route. In the 1960s that meant going to the MFA's special school, the Institute of International Relations. There I would take six years of intensive university training in diplomacy, languages, law, economics, journalism, and military science.

The Moscow State Institute of International Relations of the Ministry of Foreign Affairs was established in the early fifties and is the most prestigious institution of higher learning in the Soviet Union. Only sixty students are accepted each year and there are forty applicants for each spot. IIR consists of three faculties: International Relations, International Economic Relations, and the faculty of International Journalism, which was added in 1965 when the ideological work against capitalism got new priority on the party's list.

The Institute building is located at the bridge where Sadovoye Koltso jumps the Moskva River. It is a four-story brick structure built at the turn of the century. With its marble hallways, parquet floor corridors, and pillared main conference hall, the building is supposed to project stability and confidence to those who rule and learn there.

The Institute trains personnel for all government offices involved with foreign affairs, with most students ending up in the MFA, KGB, or GRU (military intelligence). There are several students from socialist countries, including Cuba. Almost all of them are destined to work in their countries' intelligence organizations.

The entrance requirements were stiff and I would have to follow an arduous program during four years of high school if I had any hope of entry, even with my high-ranking family connections. I got the inside track on this through Ivan Pavlovich Baikov, who was the director of personnel *(Nachalnik Otdela Kadrov)* of the IIR. Baikov had been an MFA "dip" for five years and was a friend of my father. Like my father he was a KGB colonel as well. Baikov was a soft-spoken man in his late fifties. Always immaculately dressed in English suits and Oxford shoes, he rather looked like a British gentleman. But underneath those manners one could detect the iron will and penetrating vigilance of an old Chekist. I learned later how many professors, KGB and GRU instructors at the Institute, respectfully feared him.

52

Baikov explained what I should do. Beyond having the right connections, I had to have a superior academic record, graduating with at least what in the U.S. would be an A-minus average in all required subjects—politics, history, geography, languages, literature, science. In addition, I had to have a good sports record and have taken part in competition. Naturally, I had to be a model Communist youth, with officially approved tastes, conduct, and interests. For the entrance interviews, Baikov told me, I had to develop poise, and quickness of mind, and be ready with the right answers for any situation. Finally, I had to prove I was a real Communist worker. This could be accomplished either by volunteering to do work for the Komsomol (Communist Youth Organization) or by holding a job for two years. I loathed the Komsomol, which typically was a stepping stone for *stukachi* to work their way up from the lower classes and become Gestapo-style party bosses, so I opted for the job.

Father once again used his influence. He talked to another friend who was director at a high school. For a Parker pen and one of those ties with a naked woman on the inside I landed a job there as a chemistry and physics lab technician. The job was on the other side of Moscow, but I thought I could put up with two hours' commuting for a couple of years for the sake of my bright diplomatic future. I was fifteen then and not exactly up to professional standards in my knowledge of the sciences. That problem was alleviated, however, by my mother's giving two teachers a cheap coat from Korvette's and a dress from Italy. Then they stopped complaining about my leaving too early and started doing some of my work while I studied, continued my private lessons, went out for sports, dated, and enjoyed life in general.

I had to establish a work record early because if I waited until after high school I would be drafted. Conscription was mandatory at age nineteen unless you were admitted to a university. The job was not too difficult, but because of the hours I would have to go to a night school. This last adjustment exposed me to an entirely new group of people.

Night School No. 139 for Working Youth, on Prospect Mira, was crowded with adults, most of them over thirty, who were compelled to be there by a change in government educational requirements. The law said everyone must complete ten years of school, instead of eight, so now all those rough and tough factory workers, government clerks, war veterans, dropouts, ex-convicts, and prostitutes were taking history, geometry, literature, and so on. There were twenty of us in each class. As per Russian custom there were two pupils seated at each large double desk. By coincidence I found someone from my social class to share my desk. She happened to be a bored forty-five–year-old wife of the KGB resident in England.

My new schoolmates smoked and drank heavily and were always discussing their sexual adventures. Independent and almost bitter about the Soviet system, they felt trapped and didn't have any reservations about voicing their gripes. They didn't have much to lose anyway.

Discipline—aside from grading—was loose and not a problem in any event. As with any adult night school, the students were on their own. There was no Communist Youth Organization to keep track of everyone. In order to have membership on my record, I had to join the Komsomol cell where I worked. But I escaped having to be very active in it, thanks to my being in the night school and to the rest of my busy schedule.

I couldn't imagine myself attending a regular high school with all those naïve Komsomol punks. But soon I had to learn a lesson. I got enough courage to invite a beautiful young girl out for a date. She had the worst grades in the class and was indeed rather dumb. But I couldn't stand just sitting behind her every night watching her sexy back and those wonderful legs, so I invited her to a movie. The movie was about some hydroelectric workers who were building a power station in Siberia. She was very interested in the movie, and every time I would try to take her hand in mine, she'd brush it off. On our way home she kept on talking about all those tennis players whom she knew, without paying much attention to me. But to top it all, after she shut the door right under my nose, some guy from another class grabbed me, dragged me into a dark corner, and beat me up with iron knuckles. "You motherfucker! You leave our Tamara Ishutina alone. Go back where you came from!" I was totally unprepared for a fight and assured him that he could have his Tamara and I would never try to come near his group. So I decided to concentrate on getting the best grades possible and stop chasing after people in a different class.

This experience in turn encouraged me to spend more time with a faster crowd of my contemporaries. Through my old buddy Lavrenty

Ludvigov I made friends with a group of spoiled children of the elite, who were much like myself. Usually we could get together at Vladimir Burstein's place. He was an affable young man whose father was minister of oil and natural resources of Sakhalin and the Far East territories, a key position of the type the party rarely allows to Jews. Burstein's Moscow flat was large, even by U.S. standards, with three spacious bedrooms, a large living room, and fine old furnishings. They had a large *dacha* too. Since his parents were away on business in Siberia much of the time, we had these places to ourselves for the partying. There were about fourteen of us, male and female, plus other acquaintances. I would show up with American cigarettes, Scotch and other imported spirits, American records, and my RCA Victor phonograph. All of us affected Western styles to one degree or another as our code of nonconformist behavior. This didn't mean we were dissidents or that we were pro-Western politically. We just didn't care about politics. We were simply different. Our conversations were laced with fractured imitations of American slang we'd picked up from records and books. America was the land of our feverish fantasies and unencumbered revelries, the land of parties free from the party.

5: The Party Line

"Hey man, look, ain't that jive stuff? I'm telling you, those rotten capitalists know where to get on and off." Starsky would spit out broken pieces of what passed for American slang. At this particular party I remember him sitting on the floor with a tumbler of Scotch in his hand trying to catch an express train to drunken oblivion. "I'm telling you, man, I want to split, go right down to Hollywood and pick me up a couple of broads and, while I'm at it, fuck our dear Communist party too." His voice raised in excitement at that last idea, but he got no reactions from us. We were all too busy to listen. Starsky was a fixture in our group; being three or four years older than the rest of us, he had already managed to get into trouble with the law, mostly for public drunkenness. He was always saying things like "screw the party."

Also present at this bordello party, or *bardak* as we called them, was Vladimir Kravchenko, a chubby son of the director of Moscow's Theatrical Union. It was his mother who had contributed to our youthful delinquency by getting us BB guns so we could practice at shooting neighborhood cats. To avoid purges in the 1930s, the Kravchenkos had changed their name from Levenstein to their present Ukrainian name. Burstein was there too, a tall man with fine features and black wavy hair. He had an air of detachment, and in his black suit and gray tie he resembled an undertaker sizing up future clients. Then there was Dmitri Volodin, who was on the rowing team that I had joined. Dmitri was a hardcore beatnik, in the Soviet meaning of the word. He favored dissident gatherings and prostitutes. He never wore anything made in the U.S.S.R. Like others in our group, hs used too many English words whose meanings, I'm sure, he didn't know. Dmitri would usually bring three girls to a party. They'd be dressed stylishly in Western creations, an indication of their faithful service to foreign tourists around the Metropol, Moskva, and other hotels.

That evening I was introduced to Nina, who was not one of the hookers, but the seventeen-year-old daughter of an army colonel. She was tall, blond, slim, and moved with the agility of a dancer. I was immediately taken with her because she was not only beautiful, but she also knew who Paul Desmond was, and could tell me the vintage of the Sinatra record that was playing. We shared a passion for skiing and, shortly, for each other. She suggested we continue our conversation in one of the bedrooms. The party was getting too noisy, she said.

Women in Russia have been granted equal status with men. The professions are open to them, as are the laboring jobs, and they wield tremendous influence in the family. In sexual and romantic matters, however, they are the equal if not the superior of men. Pehaps because of the five-to-three ratio of women over men, women are very forward. Most of the women I met then were very free about enjoying themselves erotically. They weren't coy about their desires nor shy about asking for what pleased them.

The bedroom was huge, with a large bed faced by an Italian dresser. I turned up the Chinese porcelain lamp on the night stand and we sat down on the bed together. "Give me a cigarette," Nina asked, taking off her shoes and putting her arms around me. I got a pack of Chesterfields out of my American-made sports jacket. I lit two at once, like Paul Henreid. When we made love it was with the uninhibited intensity of two strangers discovering each other. We professed undying love at first encounter, perhaps only to heighten the enjoyment of the moment. And eventually we did become close.

The party was in full swing when we came back to the living room, but we decided to go home. It turned out Nina lived in the building next to mine. The street was empty. Big snowflakes quietly fell on the asphalt and melted fast, leaving a film of freshly scented moisture in the air. Our footsteps echoed off the tall buildings. In this early hour of Sunday morning there were no cars on the street, the windows were darkened. We went through a park where bare trees stood up like gray mirages on the white snow between the benches, also covered with snow. Holding each other close we walked up to her home.

"Look," Nina pointed at her spike-heel shoes, "might as well throw them away." The shoes were not exactly appropriate to the weather.

"Why not," I said, "tomorrow we'll go to a store I know of and we'll pick you a pair from France."

"Oh, are you a magician?" Nina laughed. "French shoes here, in Moscow?"

"You'll see. I'll meet you right here at noon, okay?"

"Okay." Nina gave me a kiss and opened the entrance door.

"I like you, Vladimir."

"I love you, Nina."

For the next five or six months we met almost every day. We went to parties and talked in the park or on the staircase of Nina's building. One of my parents was at home most of the time. The winter was harsh and spending an hour kissing on a park bench left our lips cracked and toes frozen. Therefore we spent most of our hours on the dark staircase. We were too young to go to restaurants or hotels. No empty apartments—except for Burstein's—but that only on the weekends. Our problems were typical of those experienced by impassioned teenagers anywhere.

Heavy romances weren't on the agenda for me at that time, however, and when our meetings threatened to interfere with my work-school-sports schedule, I felt duty bound to give Nina notice with what in retrospect seems high-handed haste. We were at still another party at Burstein's when I told her we'd not be seeing each other for a while.

My rowing coach had put me on a special team which was to compete in the Moscow championships the next summer, but only on condition that I train an extra hour a day, including Sundays. This was a great opportunity to win a sports medal that would help in my campaign to be admitted to the IIR. My parents also were pressing me to put extra time into studying to prepare for the entrance exams.

"Tell me what I can do to help you," said Nina. We were sitting in the same bedroom where we'd been that first night.

"I can't see you for a while. At least until I'm admitted to the Institute next year."

"What are you talking about? That's unreasonable."

"I'm sorry, it's been decided." I was chain smoking my Winstons, trying not to look at her. I could feel her staring at me.

After a few moments she said, "I'm sorry too. I thought you were a man, not a boy with stupid ideas. It's stupid what you just said. I would not care if you were a diplomat or a factory worker anyway."

I shrugged my shoulders.

"Well then you just go on, but one day you might realize that feelings come first." She leaned down and took off her shoes. "Why don't you take this French shit and eat it?" She calmly extended her right hand and dropped the shoes in front of me. "You insensitive idiot." She walked out barefooted, but didn't slam the door as I'd expected.

I felt exactly the way she'd described me, at least for the moment. I joined the others to try to enjoy the rest of the party. I poured a slug of Scotch and drank it quickly in disgust with myself. "Hey man, where's your broad?" said Dmitri Volodin, using his best American slang. "Did she split? Jive turkeys like that always split. Latch on to one of mine here. I'll let you have one cheap. How about that flight bag you promised me? Real cheap, hey?"

I had met him a few days earlier at the gym while packing up my training suit into an Air France bag. "That's a cool bag," he'd said in English. "Can you get one? I'll pay you." I had another like it at home, so I agreed to bring him one when we got together for our next party. "Right on, salute your generosity," Dmitri said, shaking my hand and giving me a big grin. I had brought the bag to the party.

The doorbell rang and, since everyone was too busy to answer, I made my way through the long corridor and opened the door. Nina stood on the landing leaning against the wall. "My shoes, please. It's too cold." I went back and brought her the shoes.

Next morning I woke up on the bed in one of Burstein's bedrooms. The place smelled of stale smoke and liquor. I was alone and hungover. I collected my belongings and quickly went out. The first spring sun was quickly melting the ice and snow. Cars were moving carefully through the muddy slush, and people on the street looked happier than usual. No one was home when I got back to the apartment. I put on a record of Frank D'Rone singing "After the Ball is Over," lay down on the couch, and closed my eyes. I was starring in my own American film again, sopping up the melancholy of the moment by the bucketful.

I never saw Nina again, even though later she'd relented and invited me to her birthday party. I heard later that she married someone in the Ministry of Foreign Trade and that they went to West Africa on assignment. Friends told me she became even more attractive and bright and that her husband was envied by the entire male population of the Soviet colony where they were stationed.

I settled into a grinding routine. I would get up at six and quickly go out into the freezing street to wait for the trolley bus and the hour ride to the school where I worked. There I would set up the experiments for the classes which started at 8:30 A.M. The lab was very small with a desk at the huge, frozen window overlooking the Moscow Circus School. Wall-to-wall shelves were stacked with equipment, most of it antiquated. I'd put my Air France bag on the desk and get a pack of Winstons from under the radiator. As the smoke numbed my frozen senses, I thought about the long day ahead—studies, working out at the gym, night school, more studying, and then to bed. I looked out of the window at the falling snowflakes and the people dressed in black and gray moving on the street like dirty spots, acting out a dull routine. I tried to imagine what it would be like to keep on with this kind of monotony indefinitely, like so many of them below. When I'd finished my smoke I opened the window to air out the room. Smoking was prohibited.

Later in the day I'd go to my daily workout at Dynamo Stadium. I would run, lift weights, and row in the pool. Then I'd hurry through my sandwich, which was often dry—no mayonnaise; stores were almost always out of it. Sometimes you couldn't get things no matter how much money you had. At moments like these one of J.D. Salinger's short stories would come to mind: "This Sandwich Has No Mayonnaise" had nothing to do with sandwiches, but a lot to do with how I was feeling. *The Catcher in the Rye* had become my favorite novel for the moment, its sarcasm and youthful frustration spoke to me just as it did to my contemporaries in the West. I could identify with

Holden Caulfield much more than with the Dmitris on my rowing team.

I'd take the trolley car, then a bus to night school. I always disliked the subway, which was usually crowded with exhausted workers and rank with body odors. The bus wasn't much better. I'd stand, crowded on all sides, looking out of place in my baby seal coat and my flight bag squeezed between my legs.

The adult school was up two flights of redwood stairs in a large hall which many years ago had probably been used as a ballroom by an aristocrat. As soon as I'd take up position near a window, I'd go into another of the roles I had to play to fit each of my environments. I'd been the diligent worker, the athlete, the musician, the earnest candidate for the IIR, and here I had to play the part of a tough fellow who didn't give a damn. This ability to play roles was to be even more useful later. In fact, my life would depend on it.

But my resolve to keep to this Spartan lifestyle didn't last long. Within a few months I'd made enough headway to allow myself some fun. By then Vera had replaced Nina. I'd met Vera at another of Burstein's parties. She had been going with my childhood chum Lavrenti for a year, but their relationship was on the wane and he didn't seem to care that we took up with each other. Vera was not as stunning as Nina, but more interesting.

"Vladimir," she asked me at that party, "you like it here?"

"Not really," I answered.

"Then why don't we leave here and go for a walk?"

"A great idea," I agreed. And that was the last time I ever hung around Burstein's. What a walk it was . . . at least five miles in the cold of Moscow all the way to Vera's apartment building near the Ukraine Hotel. We talked all the way and got very close, to the point that I overcame my reservations and excused myself to run around a corner of an empty street to do my private business. There are no public toilets in Moscow and once you're stuck, that's it.

Vera shared my secret anti-Soviet attitudes. Her father had died two years before. He had been a prominent Kremlin physician with all kinds of honors. Her mother was a professor of medicine at Moscow University. Vera had the same relatively privileged upbringing I'd had. She hated the repressiveness of Soviet society, especially in the areas of music, literature, film, and art. Lavrenti's influence was quite remarkable there, for she loved Western music, and through him she'd become a fan of Elvis Presley. She too had read *The Catcher in the Rye* and loved Sinatra, Brubeck, Mulligan, and Count Basie. I became much closer to Vera than I'd ever been to Nina.

My parents soon made it clear that she was not for me, however. Lavrenti had told them she was sickly. She had chronic anemia, but that certainly didn't stop her from partying! Also, she was short and, they thought, not glamorous enough to impress the social circles I'd join as a member of the diplomatic corps. Her worst sin, in their eyes, was not being a social butterfly. She came to one big party thrown by my parents, for example, and acted very quiet, keeping mostly to herself and not interacting with our friends. The truth was that she was very vivacious and talkative, with a great deal of wit and knowledge, but didn't feel comfortable with our crowd of diplomats, party officials, and their hangers-on.

My father gave me a lecture about her soon after the party. "She's a very nice girl, Volodya. (My father rarely called me Vladimir, preferring this diminutive form.) She has a good figure, pretty legs, and she's polite, but if you get tied up with her she'll drag you down. She's not pretty enough, and not sociable. What kind of impression would she make if you had to take her to a big diplomatic reception? Also, she's sickly. No good. Look for somebody else."

I said, "Okay, maybe you're right." But I thought that with time my parents would come to like her better. I wasn't ready to give her up, not just yet. But my father's comments stuck with me. I wasn't all that independent-minded yet, either. I kept going with her for the next two or three years. She generally avoided encounters with my parents, and I avoided her mother, who disliked me and had warned her daughter that I was taking advantage of her. I didn't see it that way. I thought I loved her madly.

I'd go with Vera once in a while to parties frequented by artists, writers, poets, sculptors, and their friends. These were held mostly in the studios that the government built for them. They were quite poor, living off fees they'd receive when their works were displayed, performed, or acquired for government buildings. And although outwardly they were pro-Soviet, among themselves they were liberal, with dissident attitudes.

62

Vera and I befriended an artist named Zorya Russakov. He was very popular as a cartoonist, painter, and sculptor, one of the more successful of that group. I had known him when I was a child. He was the grandson of the Countess Gruenfeld. A dashing fellow, he'd been an artillery spotter behind German lines during World War II and was a real hero, as opposed to the various *stukachi* who only claimed to be heroes of the Revolution.

I felt I could be myself with these bohemians, but still I didn't feel close to them. I agreed with their gripes, but saw them as futile. The thought of living this way depressed me. They complained mostly about the government censorship that forced them to stick to socialist realism. They were sick of painting sterile scenes of earnest, heroic workers. I had taken a couple of high school classes in art myself and even *I* was sick of pictures of heroic workers. Having grown up so close to the power structure, however, I didn't need anyone to explain to me that these sculptors and painters would get nowhere with their grievances, and would continue to live a marginal existence to boot. There was no future in art. Besides, I wasn't very sympathetic toward them because they seemed narrowly engrossed in their own world. They cared little for the music I liked, for example, so I wasn't interested in their yearnings for free art, and thus we found little common ground. So I kept this scene divorced from my other activities for the most part. And I certainly never let it creep into the official Mr. Wonderful role I had to play to get into the Institute.

By 1961 I was very much into water skiing, rowing, fishing, and swimming. I found they took my mind off my schedule or preparations for the IIR. The summer of 1961 couldn't have been better. In just one more year I'd become a student at the Institute of International Relations, which would open all the avenues to an independent, rich life.

A week before my father returned from a trip to Ghana, he bought a Johnson outboard for my new speedboat. There weren't any Soviet motors except a heavy ten horsepower Moskva outboard. If you paired two up, they'd sink the boat, and one was not enough for pulling a skier. The Johnson was the first American outboard in the Soviet Union. None of the Soviets, even those high up in the government, could pay a three hundred percent customs duty on a thing like that. In this case, my father sent the Johnson with a Soviet Supreme Council member, on a special government plane.

The phone rang. I heard my father's voice in the other room. "We'll be right down, Lev . . . Just take two bottles of vodka and three of wine . . . No, Vladimir's girl is not here yet. We'll wait for her downstairs."

This was Lev Skryabin calling. Lev was Molotov's nephew and our families were very close. I heard Lev telling my father several times that he'd be forever grateful to him for not letting down our friendship during the purges against his once powerful uncle. Khrushchev's attack against the "personality cult" and his new government made it very dangerous for anyone to be even remotely connected with people like Molotov or their relatives. But my family and Skryabin's remained good friends. Lev was in the Ministry of Foreign Affairs and, as they say in Russia, "old cadres never die." His uncle would later become powerful again in the capacity of Special Counselor for the Ministry.

This Sunday we planned a trip to our *dacha* in Lev's car. Lev and his wife, Dina, were waiting downstairs in their apartment. Dina and my mother were pretty close. I wondered if there was ever any swapping going on. I'd seen my father kissing Dina passionately and, in turn, Lev hugging my mother a bit too warmly.

Vera was expected but didn't show up. She was probably hung-over from last night's party—also she didn't mix well with my family.

The day was starting out nicely. As we passed through the guarded iron gate and entered the resort area where our summer cottage was, I found myself in another world. I was looking forward to the moment when I would whisk out in my boat.

As Lev's compact Moskvich automobile stopped at our house, I helped Dina out. She held onto my hand, her eyes wandering about and then penetrating mine. With a smile she said, "I wish we'd come here last night. It's so wonderful. You party too much, Vladimir."

I didn't say anything and went to help unpack. "Well, shall we start the morning with a drink?" I heard my father asking Lev. "Surely, we'll begin the day with one," Lev happily replied. "Vladimir, why don't you go ahead with Dina. Angelina, you want to join us?" he asked my mother.

64

"Yeah, I'm kinda tired." They all went into the house.

"Well, it looks like we are going water skiing alone," Dina said. "Would you mind if I pull you?" I thought it was a good idea. We put on our swimming suits and went down to the pier.

The Johnson was a powerful motor for my boat. As Dina and I jumped in and we pulled out, I saw several bystanders watching. The American wonder picked up speed and quickly left the pier behind; I was overwhelmed with a sense of the utmost superiority.

We didn't do much water skiing. Instead, we found a deserted beach ten miles away and made love, as I suspected we would. Later Dina and I were lying on the beach listening to "Love is the Thing" by Nat King Cole, one of my favorites, on my Phillips portable tape recorder. The sky was blue and the sand was yellow, the water was crystal clear. "Johnson" sparkled under the bright sun. Nat King Cole sang and Dina's beautiful head was on my stomach. There was no one around for miles and miles.

The rest of the day went fast. When we got back to our *dacha* we found the others quite drunk. There wouldn't be a chance for Lev to drive us back to Moscow.

But I had to be back, because my schedule for the next week was very demanding. The Moscow Championships in rowing—or as they call it, "academic sculling"—were coming up next Sunday and I had to be ready. Plus, my German lessons at the Ministry of Foreign Affairs had to be attended.

So I said goodbye to the bunch and walked three kilometers to the nearest bus stop. I got to Moscow very late. As I was getting out of the Kirovskaya subway station, I noticed a drunk lying on a sidewalk, then another; a typical picture of a late Sunday in Moscow. The air was stale and hot. People were gray-faced, ready for Monday's slavery at factories, bureaus, stores. Many drinks, but not many smiles.

As I crossed Kirovskaya Street, flanked by monolithic gray building facades that concentrated the heat shimmering up from the melting asphalt, to my right toward the middle of the square I could see two long lines of people. Nothing unusual; one line was for taxi service, the other one was for *kvas*, a traditional yellow-colored soft drink brewed from rye, with a sweet and sour taste. It was being dispensed from a large metal tank by an old woman who dourly filled mugs and pushed them towards the sweating customers as they put

65

down their kopeks. The line waiting for the taxis looked the more irritated, for they had no *kvas* and there were no cabs to be seen either.

As I approached our apartment, I saw a note on the door. The note was from Vera: "I'm sorry. I overslept. Could you call me when you're back? Love."

I turned on my Grundig solid state, poured a glass of Black & White and settled at the window facing the square. Gerry Mulligan and Dave Brubeck stimulated my imagination as I was sipping my Scotch and smoking a Winston. My thoughts took me miles away, right over the ocean. I turned on my Grundig shortwave radio, turned it to "The Voice of America," and the voice of Willis Conover filled the room. "This is 'The Voice of America' studio in Washington, D.C. This program is coming to you from the United States of America." I listened religiously to the Jazz Hour.

The broadcast ended and the day was over. Next Sunday it would be the same. Somehow I felt I was missing something, but I couldn't figure out what. Maybe it was Vera I wanted to be with, and the hell with what they thought about it. Still, I didn't call her.

Next Sunday was just as beautiful. The competiton at the Khimki Reservoir in the northern suburbs of Moscow started with single sculls. Our turn—pairs—was next. Since it was my first big official competition, my partner and I were given an old scull circa 1950, bulky and unmaneuverable. My partner was very nervous. He went to the W.C. and didn't come out in time for the competition. We were supposed to be at the start in five minutes. My coach, Vera Scheremetyeva, called for a substitute, a new guy, tall and very skinny. I had never practiced with him before. She said, "Well, there's no other choice. Your partner is in no condition . . . you'll have to go with this fellow."

The greatest disadvantage was our weight distribution. I was taller, heavier, and my sliding bench was the front one, his closer to the end of the scull. When we started I felt that with every stroke the nose of the boat was about to submerge. I knew we were not going to win. But we pulled up at the finish and took the third place prize. Exhausted after the two thousand meters, I got out of the boat. A pro recruiter walked toward me. "Would you like to join so and so crew to train for the Soviet Championships?" I told him I was extremely flattered and I'd think about it.

Being a pro in sports didn't coincide with my plans for a diplomatic career. On the way back home, riding in a taxi, I decided I'd had enough rowing. I had reached just about the highest point in my amateur standings and that would do for the IIR entrance qualifications.

Several months later the Moscow winter sparkled. The dirt on the streets and the mud in the new suburban housing developments were evenly covered with snow.

At that time Khrushchev's plan to provide free housing for everyone was going full speed ahead. Scores of massive, block-style apartment buildings were going up all over the Moscow area, mostly in the suburbs. Inexperienced crews—most of them women new to their jobs—plus shortages in materials resulted in sloppy construction. Many such new apartments had developed cracks in the plaster, leaky windows and roofs, troublesome plumbing and electrical systems, jammed doors, and faulty radiators. The residents, however, happily put up with such annoyances. There were long lists of people who waited as long as six years to get into these new apartments which they would not have to share with another family.

The worst housing shortage was for those who lived in the regular state-run apartments. These were rent-free and only a few tenants paid even nominal utility fees. But one usually had to live with one or two other families in one and two bedroom apartments and wait years until new quarters became available. One way around this—for those whose status and finances permitted—was to buy a cooperative apartment. In this arrangement, a group to which one belonged—for example, the workers at an automobile plant, or a journalist union— owned an apartment building. There was a waiting list for these apartments too, but much shorter—months instead of years. At that time, in the early 1960s, one could get one- to three-bedroom co-op apartments for 2,000 to 6,000 rubles. But, if you could pay in American dollars—as could my father, who earned hard currencies overseas—the price would be roughly $1,200 to $1,800. This would be paid with forty to sixty percent down and the rest in small monthy installments. A family as a rule would live in one of these cooperative apartments and the parents could pass them on to their children. It was against the law, however, to sell one of them.

The snow blanketed new and old buildings, state-run and cooperative buildings alike. The unfinished roads in the suburbs and the wide boulevards in the city and the city lights made the white canopy sparkle in winter vignettes reflected endlessly in the windows of the large department stores along Kutusovsky Prospect. Leafless trees guarded this white desert.

6: The Time Is Short

The Christmas celebration of 1962 was just about to begin. My father had just returned from his trip to Sweden and Norway. My gifts were a new seal coat, a suit, and, most important, a pair of hockey skates. Although my knees had been injured playing hockey, it was still my favorite sport.

The day before Christmas my mother asked me to go shopping. As always, I took American dollars which my father constantly supplied me and went to a special store that had an abundance of foods and spirits not available in the stores open to the public. The people who shopped at this store were mostly those who held legitimate access to free world currencies. This included Soviet diplomats of all types—members of the MFA, KGB, GRU, party Central Committee, and trade representatives who worked in the countries whose currencies were easily convertible. They could save a part of their salary and bring it home. A certificate from customs would be issued to prove the currency's legitimacy. Currency surplus could also be exchanged by a foreign affairs' employee for special certificates—or "gold rubles" as they are nicknamed—and used for purchases in the same special stores.

Two KGB men met me at the door. "What do you have?"

"Dollars."

"Okay, come in." They were there to screen out free currency speculators, local crooks, and anyone who'd wander in there by mistake.

There were very few people in the store—some Americans and other foreigners, and people like me. From filet mignon to lobsters, from papaya to Greek olives, everything was artfully arranged on the counters.

I picked up two bottles of Scotch—Black & White as always—then some Beefeater, Napoleon brandy, and some champagne, a half-kilo of caviar, salmon, steaks; a carton of Winstons for me and two of Phillip Morris for guests, and some other items. The clerk at the counter treated me with great servility, as if I were the chairman of Politburo. I extracted the dollars from my wallet and put them on the counter in a gesture of independent superiority and walked to a waiting taxi.

We had a party at home that night. Some friends, like Lev and Dina, were there, but mostly there were KGB, MFA, and party people—all who might be instrumental in my career.

As the party progressed and the guests became drunker and drunker, and danced to Paul Anka's "Greatest Hits," Ivan Baikov, the head of IIR personnel and my father's friend, called me to come to the kitchen.

"Vladimir, I wanna talk to you a bit."

"Yes, surely," I said, lighting up a Winston.

"You'll be seventeen very soon and already it looks like you've accomplished a lot."

I said something like "Well, I can do more."

Ivan continued, "Now, listen to me very seriously. We have talked it over with your father."

I sat down at the kitchen table intending to pour some whiskey in Ivan's glass, but he stopped me. "No, I've had enough. Remember what we talked about before?"

"Sure I do," I said.

"Okay, you've followed my suggestions. Your father is proud of you. But there is something else I want to tell you." He paused and I felt my heart beating faster as his all-knowing eyes drilled a hole in my forehead. "I will help you, but you gotta watch it. Starting right now."

70

I said, "Watch what?"

"Your playing jazz records, your listening to 'The Voice of America,' your sex life, your using taxis too extensively."

I was stopped cold by his words. Not by the advice, but by the information about me. I knew it was not in my father's interests to discuss my love for jazz or the BBC. That could not only harm his own career as a double for the MFA and the "neighbors," but close all the doors to mine.

"Don't worry now, son," Ivan nodded understandingly. "I also have my own preferences and I also wear British-made suits. The thing is that you are about to be put under my surveillance. The reason—your choosing the Institute. Your application has been processed, your record is outstanding, so don't screw it up."

I was hesitant for awhile but finally decided to ask my burning question. "Did you—"

"Yes, we always have. You should know better than that," Ivan said in a fatherly manner. We were talking about bugging and tapes. I should have known that all the living quarters and telephones of MFA and KGB employees had been bugged.

Ivan carried on. "I have been given orders to screen every potential student at the Institute. You fall into this category. Listen, I know you, but a jerk who'd be checking you out doesn't know you. So, just cut down on that jazz. Later, when you go overseas, you'll have enough of it *and* everything else."

This conversation at the Christmas party proved to be very valuable. I began to notice when I was tailed, so I was on guard. In the months that followed, just before the entrance exams, I was approached by women of "ill repute," actually KGB agents. I ignored them. Some men offered me U.S. and French currencies in exchange for rubles, and once a "Western tourist," wearing a Russian-made tie, asked me for directions in English with a heavy Russian accent, after which he told me how good the life is on the other side. I told him to screw off and tell his imperialist jobbers not to disturb my Communist consciousness. Invariably, KGB agents would give themselves away by things noticeable only to my experienced eye.

Suddenly these provocations stopped and I received a message from the Institute of International Relations to come for a preexamination interview.

Trying to look good, I put on my Italian Trevira suit, which my father had recently bought in Rome. I told my mother that she shouldn't worry as much as I did, because after all *I* was going for the interview, not she. She wished me all the best and also wished that my father were there, but he was on another trip to Peking.[1]

As I was entering the room designated for the interview, I saw Ivan Baikov and two young men at the table.

"Please, sit down." One of the young men pointed to the small chair facing the table. "You are Vladimir Nikolayevich Sakharov, born in Moscow, May 3, 1945?" I said that was right. "Why have you decided to submit an application to the Institute of International Relations?" the other with the dark complexion continued.

I answered, "The reason for my applying here is my desire to contribute to the implementation of the foreign policy of our Communist party." The same one asked, "But wouldn't you be able to do that in some other capacity, say, a road builder?" I said, "Of course, but my knowledge of German, of history, economics, and my general interest in the politics of our party prompted me to try international relations first."

"Good," the other man said. "What kind of books do you prefer? Soviet or Western?" he added.

I said, "Our Soviet writers. I like socialist realism and don't care for the pseudo-intellectuals."

"Good," he replied.

"What music do you listen to?" That was the dark-haired man again.

"I am fond of Shostakovich, Rachmaninoff, Tchaikovsky. In fact, I play their—"

"Oh, what instrument do you play?" the dark one interrupted. "Piano? You know, we need a piano player for our orchestra." I picked up the cue and stated I'd be privileged if accepted.

[1] It was very rough for Soviet diplomats in China then. Mao's "Great Leap Forward" policy—disapproved of by Moscow—was widening the Sino-Soviet split as was Peking's increasing claims to leadership of world revolution. In short, China was moving further away from any possibility of either economic or political control by Moscow. Ordinary Soviet citizens could not comprehend what they perceived as monumental Chinese ingratitude for post-war economic aid sent by the Soviet Union to spur China's industrial development. Now Mao was saying China didn't want any Soviet aid, that it hadn't been enough anyway, and that it didn't want the strings attached either.

Finally, Ivan Baikov interfered. "Why don't we finish at that? He seems to be quite fit to join the Institute."

On that conclusive note, the hour's interview was over. I flew home to my happy mother for a round of celebrations. In Russia it is a custom to celebrate *any* major or minor event—like a weekend, snow falling or snow melting. In this case, the event was my successful jump over the first hurdle of my career.

The next week I was very busy with exams. The first one was an essay. Several topics were given, most of them related to the party's position on literature. I chose one of them in which the party's position would be less obtrusive, *"War and Peace* by Leo Tolstoy—His Influence on Soviet Literature." I wrote a fifteen page essay in the three hours given us. The trick was that no student could argue about his or her grade for the essay; moreover, they couldn't see their essays after they were turned in. Therefore, anyone who didn't pass through the preliminary screening, or about whom the KGB had some reservations, would be failed on the essay. An unsatisfactory mark meant: don't ever try to come around this institute again.

As soon as I found I had an excellent grade on my essay, I knew I didn't have to worry. I passed with flying colors the next exams in German, history, geography, and Russian language. A week later I was admitted and gloriously showered with gifts from my parents and grandparents.

Descending on the escalator some two hundred feet into the tacky vestibule ornamented with revolutionary statues, I heard a voice behind me: *"Wie spät ist es?"* (What is the time?).

I turned back and answered in German: *"Die Zeit ist knapp."* (Time is short.)

"What do you mean?" The dialogue continued in German. "Just what I said. I saw you coming out of that building. How come the people who emerge from there are dressed like people who live in Stockholm or Amsterdam, or somewhere like that?"

The train was approaching the platform on which we stood. The doors opened and let the crowd out. We entered continuing this ridiculous conversation. I think I said something like "I didn't see any difference between the people who come out of that building and the rest of the street fillers."

I asked the man, "Are you from East Germany?" He answered,

"West." As soon as I heard that, I wished I was invisible or, better, somewhere else. Being aware that KGB surveillance still might be on me and I'd be finished if they saw me talking to a foreigner—the worst kind possible, a West German—I prepared to split at the first opportunity.

We talked on. "Is that a school or what?"

To which I murmured, "Ah, that's what you might call it, a school of foreign languages."

The train stopped at the next station. I waited until the doors let the passengers get in and out and, just before they were about shut, I sneaked out. I felt much better and decided to take the escalator up onto Gorki Street and get a cab.

Little did I know I would meet the same man five years later. I didn't detect him at the time, maybe because of my limited knowledge of American accents. Later on I'd come to admire that man for his unabated creativity and discipline. As I learned later, one had to have guts to work as an agent of a foreign intelligence service in the Soviet Union.

That night I came home early. My father, as usual, was overseas; my mother had just left for the Black Sea, so I decided to have a party. It was high time for me to get acquainted with my future colleagues.

That morning I had asked Baikov to help me change my area of specialization. When I was admitted to the Institute, for some reason I was assigned Southeast Asia, Vietnamese language, and French. That didn't sound attractive. First, you can't get free currency in North Vietnam; secondly, who wants to go there? And as for France, it could go communist anytime. So I chose Arabic and English. The Middle Eastern specialization would get me a comfortable slot in some Arab embassy, and English would be a necessity. I must know it better. Naturally, Baikov helped. My program changed. The director of personnel called the dean of the faculty of International Relations' Eastern Division. The dean obeyed, because if he didn't follow KGB recommendations, he might find himself working in a public library or digging potatoes in the fields near Moscow.

After I'd left Baikov's office I bumped into a couple of other students. They introduced themselves as Victor Kudryavtsev and Nikolai Khlopinsky. Victor was a burly six-footer, with blond hair, blue eyes, and very fair skin. They called him "Bulldog" because of his protruding lower lip, massive face, and sloping forehead. Nikolai was a bit taller than Victor, and heavier—about 200 pounds. He had a scarred lip from a boxing injury. He was dark, with black hair, and had an oval face. The three of us became chums, an awesome looking trio who could drink enough for a battalion.

Victor's family background typified most IIR students' roots. His father, Sergei Kudryavtsev, had a high position in the government which he'd held since before the war. His posts included Counselor of the Soviet Embassy in London and in Vienna, the ambassadorship in Cuba just before the missile incident, and the post of Charge d'Affairs in West Germany. Later he was instrumental in getting the Americans out of Cambodia in his ambassadorial capacity; in 1974 he was assigned to UNESCO as Soviet ambassador. Having a KGB general's rank he was on the MFA's *Collegiya* (Advisory Council) and exercised quite a bit of power in foreign policy decision-making.

Nikolai, on the other hand, didn't have influential parents and relatives to back him up. He was one of the very few individuals who was admitted to the IIR on the basis of his outstanding record only. But even then there were certain factors in his favor. His magnetic appeal to women, which he used extensively to get what he wanted, played a major role as I found out later, in his friendly relationship with Raisa Ryzhenko, wife of the rector of the Institute. I suspect she must have said a good word for Nikolai to her husband.

The three of us agreed to celebrate our meeting. That evening we went to the Warsaw Restaurant. Sipping cognac, Victor Kudryavtsev announced he needed a woman and, since his father was now in Cuba, his apartment was free. Nikolai quickly got the message and ran out to make a phone call.

At the entrance to Victor's apartment building three girls were waiting for us. They looked like sisters, dressed very lightly and wearing spiked heels. "All right, girls, this is Victor and this is Vladimir." They smiled and moved toward us. My eyes went wild. I couldn't make my pick, all of them were so beautiful, nice, and friendly. I let Victor make his choice first. Her name was Nina.

Then, Nikolai took the second girl by the waist. Her name was Lyuda. I was left with a brunette, very slim and long legged.

"Nina," she said, stretching out her hand.

Nikolai laughed, "Just call her U-2, U-1 is Nina. This is U-2, like Powers' plane they shot down. See? I call them that so I don't confuse them when everybody gets drunk."

"Okay, U-2, let's go up." We took the elevator, the girls hanging

on our arms. I thought to myself, "This is the beginning of a new life. Everything I want, I get: girls, prestige, good friends."

We entered the apartment. It was luxurious beyond imagination. There was expensive furniture rarely seen in the Soviet Union, all kinds of things from abroad on the tables and shelves; Persian rugs, soft leather sofas, and king-size beds in all three bedrooms. Even I'd never seen anything like it before.

Victor pushed a button beneath the bar. It opened and an array of bottles appeared, bottles of different shapes with all kinds of foreign labels. We started with Cuban rum followed by Frascati white wine chasers. Havana cigars were in an ivory box on a hand-carved Chinese coffee table. They, combined with the rum and wine, began to affect me. I felt like I was on top of the world—pleasure and luxury, no worries. U-2 was sitting on my knee. Very light and beautiful, U-2 was smoking my Winston, holding it between her long fingers. I was trying to keep my cool despite my excitement and anticipation of extraordinary pleasure.

But my diplomatic awareness of protocol wouldn't allow me to engage in any wild displays of passion. I took my lips off her full mouth and was stunned by what I saw. Both Victor and Nikolai were half undressed and the girls were taking off their dresses. Nikolai pointed to the bedroom door in the hall. "Shall we?" We got up and moved into the bedroom.

The room was half dark, just enough to see the action. U-2's body was a little bony, but quite to my liking. Of course, I assumed she adored me, for who couldn't help but adore a member of the New Elite?

I don't remember how much time passed. I ended up with U-1 and Victor ended up with Nikolai's girl. Nikolai ended up passed out on the floor in the living room.

The girls were ready to leave; the taxi was waiting. Instead of joining them, I walked several blocks along Leningrad Prospect almost to Mayakovsky Square. It was three in the morning and the city was still asleep. Only the sound of street cleaning cars could be heard a bit ahead on Gorky Street. As I walked I sobered up and began to feel much better. The buildings on both sides looked like gray Roman monuments ornamented with phony decorations, like on some movie set.

As I was approaching the familiar corner of Gorky Street and

Pushkin Square I saw a phone booth. I stopped and thought about calling Vera. She must be asleep now. So if I called her, she wouldn't answer; her mother would pick up the phone—and I didn't feel like talking to her mother. I dialed Vera's number and waited for a minute.

"Da?" I was not prepared to hear Vera's voice. "Who's there?"

"It's me, Vladimir," I said, trying to sound casual.

"Do you know what time it is?" She was really irritated.

"Uh-huh," I said, "about four in the morning. Are you alone?"

"Yes, mother went to Leningrad yesterday. They have a conference or something." Vera was waking up.

"So, you are alone, my love." I was searching for a cigarette.

"Are you drunk?" Vera said.

"No." I thought I'd sobered up.

"Why haven't you called me for almost a month?" That was my old Vera.

"You know, got busy . . . Look I want to see you now."

"It's late. Where are you?" I told her where I was. "Call me in the morning when you are at home."

"But look, I want to see you now. It's important."

"Call me in the morning."

I held on to that scratched receiver for awhile, then hung it up and walked out to the corner. I would have hurried up to her, but there were no taxis around and Vera lived too far from Pushkin Square. A lot in my life might have been different if I'd made it to Vera's that night.

PART THREE

The Making of a Soviet Diplomat

7: *Knowing Your Enemy*

Ostensibly the Institute of International Relations trains Soviet diplomats for the Ministry of Foreign Affairs. The training, however, is much different than that received by someone planning a diplomatic career in the West. A Western student training to become a member of the striped-pants set pours over confusing theories and methodologies, history, political science, a bit of a language, and basic protocol. His Soviet counterpart is not only being trained in these academic subjects, but in how to be a Soviet agent as well. For the Soviet trainee, subversion is emphasized over statecraft.

It is true that members of Western diplomatic corps are involved in intelligence. Attachés, for example, provide liaison with agents. But for Soviet diplomats, there is no distinction between diplomacy and espionage. Usually the more perilous undercover work is left to KGB and GRU illegals in the field. However, all Ministry of Foreign Affairs officers in embassies, consulates, the United Nations, trade missions, and other foreign missions are monitored by and subject to the direct orders of the KGB. All are soldiers, whose job is to wage political, ideological, and economic warfare against the capitalist countries and their imperialist sponsor, the United States. The anti-United States political warfare is conducted on all levels of Soviet diplomacy. The SALT talks, for example, are a vehicle to reinforce the legality of Soviet military supremacy and to present the United States to the rest of the world as stubborn, militaristic, and imperialistic. The Middle East conflict is being used to manipulate the Arab countries vis-à-vis the U.S.

Ideological warfare includes propaganda and recruiting potential Soviet agents in the local population and facilitating their infiltration of government, military and police departments, labor unions, religious organizations, political parties, schools, and nationalist groups.

Economic warfare includes attacking imperialism at its heart. That is, using actions, direct and indirect, to weaken and finally force the collapse of the economies of the Western nations, as it was almost daily emphasized and officially expressed to the assembled classes at the Institute one day by Pavel Podlesny. This was in 1965, early in my third year, when a new directive from above was read to us.

We knew something was up because a special meeting had been announced in the morning during language classes. Podlesny, the party secretary of our class who also doubled as the chief *stukach*, entered our Arabic classroom without knocking and gave Vladimir Segal, the teacher, one of his "I am gonna get you someday" smiles. He announced with that exaggerated superiority which helped him overcome his smallness, "You are all to gather at conference hall number two at fifteen thirty for a special meeting." Most of us sighed. I hated those special meetings and expected it would be no more interesting than the recent lecture by Henry Winston. I thought I'd hear something stimulating from an American, even if he was a Communist, but he just repeated what I heard every day from my Soviet teachers.

"Sorry, class," Segal said. "I sympathize with the inconvenience of your being detained after classes, but you must do what the mother party asks you to." He smiled broadly and walked up to the window. Segal was considered the best Arabic teacher in Moscow and he knew it. He was almost irreplaceable.

The special event that day followed a lecture on international law by Igor Blishchenko, the foremost Soviet expert on the subject and legal consultant to the Soviet mission to the United Nations and counselor-minister at the MFA. (Blishchenko later became a member of the Soviet negotiating team for SALT I.) Few of my classmates were looking forward to staying after school. Victor, Nikolai, and I hung back as we walked to the conference room, trying to get seats in the last row. I hoped to pass the time reading a copy of *How Green Was My Valley* that I'd brought with me. Nikolai had a James Bond novel and Victor said he wanted to take a nap. As soon as we sank into our chairs, an unfamiliar man walked into the hall accompanied by the deputy director of the Institute and our world economics professor. The man had a rather long title, but most importantly, he was a member of the MFA's *Collegiya*, obviously in charge of the liaison with the party's Central Committee.

He started out very quietly, as though he was not accustomed to public speaking. "The government"—I caught his words somewhere toward the middle of his statement—"considers it necessary to expand and strengthen the level of preparedness of IIR students in the fields of economics—especially Western—statistics, bookkeeping, and finance." Then the man cited Lenin, who predicted there will come a time when capitalists will come crawling to us, begging us to trade—then we will dictate to them our conditions. "In light of our successful economic policy in the developing countries our government considers it necessary to begin a comprehensive implementation of our economic interests in the countries of the capitalist world. The economic and political interests of our country are inseparable. Now we are entering a new era of our economic fight against imperialism, the fight which will destroy the capitalist system and put an end to imperialist exploitation and its main source, the United States." In itself, the statement was no news to me as I often read similar words in the newspapers. It was the second part of his speech that attracted my attention. The man's voice suddenly got louder: "It's you, the students of the Institute of International Relations in whom the party and the government entrusts the implementation of this policy. You will be the ones to sit with representatives of Western corporations at the bargaining table, you will work for our government in the developing countries to help them rid themselves of American monopolies, you will show the capitalists who is the master of affairs. To do all this, you'll have to learn how to beat them at their own game. You will have to learn more specialized economic and financial disciplines. Your economics teachers have already been instructed."

"What a bore," Nikolai said, turning to me and then to Victor. "Let's go get drunk after this." We all agreed.

But my attention perked when he alluded to his instructions as coming directly from the Central Committee. There was a shift to economic warfare, he said. The emergence of new nations among the former colonies in Asia and Africa was in harmony with the Marxist-Leninist doctrine that says that the Western capitalist system could not survive without sources of cheap raw materials from colonial holdings. Following this line of thinking, the Soviet strategists believed that the emergence of Third World nationalism could mean trouble for the United States and its allies. Soviet projections showed that the capitalist powers would become increasingly more dependent on Asia, Africa, and Latin America in the future, particularly for petroleum. The Soviet Union, he said, will be directing a massive effort encouraging these new nations in policies that will disrupt the capitalist supply line and destroy their economies. I didn't realize how far-reaching this new Soviet policy would be, however, until I actually worked to implement it in the field during the years that followed. For now, however, it meant that the Central Committee wanted our training intensified, especially for those—like myself—involved in the Institute's Middle Eastern studies. This was where most of the oil was and where—the Central Committee already had decided—a major, long-term economic and ideological campaign was to take place with IIR graduates on the front line.

The directive resulted in a major shift in our curriculum. Previously, the emphasis had been on diplomatic protocol, international law, criminal codes and local regulations of foreign countries, foreign languages, intelligence tactics, and military strategy. Now there were new classes in Western currency and banking systems—with a Marxist slant that depicted the Rockefellers and others pulling the strings of U.S. government and the world capitalist conspiracy. We also learned about business procedures, corporate structure, principles of international trade, accounting, securities, marketing, and labor relations.

There was special emphasis on the relationship between the United States and its industrialized allies on one hand, and the dollar-poor but resource-rich nations of Asia, Africa, and Latin America on the other. We learned how the industrialized countries depend upon the developing nations for raw materials—oil, for example.

As a Middle East specialist, I studied the oil business and its relationship to Arab politics. I learned it was possible to plan, stimulate, and arrange for certain conditions—political, ideological, and military—that would trigger a cutoff of supplies to a Western country.

The economic training was quite thorough and was focused upon the practical, day-to-day workings of financial operations rather than on theories. We had all the theory we needed from Marxism and Leninism—*Das Kapital* and familiar works of Marx, Lenin, and Engels gave us a framework that classified all these activities and told us that all the politics in these countries were a logical extension of economic activity. Our further schooling in Western economic matters, therefore, gave us no more the reasons how they worked than why they worked.

We learned accounting and worked with balance sheets and actual records from Western corporations, including Standard Oil of California, Occidental Petroleum, Pullman, Kellogg, Bechtel, and Fluor. We studied how a U.S. company comes into a Middle Eastern nation and secures contracts, who their agents are, how they interface with the government. We studied it so that one day we'd be able to act better, entertain better, offer better terms.

We also studied the economies of the developing nations closely. The East division of our class consisted of nine small groups—Arab, Turkish, Iranian, Indian, Cambodian, Japanese, Indonesian, Chinese, and Vietnamese. My group was Arab and we paid special attention to Soviet economic opportunities in the Arab nations, and how these related to the political situation in each.

This was at the height of President Gamal Abdel Nasser's reign in Egypt (where I was to be stationed later) and the massive Soviet military, economic, and technical assistance which had made that country Moscow's leading friend in the Middle East.

Nasser, though considered more of a bourgeois nationalist than a real socialist, was the acknowledged leader of Arab nationalism and the Soviet Union was his champion. The opportunity to play this role was handed to Moscow by the United States when it refused to sell arms, provide loans, and to help finance the Aswan Dam because John Foster Dulles saw Nasser as too much of a socialist revolutionary.

Part of our economic training was to identify and exploit the many similar—though less dramatic—opportunities for economic collaboration that would present themselves in our host countries. In countries like Egypt, where Soviet collaboration was already in full bloom, we would be managing economic matters and making sure the Soviet Union would gain the most political mileage from its involvement. The Soviet Union worked hard to establish a strong foothold in the Arab world, recruiting nationals, disseminating anti-American propaganda, and encouraging development of institutions along Soviet lines. I later became very familiar with all of these activities. In countries where Soviet influence was not as yet so great—for example, oil-rich Kuwait, where I was later stationed—there were opportunities to bid on development projects—roads, ports, factories. There was never any question that we could undercut the prices offered by any Western European or U.S. company, since the Soviet government could send technicians and materials at whatever price it chose. As long as the political objections of anti-Communist factions within the country could be overcome, a deal could be made.

We learned how to be good salesmen for the Soviet Union. We practiced on hypothetical, but very practical, situations. Here's an example of such a problem. A U.S. corporation has proposed to build a pipeline in a country. The local government has given that corporation a guarantee to develop the project, but the government is reluctant to guarantee financing and the corporation will have to put up the money itself. The corporation therefore is negotiating with the banks for financing. The bank demands a performance bond, but the party who would put up a bond demands the host government guarantee, and the latter procrastinates. The corporation is very unnerved about the performance bond because by law the amount of the bond is applied against the corporation's line of credit. Country X also happens to be a developing nation with a socialist-type regime. Given this scenario, we would then be asked to demonstrate how we would push the U.S. corporation out and get the contract for the Soviet Union. The correct answer would be to approach the government with a similar package, but offer to do it more cheaply and finance it ourselves, with minimum government guarantees and no investment needed. We would offer to bring in Soviet technological assistance and let advisors remain there on a long-term basis free of charge (the better to establish cadres there, of course). We also would offer easy, long-term payment, or payment by barter. Then we would act on the political front, finding out which key government

86

officials would be most appreciative of our support and promising them backing if they cooperated.

We knew we had an important weapon in political support. It could be an invitation to a high level official to meet the ambassador, or a trip to Moscow publicized by the press, or a demonstration of support organized by Soviet operatives among the locals. Or it could be a high level reception with all the local authorities invited, as was the case in Kuwait during the negotiations for the sale of fishing ships in 1971. The budget for such activities would be virtually unlimited, and no one would have to pay for it out of his own pocket, as sometimes is the case with tax-ridden Americans and poor ambassadors.

From what we were taught, it appeared that Western European and Japanese corporations would be giving us tougher competition overseas than their American counterparts. The Americans, particularly contractors bidding on building plants, roadways, and other industrial and transportation facilities most desired by newly developing nations, get little direct help from U.S. embassies and consulates. They get no guarantee bonds from their government, as do most European and Japanese corporations. U.S. business executives overseas also have an "ugly American" reputation for being boorish and pushy. U.S. companies go into a country without any coordination or direction from Washington. This was the opposite of Soviet strategy, in which Moscow's international political objectives were the primary goals in any economic enterprise overseas.

In short, the principles of taking business away from Western companies involved (a) offering better terms, (b) providing easy credit, (c) using barter whenever possible, (d) providing Soviet specialists cheaply or gratis, (e) offering long-range technical training for locals, promising that they will be thus enabled to run their own projects in time, and (f) most importantly, gaining and using political leverage with the local regime. Furthermore, the winning of a project isn't an end in itself, as it might be for a Western company, but a take-off point for a long-range campaign of increasing Soviet influence over the host country.

Each project is, in fact, a KGB Trojan horse. Once a contract is underway a group of specialists arrives. It resembles an army unit, but at its head is the KGB. Since the group has to do a good job, qualified engineers and technicians are involved. However, their work load is above their manpower distribution, for a quarter of the people would be concerned primarily with intelligence and internal security. These KGB officers would keep contact with their superiors in the embassy or trade mission, Morflot Merchant Marine office, or economic counselor office to channel information and report on recruitment activities. Their importance is in their free access to local and foreign contractors, ease of movement, and relative freedom from local surveillance.

If a contract is in trouble, the ambassador himself might talk with top leaders, or even request someone from Moscow to straighten things out. All communications are fast and there is little red tape.

This transcended mere opportunism and expediency in any one country, we were told. It was an important part of a worldwide strategy to promote Soviet hegemony that was developed by the party under Khrushchev in order to adapt to the realities of the post-Stalin era and now has been refined to great effectiveness under Brezhnev's leadership. This strategy is a perfect solution to an old Soviet dilemma, one that harks back to the split between Stalin and Trotsky. That is, whether the Soviet Union should concentrate its efforts on internal development or on exporting world revolution.

The cornerstone of this solution was peaceful coexistence—later, détente—which minimized cold war pressure from the United States and, more importantly, opened up trade with the industrialized Western nations.

With détente, the Soviet Union increased purchases of food and technology from the West, making it easier for Moscow to fulfill its domestic five-year plans and to meet the rising expectations of the Soviet population for a better life. The U.S.S.R. could have produced much of the technology independently and gotten by without the imported agricultural goods, of course, but it would have meant sacrifice and a much greater investment of domestic manpower and resources. As further incentive, Western countries—anxious to export to the Soviet Union—offered competitive prices and easy credit, even though the Soviet Union had a history of reneging on foreign loans— World War II lend-lease, for example. It was taken for granted among the MFA and other government officials I knew that the Soviet Union felt free to default on any current loan obligation if the party leadership deemed it in Soviet interests.

This easy access to Western industrial and agricultural wealth, in turn, gives the Soviet Union a free hand to further strengthen its military might, move into developing countries, and increase its global economic and political influence. The government sends technicians into a country like Afghanistan and helps build roads, pipelines, and schools, exchanges cultural and technical missions, and all the while establishes pro-Soviet elements in the armed forces, political parties, and religious groups. This is followed by a Communist takeover that makes the country a Soviet satellite. The process has many variations and proceeds at varying paces in different parts of the world, but nevertheless, the end result is the same.

The goal, as we were often reminded at the Institute, is two-fold: one, to bring the developing nations themselves into the socialist camp; two, to gradually cut off the industrialized capitalist countries from their sources of fuels and raw materials. Long before Americans were thinking about the possibility of an oil crisis, for example, we were learning about the dependence of the United States, Western Europe, and Japan on Middle Eastern oil.

To this end the organization of the Institute and the chain of command—from students and professors to KGB supervisors and directors, to the Ministry of Foreign Affairs *Collegiya* and the party's Central Committee—was slightly altered by orders from the Central Committee. A new IIR division was established, namely the Faculty of International Journalism. Again we had a meeting; this time about the increased importance of ideological warfare against capitalism and the defense of Soviet ideological positions in developing countries. Emphasis on propaganda through radio, television, and press and work among local political leaders, religious organizations, and correspondents was to be elevated to a new high.

This new faculty was directed by a Central Committee official, bypassing the KGB chain of command. Only the best of the brightest were being considered for admission. The first class consisted of only a dozen students. Even the chain of command for that faculty seemed different—students to faculty and faculty directly to the Central Committee. I am sure they even had less of a *stukach* element. There was something special about those young guys, an aura of mystery and superiority—like some sort of SS, I thought to myself. It dawned on me they were not afraid of anybody. I met some of these people later in the embasssies and consulates. They represented a new force in Soviet foreign policy conduct, less involved with conventional material gathering and more engaged in direct political subversion and liaison with local political, religious and media figures.

In 1966, in my fourth year at the Institute, I wrote a paper on the operations of Western oil monopolies in the Middle East and the problems of Arab independence from these monopolies. My professor, Pyotr Vladimirovich Milogradov, the top Soviet authority on the Middle East, invited me to his office to discuss my paper. I knew the old man liked me, because he once tried to fix me up with his daughter and generally didn't demand much from me.

"I like your paper," he told me after I sat down. "However, I must make some remarks. You missed an important point," he continued, looking at the pages, "the downstream operations."

"I'm sorry. What do you mean?" I politely asked.

"I'll explain. You describe well how Western corporations steal from the Arabs, how they fix oil meters, how the Arabs will take control of crude oil production." I kept on nodding. Milogradov offered me a cigarette. I took it.

"Vladimir, you have not suggested in your paper how the Arabs will take complete control and how we should help them." I got ready to listen. Milogradov took a long drag on his cigarette and raised his eyes to the ceiling. "The key is the downstream operations; that is, refining the crude, transporting it by land and by sea, and establishing the prices. The process of nationalization will be completed by 1970 and then we will see the oil-exporting countries getting together and saying, 'Enough, we will tell *you* what the price is.' You know the basics of the capitalist economy, its almost total dependence on cheap labor and Third World natural resources. So, if Third World countries, in this case, the oil-exporting countries, became independent and raised the oil prices, the Western world would get hurt."

"How would we go about it?" I asked moving my chair closer to his desk.

"That's what you were supposed to think about, and you didn't this time. I will tell you." He leaned back in his chair. "First, we'll raise the Arabs' awareness about imperialist evils. That is your first job. Then we'll get OPEC on our side and offer to the member countries what the capitalist can't offer—our sincere, profit-free friendship. Then we'll help them develop their downstream operations. Then they'll see they've been robbed blind by oil companies before and begin to retaliate by raising prices."

"But wouldn't it be dangerous for us? Suppose we need oil—we'll have to pay a lot for it," I hesitatingly interrupted.

"Vladimir, are you joking? We have probably as much oil as the rest of them all together. The only time we'd need it would be if we wanted to resell it right back to the oil companies." Milogradov burst with laughter.

I had no way of knowing if Milogradov was exaggerating about Soviet oil reserves; the Soviet government keeps this secret. But the Soviet Union certainly always had enough to be self-sufficient in petroleum and may have a sizeable surplus in untapped fields. Western experts estimated Soviet proven oil reserves in 1979 to be 71 billion barrels, second only to Saudi Arabia's 165.7 billion, but Soviet officials I encountered while I was there—including those working directly in managing oil production—said Soviet reserves were much higher than Westerners suspected. Most present production is concentrated along the Iranian border in Azerbaidzhan and Kazakhstan, but there are also large deposits in Siberia, including new finds in the Arctic regions.

Milogradov went on, more earnestly. "You know, I'll tell you more. Wouldn't it be great to have some kind of a problem, say, in the Middle East, like between Jews and Arabs. You probably don't know, Americans will always be on the Israeli side. You know whose side we'll take."

"Sure," I answered, "the Arab side."

"Right! We'll support them all the way against the Jews. Gradually they'll take control of oil production and Americans will be isolated." He looked at me seriously.

"Well," I mumbled, "what if the Arabs make a deal with the oil companies, no matter what the official position of the American government would be? Sort of a private arrangement."

"It would happen in some cases. But then with the rising prices the companies will also have to increase the prices. Who's gonna pay? People, ordinary working people. For us, either way it will work to our advantage. For them," he pointed out of the window, "how long

91

will the working class tolerate its increasing poverty at the expense of a few capitalists who get richer? That's the question. See, it's not *how* anymore. It's *when*."

"When is *when* would you say?" I asked, looking at my Omega. It was getting late and I had to get ready for an exam.

"Let's see. Nationalization by 1970 . . . a possibility of a conflict before then, or just about that time. Israel also needs oil and land, you know. If arranged with care, there should be a continuous conflict. Then in the mid-seventies the oil prices will skyrocket and by 1980 we'll have a recession and maybe an economic depression of the Western world. I'd say between 1985 and 1990 or maybe sooner the capitalist system will collapse or undergo drastic changes. You'll live to see it. In fact, you'll probably be a part of the machine which will help to make those changes." Milogradov sighed and said very quietly, "You are lucky. I probably won't see it."

"No, Pyotr Vladimirovich," I said reassuringly, "of course, you will. It's not too long from now."

"In any case, I am giving you an 'excellent' grade with a minus."

He handed my paper to me and I said goodbye, having put together in my head a picture of the operations I would get involved in. But I still couldn't believe that Americans would let something like that happen. I thought they were smarter than that. But soon, events would bring me to doubt this.

Soviet military might is seen as a way to check any threat from the West and, more importantly, to use as a political lever to scare Americans into submission and convince the rest of the world that it should take the side of a stronger ally. It serves to consolidate gains, as in Cuba, and make sure that once a country is in the Soviet camp it remains there. In the end, military supremacy will enable Moscow to dictate terms to an economically and psychologically debilitated United States, if Washington continues to allow its power to decline.

Much has been written about the comparative military strength of the Soviet Union and the United States and about how the Soviet Union has greatly increased its might over the past decade. As I had learned Soviet military science during my IIR training, and later worked with Soviet commanders and military intelligence officers, and saw Soviet weaponry firsthand, I had no doubts that Soviet military strength was second to none. In 1969 we had all become convinced that Soviet military power had far outstripped the West. That was the time when I became privy to new Soviet weapons, such as *shchuka*,—or the "Pike"—a missile capable of hitting ships over the horizon with a cruise altitude of only three to six meters, undetectable by radar and able to submerge just before hitting its target.

American leaders do pay close attention to Soviet military strength. How accurate they are in assessing that power is another matter and the subject of continual debate in Washington. Where American policymakers fall down badly, however, is in assessing the Soviet Union from a political point of view. Every move made by Soviet leaders has some political objective; whether the moves are military or economic, they must serve Marxist-Leninist political objectives. This has been intrinsic to the Soviet system since Lenin established it.

The U.S. approach to SALT negotiations is typical of this oversight. As a Soviet diplomat, I was trained to use treaties as political tools to carry out Soviet revolutionary objectives, not as ends in themselves. There was no compunction about making any kind of expedient agreement for propaganda purposes, with every intention of breaking it. The Soviet approach to SALT negotiations, I suspect, is in line with what we were taught was the correct Soviet strategy in all disarmament negotiations—namely that arms limitation treaties were to be negotiated for purposes of presenting the Soviet Union as progressive and peace-loving as opposed to the imperialistic, militaristic Yankees.

Moscow, in the view of this policy, has nothing to lose. If negotiations fail, it would be blamed on the imperialists. If they succeed, the Soviet Union could take the credit, but with every intention of continuing to do exactly as it pleased. If the United States complains that the USSR is not living up to a treaty, Moscow can accuse the imperialists of seeking to get out of the agreement as a pretext to continue their militaristic policies. The view in the Kremlin is that this is just another show for the benefit of the Third World, whose political conversion to Marxism-Leninism the Kremlin sees as the eventual key to destroying the capitalist powers.

Another factor that is generally overlooked in the arms debate is the sense of invincibility that everyone in the Soviet Union shares. There has never been any doubt in their minds that they are the most powerful nation on earth. This confidence even extends to believing

93

that nuclear war is not unthinkable and the Soviet Union would emerge victorious and still able to survive after such a holocaust.

Their twenty-five million people killed in the Second World War shows that they would make any sacrifice to protect the motherland. Such ingrained willingness to die for the country doesn't mean, however, that the Russians like war. Indeed, they abhor it, but they'll fight if they must.

This sense of confidence has been fostered by continual reminders from the media and by the extensive civil defense preparations that have been a part of every Russian's life for a generation. I was six years old when I took my first trip into a bomb shelter. It was five minutes away from our school. It was a cavernous structure, six stories below ground. We entered through a huge steel door and walked down wide, dimly lit stairs. There were steel doors to seal off every level, and the rooms on each level were similarly sectioned off like a ship. We went down to the fifth level where there were ample stores of water, dried and canned food, wooden benches, tables, and cots. There were forty such rooms, each of which could comfortably accommodate about twenty-five people. There are similar shelters near every large building complex in Moscow, so one is never very far from a shelter.

In addition to this, there is a system of highways that circles Moscow with all major thoroughfares feeding into it. This large circumferential freeway was built in the early sixties. (I spent the summer of 1963 as a laborer on the construction gangs, my stint with the proletariat.) A network of underground bomb shelters was constructed along with the highways and strategically placed at regular intervals. Most of Moscow's population could get into shelters within the twenty minutes it would take for land-based U.S. ICBMs to reach Russia. Missiles launched from submarines closer to Soviet shores—or for that matter from China—would arrive more quickly, however.

In the event of nuclear war, it is likely that these precautions would result in there being more survivors among the Soviet populace than there would be among the unprotected Western populations. This diminishes U.S. counterstrike capability, an important advantage that is not calculated in SALT negotiations.

It is probable, however, that a good part of these shelters would become tombs for their occupants in the event of strikes with 50 and

100 megaton bombs. Nor would survivors of initial blasts emerge from their shelters after a few weeks with much chance of long-term survival in an environment saturated with fallout that would remain radioactive for hundreds of years. Prognostications along these lines, however, are conveniently omitted from state-controlled public commentary in the Soviet Union.

From what I saw, the degree of real protection offered by civil defense aside, the shelters do have a strong psychological effect. The public, by and large, believes in them and is therefore much more sanguine about the prospects of surviving nuclear war than are people in the non-Communist nations.

When their leaders say that the Soviet Union could emerge victorious, the people believe it and suffer little anxiety about the Bomb. This, in turn, gives Soviet leaders a free hand to take what risks they see fit in foreign policy. Khrushchev, for example, didn't have to answer to public opinion about the 1962 Cuban missile crisis.[1]

I studied nuclear war tactics at the Institute. The training was quite thorough, and with graduation, I automatically was commissioned a lieutenant in the Soviet Army and became an officer in the GRU (army intelligence). Next to languages and area studies, the military training occupied, in terms of time spent, third place in our busy schedule. The department was located in a restricted area on

---

[1] During the Cuban episode, in fact, there was little feeling of crisis in the Soviet Union. At the time, I was sitting at one of my first lectures at the Institute, next to Victor Kudryavtsev, whose father was ambassador to Cuba. No one noticed the events as anything important; in fact, most people didn't know anything was happening. For us, it was a joke which our government and Nikita were playing on Americans, to see how far they could be pushed and how that young, handsome Kennedy would react. Nikita backed off and the incident was soon forgotten, although he was criticized for recklessness in general by the Party Central Committee when it ousted him in 1964. But that was mostly about his agrarian adventures. (For example, Khrushchev ordered a sweeping but poorly planned program to farm vast tracts of virgin lands in Siberia and elsewhere. The climate and soils of these lands were inadequately studied, and there were numerous crop failures, not to mention the wasteful diversion of labor and machinery from already productive lands. Another of Khrushchev's harebrained schemes to increase food production was to centralize management of agricultural machinery for collectives. Then he combined collective farms themselves into even larger "Soviet" farms and decreased the size of private plots which still produce about half of Soviet farm products. All this added centralization and collectivization further reduced incentives for farm workers, increased red tape and corruption, and lowered production.)

the second floor and consisted of four rooms with the walls covered by all sorts of diagrams and classifications of American, English, French, and German tanks, rockets, airplanes, and military maps. Our military instructors were all veteran colonels from the KGB, GRU, and the armed services.

Military translation is a special study of a foreign military language. While our classmates from American, English, and French groups simply studied related military jargon, we, the Arabists, had to study the military Arabic, because this language had a special vocabulary and word applications for military use.

"You will encounter situations when you'll have to interrogate Arab or Iranian officers and soldiers who don't speak English. They all will depend on your craft," I heard once from my military instructor, an old fox named Colonel Vitvitsky.

By my fifth year at the Institute I had learned how to handle most Soviet and some Western light weapons and was able to take them apart and assemble them with my eyes closed. We had to pass an exam on that. We also went through several survival sessions which took place in the woods a hundred miles north of Moscow. I learned how to communicate via field transmitter and shortwave radio.

Special attention was devoted to the study and simulation of tactical warfare. On all terrains, for all purposes, we conducted our little war games. This was in preparation for working as consultants and advisors to various factions of national liberation fronts.

And since almost none of us were later to become career army officers, the studies didn't concentrate on global nuclear strategies from the standpoint of military planning. Instead, we zeroed in on recognizing the types and the makes of the enemy's weaponry, so we'd be able to accurately report on its movement while abroad.

The strength of Soviet foreign policy is in its relentless pursuit of long-term objectives, so that occasional setbacks don't mean much. For example, in the Middle East, Egypt turned away from the Soviet Union and to the United States under President Anwar Sadat. Overall, however, developments in the Mideast are going according to Moscow's plan, a policy that was being shaped while I was at the Institute preparing to be a Soviet Arabist.

The long-term objective was to cut off the U.S. from the Arab world and its oil. The tactics involved continually fanning the fires of

Arab-Israeli conflict. With U.S. support for Israel, and Soviet support for the Arabs and its strong influence over the Palestine Liberation Organization, Moscow made friends while the U.S. was maligned as a colonialist enemy.

We were taught at the IIR that with this strategy, time would be on the side of the Soviet Union. One by one, the countries of the Middle East would come into the Soviet camp. The first would be the ones more inclined towards socialism—Iraq and Syria for example— where pro-Soviet political forces could be more openly supported. Later even the most avidly pro-U.S. regimes would either fall or come around—Iran, Saudi Arabia, and the Emirates. It is a policy calculated to keep Moscow on top of events in the Middle East and always in a position to take maximum advantage of the deep, long-term political currents there—counting on American ineptitude to do the rest.

A recent success of this approach was demonstrated in Iran. Moscow had cultivated good relations with the Shah but at the same time aided anti-Shah elements. Moslem revolutionaries had received cooperation and arms from the Palestine Liberation Organization, which in turn receives arms from the Soviet bloc. The Soviets also had ties to Iranian nationalists among the oil workers, whose strikes helped topple the Shah's regime and precipitated a new oil crisis for the West. When the Shah was overthrown and the Islamic republic established, Moscow was in a position to pose as champions of the Moslem revolutionaries, conveniently forgetting its relationship to the Shah. Only the United States, which blindly supported the Shah to the end, looked bad.

The lowering of production and the steep raising of petroleum prices is the fruit of this policy. Not that the Soviet Union ordered Middle Eastern nations to get control of their oil and raise prices. They didn't need to be instructed as to what was in their own interest. But through the pro-Soviet nations, Moscow could encourage price increases well above what the more conservative factions— namely the Saudi Arabians—had in mind. Outnumbered, the Saudis eventually went along with the policy. This was no accident. The strategy was formulated by the Soviet Union years before Washington realized it had an energy crisis on its hands. And what I was taught about it at the IIR was only the beginning. As I graduated to become a Soviet diplomat working closely with Soviet intelligence in the Middle East, I saw this strategy being implemented very thoroughly in the field.

The United States has yet to achieve a comprehensive, long-term strategy for dealing with the many-faceted Soviet juggernaut. The best effort Washington can muster is to react clumsily to crises. The Soviet Mideast oil gambit was already in play in the early 1960s when the United States was becoming mired in a Southeast Asian war that Moscow was to use to its advantage throughout the Third World.

As a student at the IIR, I was not aware of these U.S. weaknesses. Through press and classroom instructions, the United States—and particularly the CIA—was presented to us as being an ever-vigilant enemy disrupting the forces of socialism everywhere. The CIA was a bogeyman trying to overthrow our good friend Fidel Castro, manipulating governments, infiltrating, stealing socialist scientists, fostering imperialism, and spreading the bourgeois culture.

I fully believed that the CIA was a potent force, but as someone who despised the Soviet system, I thought to myself that anything that the KGB hated and seemed to fear so much must be good. So, the CIA represented the only real possibility of defeating that system. I only wish that the United States was as formidable an adversary as I'd been taught.

8: Nashe *and* Ne Nashe

The Press Club ballroom in the Moskva Hotel glittered with a *dolce vita* gathering of international celebrities, news correspondents, KGB, Soviet cinema brass, and other party bigshots, just as it had every other night during the 1963 Moscow International Film Festival. Tony Curtis was in front of me explaining something in English to a young woman. Not far away sat Claudia Cardinale speaking animatedly in Italian to some friends. At another table sat Simone Signoret and Yves Montand, both looking a bit glum. Montand was one of the most popular foreign personalities in the Soviet Union, and my mother, who adored him, would have been excited about seeing him, had she been there.

It was easy for me to tell Western celebrities from their Soviet counterparts, who were more conservatively dressed and appeared restricted in their communication with foreigners. I noticed Westerners mingling very freely among themselves. Not so with the Soviets. There were two types of KGB in the room—polished Soviet journalists, and the guys who seemed totally out of place. These were local KGB *stukachi* strategically located to keep an eye on their compatriots. They were easy to spot by their clothing: "Made by Novgorod Textile Factory," their clothes announced.

It was my second night at a festival cocktail party and I was blasé by then, trying to look as if I were a little bored. I had seen several of the films—many of the entries that year were Italian—and some postwar Soviet films that didn't insult the intelligence. One Soviet film, *Ballad of a Soldier*, was among the Russian "new wave" being fawned over by the attending Western critics in the mistaken belief that it presaged some loosening of Soviet censorship.

I had no trouble getting into the ballroom. I simply showed the guards my Institute of International Relations red card, with a heading that read "Ministry of Foreign Affairs." This door-opener worked again, as always. Besides, the guards recognized me from the previous night and waved me into the room.

Mercifully, this time I was alone. The previous night I'd gone with Nikolai Khlopinsky and we'd told the guards we were MFA officials assigned to a group of British filmmakers. Nikolai and I had left an earlier party to go to the festival. He was crazy for anything cultural, doubly so if it were Western. The trouble was he'd become too drunk to enjoy it—nothing unusual for Nikolai. He'd gotten to the point of making passes at the starlets and generally making a spectacle of himself. I decided to leave when he asked an Italian beauty to buy him a drink in exchange for showing her his apartment. I had quietly slipped away as he drew stares from the KGB men in the room. The next night I came alone.

I blended right into this glamorous crowd and I liked it. My latest Trevira suit was perfect. No one could see the naked lady printed on the back of my otherwise conservative silk tie.

It was a welcome break from the routine at the Institute. This gathering, I thought to myself, certainly would be classified as *ne nashe* by the Komsomol lickspittles who were the guardians of our Communist consciousness. From the official point of view—the *only* legal point of view—anything that smacked of unorthodoxy or of Western capitalist origin was non-Soviet, or, in common parlance, *ne nashe*—"not ours." This, naturally extended to disagreement with anyone in authority. Suggesting that your instructor was a senile pedant was *ne nashe* for example, as was abstract painting, not to mention hobnobbing with decadent Hollywood film stars. But here I was among them.

When I got to the bar I ordered, in my best American-accented English, an à la mode *nashe* drink called *Mayak* ("guiding light"), which was a concoction of brandy and champagne with an egg yolk floating on top. Then I began circulating around the room. As I headed toward the back, Simone Signoret and Yves Montand again caught my attention. They were arguing loudly in French. Montand got up and after some more shouting, which I could not understand, he turned and marched down the stairs, leaving her alone at the table. She sighed and turned again to look at the dance floor. Her expressions seemed weary, the way she looked in *Room at the Top* when Laurence Harvey jilted her. I made my way over to her table and asked her in English if she'd like to dance with me.

She seemed surprised, then smiled, "Sure."

I set down my drink and we took the floor. We made a bit of small talk. It was a slow dance. After a while I ventured, "Too bad about your argument; I hope it hasn't spoiled your evening."

"Ah, no," she said, with her inimitable tone of ennui. "These are things that happen."

We danced and I felt very classy, until I glanced over toward a darkened corner and noticed something that made me go cold. I escorted my glamorous partner back to her table after the dance and thanked her. As I walked away, trying to act nonchalant, I glanced toward the corner again. Standing there, talking to a strikingly attractive woman, was my old "German" acquaintance, to whom I had spoken in the Moscow subway two years ago. I caught his eye for just an instant and realized he had noticed me too, but he didn't register any sign of recognition. He was in an elegant black tuxedo. His companion looked Latin, probably Spanish, I thought. Her figure was stunningly draped, she had short black hair, full lips, and she projected a vivacious energy.

I didn't know what to do. I dared not walk up to him. With KGB all over the place, I could be noticed and tied in with this foreigner— that is, if I hadn't been fingered already. I made my way toward the door as unobtrusively as possible. I took the marble stairs down to the street level, all the time looking back fearing to see one of those guys in made-in-Novgorod suits behind me. As I approached the heavy exit doors I looked back again. I thought I made it out safely. No one was behind me.

I left the building, stepped out into Gorki Street, and checked again to see if I was being tailed. There was no one in sight as I walked down the dark street. I began to breathe easier. Perhaps it was a coincidence.

After I'd walked awhile, a taxicab came past and stopped in the middle of the block ahead of me. The woman I'd seen with my German at the park stepped out and the cab pulled away. She started walking toward me. I was becoming more and more excited as we came closer.

I stopped at the corner, next to a newspaper kiosk that was closed for the night. I took a Winston out of my pocket and lit it with my gold Ronson while she crossed to my corner.

"Do you have a cigarette?"

"Oh, yes, here," I mumbled, fumbling to get the pack out and offer her one.

"I don't believe it, a Russian smoking Winstons. I haven't been able to get these for a week, since I left Mexico." She was speaking in English. "Are you a Russian or not?"

"Of course I am." I was trying my best to speak proper British-accented English this time, the way they taught me at the Institute, instead of the American idiom I favored. I figured somehow it was safer that way, and almost pulverized my teeth trying to look and sound cool.

"By the way, your German friend says hello to you and sorry for not being able to chat with you. Do you remember him?"

I made a vague allusion to the many wonders of the world.

The woman said, "By the way, my name is Rita, what's yours?" And then all of a sudden, the words came out of my mouth as though I didn't have control over them.

"Vladimir . . . Vladimir Sakharov," I said with a pause and felt my heart drop. I knew what I'd just done was a mistake, but something told me to take a chance. My mind started working quickly, as always, when I got into a pressure situation. She giggled at my consternation and took another puff on her Winston.

She patted my arm. "Don't worry, no one else will know except me and my friends."

"Who are your friends?"

"One day you might want to get to know them. It's up to you. In any case I'll say hello from you to George. That's the name of your German friend. And this message is from him to you. Study hard, learn English and Arabic. That's your specialty, right?" I nodded. Without another word, she walked away. I just stood for a while beside the kiosk, confused and enchanted. But my fear came instantly, the fear of being seen.

I walked on in the opposite direction from her, turning corners and stopping and doubling back to make sure I wasn't being tailed. I hopped a trolley bus to the outskirts of the city. Then I took a cab, then another one. Finally, to test fate, I walked around Dzerzhinsky Square, right in front of KGB headquarters. Then I took a subway home. No one followed.

The episode preyed on my mind for several months. As far as the procedures were concerned, I was required to report it to the authorities immediately, as any contact with a suspicious foreigner must be reported. But I didn't, because I didn't want to. And nothing had happened to me. Even though I hadn't mentioned my first contact in the subway to anyone. Now the incident with Rita proved to me further that George couldn't have been a KGB plant, because otherwise why would Rita be asking me about my name? At least that was a relief.

This led to a more sobering deduction, however, that George was a foreign agent. With Rita's more overt suggestions, there was almost no doubt about it. In fact, the episode with Rita was almost comically reminiscent of the exaggerated warnings we had often been given at the Institute about how we might be approached by the CIA or some other Western spook outfit. These warnings would usually be delivered in the form of a lecture and a film at the Institute, presented by some old KGB officer. One film showed an unwary young Soviet diplomat being asked to help change a tire by a couple of sexy women, who would then proceed to seduce him for purposes of blackmail and eventual recruitment. My secret reaction to that one was, well, I should be so lucky. There were many variations of this theme—warnings of being offered money, against talking to the wrong persons, against sexual liaisons, or even worse, romances on candid camera, against nurturing *ne nashe* attitudes that could lead one to perdition. One had to be ever watchful.

And one was ever watched. Someone in my position was subject to constant scrutiny. First of all there were the *stukachi* among my fellow students, and then I never knew when I might be under direct KGB surveillance. The KGB had a dossier on me, as it did on every IIR student, and a few bad reports in it could instantly destroy any hopes I had for a career. If I voiced my opinion about the system to the wrong person, for example, I would certainly be thrown out of school, and probably sent as an army private to freeze my *Yaitsy* (balls) for two years on the Chinese border and maybe even catch one of the mortar shells that Mao's militiamen sent over periodically. For talking to Rita and George and not reporting it, my fate would be much worse.

But the awareness of danger—a midnight arrest, or a call on the carpet before the chief administrative assistant to the IIR director, or even a thought of spending the rest of my numbered days in a labor camp—didn't come to me then. The fear about fingernails ripped off, genitals smashed with a hammer, and an hallucinogen called Andaksin[1] pumped into my veins to make me fear everything around me and finally go insane came much later.

George and Rita left me with an impression of comforting reassurance. George was a man I came to admire for his courage and intelligence, a man who operated with a great deal of wit and style as if he were a character in a spy novel instead of a real agent whose life could have been on the line. Those who take issue with the U.S. intelligence community should nevertheless be appreciative of the enormous courage of agents operating abroad, especially in Communist countries. One has to have lived in the Soviet Union to fully understand the immense peril of operating undercover there in a society where everyone is watched and even the suspicion of subversion is enough to bring swift and terrible punishment.

The contacts with George may have appeared minor, even frivolous, and they certainly were brief. Even though they were two years apart and I was not to meet George again for quite some time, the incidents remained vivid to me. This is because an important message had been exchanged. Although I didn't fully recognize it at the time, it was the most important and necessary act in establishing our relationship. We had exchanged messages of trust. He had

[1] Andaksin, in small doses, is a depressant drug used as a sedative in the Soviet Union and Eastern Europe. In large doses, it can cause hallucinations and extreme anxiety, leading to paranoia and finally to permanent loss of memory. It is used to tranquilize Soviet mental patients. It didn't take much imagination to realize that many of these "mental patients" were judged insane because of their opposition to the system. As I was to hear later, they were treated heavily with Andaksin to help them change their ways. Although being treated as insane was considered a more lenient way of handling the politically deviant than executions or jail, I much preferred the idea of facing a firing squad to being slowly tranquilized into being a vegetable once I had been made to reveal all I knew and confess all my anti-government sins.

gambled in his approach to me and I had assured him his risk was justified.

By telling Rita my name and not reporting this second incident, I had taken a risk that George, with his sophisticated knowledge of Soviet ways, must have appreciated. Although we had said only a few words, we had signaled to each other that we were on the same side and willing to trust our lives to each other and cooperate against a common enemy. From the moment Rita walked away from me, George and I were allies.

This bond of trust did not exist among my contemporaries at the Institute, where the order of the day was betrayal. I learned quickly there that to survive you must trust no one, keep a low profile, act like a good member of the *kollektif,* but not to be too active in Komsomol. Still you never could be sure you would not be denounced at the next semi-annual evaluation session.

Every six months we would assemble in a classroom. There, the secretary of the Komsomol organization would read reports to us. We never knew what those reports would say. They contained very private information on each student's lifestyle, academic record, work in the Komsomol, etc. The reports were prepared by the Komsomol's secretary on the basis of the information which he picked up here and there, including from *stukachi.* I didn't mind the academic part, but the part where it said "he has a good socialist consciousness" or "he must raise his socialist consciousness" was bad. If someone had to "raise his socialist consciousness" he wasn't ready for a diplomatic career. The reports, read out loud, would make each student shake and tremble. Then they disappeared into the ever-swelling dossiers on us. These sessions were an extension of the institutionalized snitching that I had seen since elementary school, except that the game now was real and deadly. The victims didn't just receive demerits or have their parents summoned—their lives were destroyed.

You might think that as the Soviet Union's best and brightest young soldiers, we would have the trust of our superiors. On the contrary, I learned that the higher one climbs in the Soviet Union, the more one is watched. And since we were candidates to go abroad, automatically we were even more suspect. The Institute of International Relations turned out to be a luxurious, highly-touted military barrack. There was no barbed wire, the accommodations were comfortable, the privileges were better than those allowed the average person in the Soviet Union, but for me these advantages only heightened my awareness that in reality the Institute attempted to control every thought I had. The system told me, "you are wonderful." Therefore I was encouraged in my belief—derived from family and cultural influences—that I had rights, dignity, worth. At the same time I found myself subject to a psychologically dehumanizing environment. Just because I was fortunate enough to circumvent this system didn't make me like it.

On the contrary, I hated it even more. I found, conveniently, that I could embody that hatred in Anatoly Kuznetsov, the person who sat next to me in class. He was the arrogant son of a KGB internal security colonel. Kuznetsov was five years older than me, dark complected, thin, nervous, and not very bright. He went through with flying colors, however, because he had one quality prized above all others by our keepers: he was a *stukach*.

Anatoly enjoyed being a *stukach*. I was sure he took pride in being a part of a well-greased snitching machine. The system was organized simply and efficiently. In each group of five or six students there was a *stukach*. He reported on students to the larger academic group's *stukach*. Academic groups consisted of ten to fifteen students. That more important *stukach* reported to the class *stukach,* who reported either to the faculty *stukach* or directly to the deputy administrative director of the faculty. There were many *stukachi,* about fifteen in our class of sixty students.

Despite his *stukach* status Anatoly was no threat to me. In fact he attached himself to me whenever he could at parties and other get-togethers, tolerating my taste for jazz and Western apparel. This must have been due to my family influence, my high achievement in Institute studies, and my ability to gain commendations from the staff. In Anatoly's eyes, I was a man who was going places and would someday wield power. Therefore I was an ally to be cultivated. I could not afford to alienate him. I tried not to indulge him too much—in fact my aloofness only reinforced his perception of me as a member of the elite—but I had to play along with him to some degree, so I could find a way to neutralize him.

The duty of the *stukach* was to get something on everyone. The most common ploy was to provoke the naïve student into making ill-considered, controversial statements, especially about politics or culture. The *stukach* doesn't necessarily approve or disapprove, he only passes on the information. It goes into the student's records, and this information enables the KGB to manipulate him throughout his life. If a diplomat would refuse a secret KGB order, the black marks on his student record would be brought to his attention. This would persuade him to carry on. But as a rule, no diplomat would even think of refusing a KGB order, for everyone knows how that merit system works.

On the other hand, if a diplomat defects or otherwise misbehaves, there is always something in his KGB file to show that he was no good anyway. "Aha, we knew all along that the parasite liked to carouse with women, listen to American music, eat Viennese pastries, and drink cognac."

This was the situation I had to live with for years. It is difficult for me to communicate the anger it engendered in me. My goal in working so hard to enter the Institute didn't stem from any particular sense of commitment to the Soviet cause. It was just taken for granted. Turning the rest of the world into a giant Soviet concentration camp was the furthest thing from my mind. In fact, if there was any way possible I would have liked the KGB yoke removed from my own people. This being highly unlikely, my goal was to live a better life and travel outside the Soviet Union. It was like the young man who wants to go to sea to find adventure, though the process was far more complex.

Once I had entered the Institute, however, I found that instead of things opening up, my life became more constricted. I didn't like the fact that I was under the KGB thumb. But I had no choice, at least not until George came along. I hadn't made any rash commitments, but the possibility of fighting back had insinuated itself, ever so subtly, into my consciousness.

As time went on and I discerned the real nature of George's and Rita's contact, I found that I began to feel better. Instead of worrying about the dangers or feeling guilty about the disloyalty, I felt that I had seized upon a small way to ease the frustration of my anger. The thought of having such an important secret from the *stukach* pleased me.

The advantage of secret rebellion became obvious after what happened to my fellow student Klyushin.

Every so often the Institute's Party Committee (Partcom) had to make an example of someone. Klyushin always had been very outspoken. He once invited an abstract artist to exhibit his work at the Institute. Somehow he managed to fool the administration and get permission for the exhibition. The exhibition was cancelled as soon as it was opened and soon it was clear that the head of the Partcom, the obnoxious little tyrant Pavel Podlesny, had nominated Klyushin to become a fall guy.

The final straw was an article Klyushin wrote in the Institute's monthly newspaper. It was tame by non-Soviet standards. It just hinted at the lack of freedom of artistic expression—the kind of opinion that some freethinking types were encouraged to make during the brief and phony liberalization of the early 1960s.

Benny Goodman, the Harlem Globetrotters, and Holiday on Ice, which toured Moscow and Leningrad in the late fifties and early sixties, and other cultural exchanges of the period, inspired in the public what the Soviet authorities perceived as an "unhealthy interest" in American culture. The party corrected this situation quickly by again shutting the door to the West. But the brief exposure misled some of the more naïve among us into believing that there was a new spirit of tolerance that would allow more open expression of beliefs and more experimentation, especially in the arts. The party made it clear no such deviations would be tolerated. Socialist realism would remain socialist reality.

Because of this, Klyushin's article came under the local Partcom's scrutiny which in turn sent Podlesny to do the dirty work. Podlesny and the deputy administrative director launched into their attack as twenty of us watched, compelled to cheer as he destroyed Klyushin. Pavel was a short Ukrainian with small gray eyes, a baby face, and a cowlick of dull brown hair. Just by looking at you he could make you feel uneasy. He was dangerous and he liked it that way.

Podlesny's voice was charged with sadistic excitement as he launched into his tirade: "Don't think you are going to get away with your shit!" he yelled. "Where's your Communist consciousness? Where's your head? Did you lose it in your hurry to be anti-Soviet? Do you know what the party used to do with the likes of you?" Pavel chopped the air with his right arm. "The party shot traitors like you and your friends. You are not fit to be a student here. You are not worthy of representing the Soviet motherland abroad." Pavel turned to the audience. "I recommend to dismiss Comrade Klyushin from the Institute and forward his case to the appropriate authorities!" That last phrase meant certain imprisonment.

Everyone applauded loudly and I had to move my sweaty hands too. Klyushin was beyond anyone's help.

After the meeting I ran into Lyuda Boltina, the only woman student in my Arabist group and a close friend of Klyushin. Lyuda was a daughter of a colonel general in the party's Central Committee. The general was very rich and influential. Lyuda was one of my favorite people in the school. She was quite intelligent and capable, but a woman without her father's hefty influence would never have been allowed into the Institute. Outside classes, Lyuda led the freewheeling life of a rich hippy. Her large apartment in Moscow was always open to me and very often I'd drop by to have a drink and play on their Steinway grand piano. Lyuda was a nice looking girl, blonde, not too tall, not too short, with a warm round face always charged with energy. She constantly thought up things to do— parties, trips, concerts. She had a sexy, soft voice that reminded me of Doris Day's.

When Lyuda saw me she must have realized she missed the meeting. She searched my face. "Was it really terrible?" she said quietly. "Did they do him in?"

"Yes. What else can you expect? That cretin made a glorious speech. Made Klyushin look like a CIA agent." I reached out to try to console her but she burst into tears and ran into the street to where her chauffeured limousine was waiting.

The streets were empty by the time I left; the dark, chilly autumn evening already had chased most people home. I didn't take a taxi at the corner stand as I often did. I wanted to be by myself. Somehow, even the traffic didn't seem to exist. The wind swirled dead leaves along the gutter and there were almost no lights from the gray brick buildings to my right and the old mansions to my left. I could hear only my footsteps. Is this what it would feel like to be the last man on earth?

Why did they all approve of Klyushin's expulsion? Didn't they know they had sentenced him to death? (He ended up in a prison camp.) They would do the same as readily to me, surely, just so they could look good. This was the ruthless system I had to become part of in order to live well. I had to learn to keep my thoughts to myself. Even outbursts like I had just made to Lyuda had to be curbed lest they be overheard by the wrong person. I felt like the last of an endangered species prowling the street unable to reach my own kind.

That was 1964, a bad year for people I knew at the Institute. They were weeding us out, and they were coming down hard on the ones who remained.

Also in 1964 there was the defection to the United States of Colonel Yuri Nosenko, which resulted in his younger brother being expelled from the Institute. I saw the younger Nosenko just after he got the news of his ouster. "I tried to convince the administration that I had nothing to do with my brother's activities, but they wouldn't hear of it." I never saw him again, but heard a year later that he had become a heavy drinker. I found out years later when coming to the United States that there was a dispute in the intelligence community about whether Colonel Nosenko was a real defector or a "mole" and, in turn, whether Nosenko's information that Lee Harvey Oswald was not acting as a KGB agent in Dallas is accurate or a plant.

The dismissal of Nosenko's brother and the disgrace of his family, however, seems to indicate that the defection was real. The Soviets probably would have picked someone more anonymous to be a "mole"—certainly one whose brother was not an IIR student that they would then have to dismiss just for show, thereby losing two men instead of one.

1964 was also a year of uncharacteristic turmoil at the IIR that occurred when the school's contingent of Polish students went on strike. Twenty of them sat for three days in front of the dean's office. None of the Soviet students could figure out what they were protesting and we were all too wary of asking. The Soviet press said, of course, all was peace and joy in Poland and this convinced most Russians. We Russians had saved the Poles from the Nazis, given them security and money, and brought their students here to educate them at the IIR—what more could they want? That was the general attitude. The mini-crisis was resolved as suddenly as it began. The Polish consul general brought some men who dragged the students to Warsaw, where, we heard later, they were all sentenced to labor camps.

And then, Aleksander Karmen was kicked out for a much lesser crime. He got a girl pregnant. One day she stormed into a Komsomol meeting and denounced him. Karmen was the son of Roman Karmen, the Soviet filmmaker who worked on, among other things, a documentary called *The Unknown War* (recently shown in the United States) and was also noted for his Spanish Civil War films. I'm certain the whole thing was a setup and the girl was encouraged to denounce him publicly rather than getting an abortion or quietly marrying him. That's what usually happened under those circumstances. Because he was a Jew, Karmen was allowed no mistakes. Again the prosecutor was the hated Pavel Podlesny. "You are jeopardizing the principles of our Soviet morality," said Pavel, which coming from him was the height of hypocrisy. "You should marry the poor woman after committing such an outrageous crime." But Aleksander quietly stated that he didn't want to marry the woman and didn't think she was actually pregnant by him. Pavel thereupon called upon us for a vote—which was really an order having nothing to do with parliamentary niceties. Dutifully we all voted to exclude Karmen from the Komsomol membership and insist upon his dismissal from the Institute.

Later on at a party, Pavel was getting drunk and no doubt thinking about who his victims would be in 1965. I found myself in an unwelcome conversation with him about Karmen. "I never liked the sonofabitch," Pavel confessed. "He's a Jew and he got what he deserved."

I knew he was trying to provoke me into coming to the defense of my classmate. I said, feeling queasy, "Yes, I agree with you. That pregnancy business was very immoral."

Then an idea came to me.

I walked over to the record player, which was idle for the moment, and selected a very *nashe* record of Soviet popular music, the kind I hated most. I thought to myself, "Fucking *stukach* swine, you aren't going to get me!"

Turning back to him, I said, "You know, I think your party committee should pay more attention to the cultural aspects of the students' lives. I've noticed a very dangerous trend toward love of foreign music and foreign clothes." Pavel nodded.

"Why don't you consider putting me in charge of the Institute's orchestra?" I proposed.

"Good," he said, "it'll be your responsibility."

The reason I wanted to do it was that I'd wanted to meet a saxophone player, a trumpet player, bass player, and a drummer who were in the IIR orchestra. In three days I met with the

111

musicians and suggested that we go to somebody's apartment, have a drink, take along some girls, and maybe play together.

We went to Leonid Dmitriev's apartment, which was vacant since his father had assumed the responsibilities of economic counselor of the Soviet Embassy in Finland. The apartment was in one of those older buildings built in the Stalin era along the Moskva River. It was furnished with Finnish furniture, Persian carpets, and a cozy Polish bedroom set. I sat down at the piano and put my Courvoisier on top of it. Vera, whom I was still seeing at the time, stretched out like a kitten on the couch near the other girls. As I began playing a heavy blues number, Leonid joined me with his tenor saxophone; then the drummer, a young Jewish student from the Department of Economics, stepped in and, finally, an immensely fat and short bass player began shaking up the room. I'd say he was the most professional of us all.

Of course, in the beginning I didn't know whether they'd be receptive to what I was going to play, but, to my astonishment, they adroitly followed the blues harmony and rhythm. I was not alone anymore. We didn't say a word, just exchanged smiles. We finished simultaneously, as though we had rehearsed many times before. Nobody said a word. Then Leonid, imitating King Curtis, very coarsely began "The Birth of the Blues" and, again, each one of us knew it. I could see the white snow down on the streets and the Moskva River half grasped by ice. But playing that piece, we all felt far away from that bitter cold.

The session, interrupted frequently by drinks, lasted for several hours. We agreed to meet again the next week. In the morning between my Arabic class and the History of the Communist Party, I ran into Pavel, the party boss.

"How did it go? I mean, your getting together with the orchestra?" he inquired.

"All right, I suppose. I'll take this responsibility. They are very knowledgeable guys and play many Soviet songs," I stated in a tone of voice I thought would appeal to a party leader.

I wasn't a party member, and I didn't want to get on a blacklist. But I was a member of the Komsomol in good standing, and could discharge my obligations to it rather easily by volunteering to do various jobs around the school—sweeping the halls, for example— and thus earning enough merits to avoid having to take part in the youth organization's political activities. One was allowed to stay in the Komsomol until age 28, so I planned to keep my membership for another seven years rather than joining the party early as did some who were more eager. There was no onus to staying on with the Komsomol and I found it an easy way to keep up appearances. Pavel asked me to prepare several music numbers for an upcoming concert which was to be held around the first of May.

"I trust you can arrange the music so there'll be no foreign influences. Just before the concert we'll call on you to be censored by our committee."

I agreed, of course, but had no idea how we would perform Russian balalaika music, or how to sound authentically Soviet. I had to find a solution because the quartet members would rather quit than play what they were told to play.

The solution came from the bass player who said, "Let's announce just when we stand before the censorship committee, that we'll be playing tunes by young Soviet composers. Those suckers on the committee have never heard anything except the Volga River hardship song."

The censorship committee gathered in the large room with a Steinway grand on stage. The committee consisted of various KGB, party and Komsomol functionaries. After everybody sat down, I looked out to where the party and KGB were supposed to be, and said, "In preparation of the celebration of the First of May, the day of International Solidarity of the Working Class, our group has prepared several numbers for the concert at the Ministry of Foreign Affairs. The first is 'Moskva Today.'" As soon as I finished, I turned to the piano and nodded. We started with "You've Changed," a mellow piece, going into "Lady Be Good" à la Charlie Parker.

We were approved for the big concert with an enthusiastic commendation. For the first time in my life I was at the center of the attention of the party and Komsomol bosses. They liked our group and our music. They did not recognize the music we played, or that it came from across the ocean via "The Voice of America."

About a week later, when I was sitting at a lecture, lazily drawing pictures of various ugly faces, someone tapped me on the shoulder. "Vladimir, as soon as this is over, you are to report to the party committee's office." I was scared out of my wits. My face turned red and ankles cold. I thought they'd found out they had been tricked.

113

"Come on in, Comrade Sakharov, we're waiting for you." Two men were sitting at a desk covered by a green cloth. The others, whom I didn't know, were strategically placed in two chairs near the table. Their eyes were penetrating, and testing, that's all I could see.

"Sit down, please." I sat down on the only remaining chair near the pink wall. I never liked pink and green, maybe because green is one of their favorite colors and covers every table in every room where a party or Komsomol meeting takes place. And pink didn't go with it. One of the men addressed me in typical party jargon.

"We called you to express our sincere gratitude and appreciation of your excellent work in the field of mass propaganda. Soviet music is one of our party's tools to nourish in the Soviet citizens their love for our homeland and the Communist party. You have demonstrated your great capacity to honorably bear the flag of Soviet propaganda and fight the foreign influences still encountered in our society."

They ended up giving me a citation in my file (read KGB file) for outstanding achievements. I was relieved. Who'd think that "Lady Be Good" could do a trick like that?

The citation meant a lot to me. Now I was established as a responsible son of the motherland in official terms and this was written into my personal dossier. My loyalty was impeccable, or that's what they assumed. Anything that improved the security of my position was welcomed.

Looking back, the jazz hoax was risky business. It involved more than college high jinks, since being booted out of the Institute would have been extremely damaging. If ouster didn't mean jail, it would mean ruin, and none of us needed to be reminded what kind of life awaited us in the Soviet workers' paradise should we lose our privileged status. That was underscored strongly for me that autumn of 1964 when Pavel marched into our classroom and announced: "Everyone be at the entrance at 6:00 A.M. tomorrow with clothes enough for two months. We are going to dig potatoes."

The next morning fifty of us were transported by bus to a ramshackle village consisting of a dozen ancient huts, so primitive it was hard to believe we were only fifty miles north of Moscow. This potato picking measure was supposed to further strengthen the link between us and the working people.

We were settled in huts with dirt floors, six to a room. There was no indoor plumbing. The site was picturesque, located on the banks of a stream with potato fields on one side and woods on the other. There were few male adults in the village—most had found ways to escape by working in factories. Those who remained were old women and children, members of what passed for a collective farm.

The potatoes were planted in the spring by the workers from a nearby textile factory; we were supposed to harvest the crop. We would go into the fields each morning and dig them up by hand since the farm lacked any agricultural machinery. We would return to our huts late in the evening, eat boiled potatoes, drink milk, and swill vodka until we passed out, wake up the next morning with hangovers, and repeat the cycle.

By the end of the month, our party boss decided to placate what had by then become a tired and mutinous group of students. He said we were going to get some meat to make a big stew. The meat turned out to be spoiled and ruined the stew.

Everybody except Pavel Podlesny went on a wild strike over that meat, just like in Sergei Eisenstein's classic movie, *The Battleship Potemkin*. We didn't go to work for two days and I had a chance to ride a horse for the first time in my life.

Since there were no roads and no cars, we found an old horse without a saddle. My colleagues delegated me to ride that old horse to the nearest store, which was almost five miles away. I had a KLM flight bag on my left shoulder, SAS on the right, and a BOAC across my back.

It was raining hard. When I finally arrived at the store I saw a bizarre scene. There was vodka all over the place, some canned fish, a motorcycle, and a piano. Who would need a piano in this place? Obviously no one. The trademark on the piano read *Krasny Oktyabr* or "Red October," manufactured twenty years ago. I tried it and was surprised to find it in rather good tune. I gave a ruble to the fat salesgirl and pointed to the piano.

"May I?" She nodded without interest. I sat down and started "I'm gonna sit right down and write myself a letter . . ." similar to Erroll Garner's version of it, then got on with "A Foggy Day in London Town." I felt much better, but weird. Music always brought up a lot of emotions in me. This time, playing those tunes, I experienced a tremendous longing for someone and something completely different from the people and places I had experienced until then.

115

The rain was loudly knocking on the store's roof. The fat girl at the counter didn't move an eyebrow. This kind of music must have been totally mystifying to her since she'd probably only heard Russian folk music. Eventually I stopped playing, got up, and walked towards the counter.

"Twenty bottles of vodka and three loaves of bread, please."

The girl put the bottles on the dirty counter and said, "That would be fifty-eight rubles and fifty-five kopecks."

"Fine." I gave her another ruble. "Go buy yourself a ticket to a movie." My sarcastic remark was quite out of place. I felt instantly ashamed of it, and left head down.

That poor old horse was waiting for me in the rain. The mud in the dirt street of this godforsaken village just about reached my shins as I stepped down from the porch. The air was fresh and it smelled like freshly gathered mushrooms. I was wearing my Swedish windbreaker and Turkish jeans; all got wet through and through. Foreseeing a rather long ride back to the potato diggers' headquarters, I sipped from one bottle of vodka and tried to preserve my balance on the horse.

The vodka was of a really terrible quality—one of those specially made for consumption in the provinces. But I had to drink it, not only to get over the chill but because it made me feel better once it hit my head.

Progressively getting drunker, I thought how stupid the whole thing was. We were of no help to anybody, just a bunch of sissies, following the directives of the party organization of the Institute. I felt the intensity of hate towards us by the remaining villagers. Once farmers who possessed marvelous agricultural lands and loved to work them, now they had turned into indifferent slaves of the regime—a regime which took everything from them. I liken this to the process by which people are turned into animals in mental institutions. They eventually turn because of the hopelessness and insane environment in the institution.

The despair of those Russian peasants is fathomless. While someone in Moscow spoke about the progress and prosperity which socialism provided for all the Soviet people, fifty miles away (that's why foreigners are not allowed beyond a specific area) you'd find the following picture: A family of four—two children, a mother, and a grandmother living in squalor.

116

I had seen this picture countless times during my youth as I explored the countryside with my grandfather on fishing trips and mushroom hunts during which we often would stumble upon squalid settlements like this one. It was no surprise to me nor to any of my classmates to see Russian peasants living such dismal lives; we'd all seen it before in many parts of the Soviet Union and knew that it was the Russian peasants who had it worse than those in the other Soviet republics. I wasn't shocked that the peasants were so miserable; what jolted me was experiencing this kind of life firsthand so that it confronted me and made an inescapable contrast with the pampered existence of an IIR student.

This is the Russia that Western journalists don't see and not an image that the Soviet government wants projected, especially to the developing nations to whom it presents Marxism-Leninism as the key to social justice and material progress. Certainly there has been great progress; I witnessed postwar rebuilding and technological advances and all the other things reported in the Western press. But I also know of millions on the land for whom things are no different than under the Tsar sixty years ago. The people of that potato village were typical. And after the past weeks of picking potatoes with them I had a strong desire to do something for them, though I knew there was little I could do. At least I would have a drink and share some food with them, I thought, as my horse finally carried me into the village. My classmates greeted me as though I were a prophet. As the party began in our quarters I went to go next door to invite some of the villagers to share our food and vodka. The family next door lived in a one-room, hundred-year-old shack. The floors were dirty. Electric power was very irregular. The only cow owned by the family was taken away from them by the chairman of the agricultural cooperative to which they were attached. On a rainy cold day the blinking light of the only bulb made the dirty room ever more gruesome. Two children sat on the floor playing with a bony, flea-infested cat. The mother was boiling frozen potatoes on a clay wood-burning stove. The grandmother was too old to get up from the bed. Her dried up body rested on a World War II partisan stretcher. The father had died a year ago from too much drink. The smell of urine floated heavily in the air. All two windows were sealed to prevent the cold from getting in. No television, no radio. I knew that the nearest school was ten miles away. Probably, they have almost forgotten how to talk. Haven't bathed in many years. Potatoes were their only food.

The woman at the stove turned slightly towards me as I walked across the room. She was wearing a soiled satin dress and coal miner's shoes.

"What do you want?" she asked coldly.

I invited her next door.

"No" she shook her head. "But you could bring us some vodka here," she said.

There would be no use pressing her. I went back and brought her a bottle. She took it without saying a word. I returned to the party.

The next morning was terrible. There were hangovers, vomiting. But our stay was coming to an end, and I was looking forward to it. The only valuable experience in the whole thing was my realization that I didn't have much in common with my "roots" and I didn't care anymore for my motherland. The contrast was too striking—on one end were the power, wealth, and arrogance of the elite, and on the other, poor people. I had to accept this and live by the rules of the class to which I belonged. But later I found I did not accept such things lightly.

9: Blues in the Night

At least I could still call my social life my own. The clandestine jam sessions, the parties, my relationship with Vera, my circle of friends, my forays into Moscow's bohemian *demi monde,* my amorous escapades, all were fairly typical for a twenty-year-old university student anywhere. Except that I was not just anywhere and the contrast between the pressure for conformity in every other area of my life and the relative freedom of my social life greatly inflated the value of the latter. I indulged myself often and felt fairly safe in doing so because my parents and the authorities were tolerant of liberal amounts of carousing in the name of letting off steam. Like my classmates, I was pretty much on my own in deciding what pleasures to pursue in my leisure time. I knew the limits of what was allowed and had no problem keeping within them. For example, drinking was liberally permitted; beer was even sold on campus, and one could imbibe to the gills, but only in private, or at student parties. Public drunkenness would be frowned upon. Likewise, one could have affairs, so long as one was discrete about them and, more importantly, one's female companion was of good background, manners, looks, and able to keep her mouth shut on political matters. Hookers were taboo, as were *ne nashe* anti-establishment political friends of either sex. Neither were illicit drugs tolerated, but then, they were unheard of anyway. In general, the partying was fairly conventional by the standards of university students anywhere, but for me the merrymaking was more than an outlet. It was what passed for life itself.

The suddenness with which I was plunged from that hedonistic life to the squalidness of the potato farm had effectively demonstrated the absolute power of those who controlled my existence. By sending us to pick potatoes, the party bosses hadn't raised our proletarian consciousness, as was their stated intent. They had demonstrated their authority. Dostoyevsky once was marched before the Tsar's firing squad, then reprieved at the final moment. He knew what it felt like to be at their mercy. He also knew how the victims of the Tsar felt.

I had been warned too. I knew, from experience rather than imagination, what life was like for so many Soviet peasants—those "real people" my father used to love so well. Rather than making me thankful for my privileged status, however, it increased my rage at the hypocrisy and injustice of Soviet life.

Upon our return from the potato fields I found my Sybaritic pursuits had lost much of their zest, even though I plunged into them more desperately than ever. I felt claustrophobic, and to add to my depression, I was getting increasing pressure from my parents. They nagged me continually to find the right woman to marry. I'd need the right wife to help launch my diplomatic career when I graduated, and that was less than two years off. The party would give overseas posts only to stable, married men. This woman would have to be attractive, of good birth, but not be a troublemaker, nor an intellectual, nor Jewish, nor sickly, nor have relatives abroad. She should be tall enough for me—"After all Volodya, you are big and tall (I'm six foot three), how would you look with a little shrimp of a wife?" She mustn't be Vera, in other words.

I was not madly in love with Vera, but we shared friendship and affection and there could have been more, perhaps, if I had believed in romantic love. But I might have been unaware of my true affection for Vera. The thought came to me much later, as I often recalled the summer night we spent together in my place in Moscow. My parents were away in Sochi on the Black Sea, so we had the apartment to ourselves.

That night we went out for dinner and walked home along the

warm and friendly streets. When we arrived back at the apartment, Vera opened her purse and handed me a package wrapped in gift paper.

"This is for you." She looked at me and smiled.

"What's the occasion?" I was surprised.

"Nothing, just thought you might like it."

She stepped back into the darkness of the room as I unwrapped her gift. It was a book, a paperback, *For Whom the Bell Tolls* by Hemingway. She must have gone through a lot of trouble to dig up the book.

"Look inside the cover," she said very quietly.

I did. It was her dedication: "I Love You, Vladimir. Always. Vera." I didn't know how to react. Should I propose or run away? In confusion I thanked her. Now I had two copies of *For Whom the Bell Tolls*. We spent the night together. We smoked in bed and listened to Nat King Cole's "A Cottage for Sale" on my tapes. I almost decided to tell her I loved her and wanted us to be together to live the way we wanted to. But I didn't.

As it was, I began to play the callous youth and think about dropping Vera soon. And I started looking for a likely candidate to replace her, a woman who would be more marriageable than she.

Still, I was in no hurry. There were plenty of candidates. As soon as I told them I was a student at the IIR with a brilliant future ahead of me, most of the eligible women would immediately show a great deal of interest. The trouble was, that isn't the way a young man wants to attract a woman, particularly not someone who thought so much of himself as I did when I was twenty. If I had to find myself a wife, she would at least be one that was interested in me, not just in my position.

I was going to call the shots, at least so I thought.

If Nikolai Khlopinsky hadn't gotten drunk one night at an MFA party, things might have worked out differently. It was an official gathering, not one of our private parties. There had been a concert and some boring ceremonies, followed by a cocktail party that we were obliged to attend. I had planned to enjoy it as much as possible then go home to study. The party was held in a great MFA ballroom with huge marble pillars. As usual, the tables were lavishly set with cognac, caviar, and other delicacies.

It wasn't long before Nikolai was drunk. I thought he must have been drinking beforehand. Victor Kudryavtsev and I were constantly keeping Nikolai out of trouble, so when I pointed at Nikolai and then at the door, Victor immediately knew what to do. We got up, holding the staggering Nikolai between us, trying to make him look like he was self-propelled. The three of us, smiling and talking, made for the exit.

We walked Nikolai's lurching body past the guards, through the glass and brass door of the Ministry of Foreign Affairs Building, and stuffed him into a taxicab.

I turned to go back inside when Victor said, "Vladimir, I'm sick of this party. Let's do something else."

It was a beautiful evening, with the warmth of harvest time still lingering. Why not? The smell of autumn leaves, moistened by recent rain, was wafting across the Moskva River. I felt as though the whole world was mine.

"All right," I said, "I'll call Vera. She told me there'd be a party at one of her girlfriends' apartments tonight, only a few blocks from here. Let's go."

We crossed Smolenskaya Square and stopped at a telephone attached to the wall of a building. Vera came down and we headed to the party. Five minutes later the three of us were walking down Kutusovsky Prospect. We entered a nine-story apartment building across from the Ukraine Hotel.

We went upstairs to a small apartment on the eighth floor. We could see the party was already winding down. The room was crowded, but the conversation seemed subdued. Not much of a find, I thought; maybe we could check out someplace else. Still, we might as well stay for a drink. Assorted bottles of liquor, Georgian wines, mineral water, smoked salmon, *basturnma* (marinated, dried meat), *lobio*,[1] jellied fish, and kebab were sitting on a table. I helped myself to some vodka.

I could tell this wasn't our type of crowd. A warbly, domestically produced tape recorder played Russian songs by Vysotsky that didn't do anything for me despite their anti-Soviet lyrics. Vysotsky at the time was an "in" folk singer, popular both among high party officials and dissidents, just as Pyotr Leshchenko was during Stalin's times. The people who filled the room were smoking, drinking, talking. No one was dancing. They were neatly dressed in what plainly were

[1] Blackeyed peas simmered in broth with garlic, walnuts, and spices.

Czechoslovakian-made clothes, by which I immediately concluded they were local party bureaucrats and journalists.

It's easy to tell social status. At the top, KGB, MFA, and other party brass wear fashionably tailored Western European, American, and Japanese suits and dresses. At the bottom, ordinary Soviet citizens wear tawdry, Soviet, mass-produced gabardines. Local bureaucrats, party secretaries and other middle-level officials usually wear Czech- or East German-made clothes, which, though not as elegant as the Western imports, are a cut above the Soviet threads. These East European imports, though meant for the Soviet public, invariably reach no further than the local officials.

I was beginning to wish I were home playing my piano, when Vera introduced me to our hostess. Natasha Palladina was her name, an old school chum of Vera's whom Vera had mentioned occasionally, but whom I'd never met.

"So this is your Pharaoh," she said, glancing at Vera and giving me a teasing smile. She had large green eyes, with long lashes—cat eyes, I thought.

"Just a poor student," I said. Vera, already tipsy from hitting the bottle earlier, stepped away to pour herself another libation. "And you are the ballerina," I said to Natasha.

I wanted to talk more with this strikingly attractive woman. She was slim, with fine, long, silky, ash-blonde hair tied in a pony tail. The simple, tight-bodied blue dress she wore showed off her lean shapeliness. She moved with a ballerina's gracefulness and command of the space around her. She was tall for a dancer, about five foot seven or eight inches, with long, smooth-muscled legs. I tried to think of something else to say to her, but for the moment her attention quickly moved back to her date, a dark-haired, boyish-looking fellow whom she briefly introduced as Yevgeny before resuming her conversation with him. It was as if to say, "Your audience is over, Vladimir."

Not to be denied, I struck up a conversation with Yevgeny. We started discussing American music, movies, and culture subjects on which I could go on at length and in which Yevgeny displayed great enthusiasm, but naïvete. This gave me an idea. *All's fair,* I thought.

"Let's have another drink," I suggested as I saw him emptying his glass. "I'll fix you a special drink that my father tells me is very popular in the States."

"Great," he answered.

I put together a concoction of vodka, cognac, gin, vermouth, cherry and mint liqueurs, a Riesling, and a little espresso.

"That tastes good. What is it?" Yevgeny said grinning.

"This is what they call in the States *sarsaparilla,* a cowboy drink," I said authoritatively, thinking of the saloon scene in the classic western movie *Shane* in which Alan Ladd orders sarsaparilla for little Brandon De Wilde and is ridiculed for it. I'd seen the film at an MFA screening.

"Ah, *cowboy* drink, sarsaparilla." Yevgeny giggled, mimicking my mispronounced English. With that he took a few more swigs, then gulps.

"Good, God. We'll be cowboys, yes."

It wasn't long before, with the two of us talking and laughing, my refilling his drink, and nursing along a light one for myself, that the Soviet "cowboy" had downed two more "sarsaparillas" then had to gallop to the toilet, or, as our in-crowd called it, "the double-you-see," feeling superior for making an English pun.

The party meantime had come to a close. Natasha was bidding goodbye to the last few guests and Vera and Victor were ready to go home too. I volunteered to take what was left of the sotten Yevgeny back to his place and asked Victor to escort Vera home. Vera gave me a hard glance, but agreed.

The four of us made our way to a taxi stand. The rain was coming down in earnest now. Vera and Victor took the first cab and as they pulled off, I put Yevgeny into the next one, closed the door and waved the driver on. Then I walked back to Natasha's place.

She let me in without a word and we walked back into the half-lit kitchen. "Too bad your boyfriend got drunk," I said, thinking I was so clever.

She gave me that teasing smirk again.

"He's not my boyfriend, he used to be, but that was a while ago. You want to make another sarsaparilla, cowboy?" She spoke with a rapid, self-assured tone and precise diction.

"Thanks just the same, I'll have a vermouth and soda," I said. She made us drink. Smart, I thought, but didn't take her bait.

"How come you came back alone? I thought you were with Vera?"

"That old black magic's got me in a spell," I said, shifting to English, but got only a puzzled look for my allusion. I added quickly, in Russian, "Well, she and I are on the outs too." A small lie but for Natasha I'd have said anything.

"Is that so? She was telling me tonight what a great guy you are."

"Don't believe it." I was trying to get past the fencing and put my arm around her, only to knock over the drink that she'd set down on the kitchen table. "See what I mean?" I said as she proceeded to towel up the spill.

When she'd finished, she moved close and put her arms lightly around my neck. There was that smile again.

"You go through a lot of trouble, Mister sarsaparilla," she said, and planted her lips teasingly on mine.

I kissed her.

Now, looking back across the chasm of time to the twenty-year-old youth who was me in the arms of Natasha Palladina that night, I holler, "In over your head, Vladimir, *way* over your head!"

"And loving every minute of it," the boy seems to answer.

If I had any thought of deciding between her and Vera, Natasha disposed of that option with what I came to know as her usual dispatch. The next day she told Vera all about my after-the-party visit. The two had words at Natasha's place, after which Natasha telephoned me.

"Vera's been here," she said, "and made a terrible scene. You told me the two of you were breaking up so I thought it was okay to mention about your coming by last night. It was awful. My best friend. She's heartbroken. You're a real bastard. I think you should call her and apologize." Had a sarcastic note crept into her voice? I couldn't tell.

"Look," I said, "if you want to know the truth, it's you I want to see, not her. She's a nice kid, but it's going nowhere with us, she won't let go, so what am I supposed to do?"

"I don't want to be competing, especially not with Vera."

"That's not the way it is at all."

The way it was, if I had been entirely candid, was that I was thoroughly consumed with desire to make love to this blonde goddess for a hundred hours straight or until I needed a transfusion, whichever came first.

"Let's go out this week. I'll explain everything," I ventured.

"No."

"I want to see you again, when are you free?"

"Well, come over now and we'll talk about it. But not at my place. We'll take a walk."

125

Later, as we walked along the Moskva River in a stiff breeze, Natasha laid out her non-negotiable demands: No Vera, and nobody else. If I wanted to go out with her, we could try it for the next few months, but only once-weekly dates, every Friday. The rest of the time she would be busy with her work and ballet school.

Sarsaparilla cowboy eagerly consented to being thusly hogtied.

Our relationship in the next several months worked out to be sort of a cultural exchange. On our Friday dates she would drag me to a ballet, a concert, or the theater, forays into high culture that I endured mostly for the literate conversations and the ardent lovemaking that usually followed. Natasha was an intellectual. She was working toward her degree in linguistics at the Russian Language Institute; she also held a job in the foreign languages section of the Higher Party School in Moscow, her specialty being German, which she spoke fluently. She knew a lot about German culture, to which she was partial. She enjoyed German music, both classical and popular, and had a special fondness for the schmaltzy *schlagers*, German cabaret songs, sung by Catarina Valente.

Her father, Vladimir Palladin, was the minister of oil industries for the Soviet Republic of Kazakhstan and a very powerful man. He would send his chauffeur-driven limousine for her whenever they got together, which was only once every few months because he was continually traveling. Sometimes he would have her flown to Alma-Ata or Leningrad when he couldn't get back to Moscow. He had a palatial flat in Moscow, which was empty most of the time. He was a tall, distinguished-looking man with, it seemed to me, a condescending air. There was instant dislike between us when we met over dinner at a fancy Moscow restaurant. He talked down to me and I got back at him by asking him, as the conversation progressed, how he could have left Natasha's mother. That didn't make much of a hit.

Natasha's parents were divorced when she was very young and she'd done most of her growing up with grandparents in the small Cossack town of Labinsk in southern Russia. Labinsk Cossacks are known for their free spirit, big heart, stubbornness, and a history of survival under all kinds of regimes. The experience of coming to Moscow from that remote place more than likely gave Natasha much of her drive. She was going to make it in the big city and somehow redeem her birthright as the daughter of illustrious parents.

I got on better with Natasha's mother, although I didn't like her much either. She was a psychiatrist at the Serbsky Institute, a mental institution that serves the party and military but became notorious in the sixties as a place where the party stuck dissidents. This was part of the so-called liberalization of the post-Stalin era. If you were lucky, the insane asylum replaced the prison camp. Since I knew that liberalization was always more visible than real, the fact that the KGB was disposing of its victims in this new way made little difference to me. Whether they put you in prison, sent you to dig potatoes, put you in a strait jacket, shipped you to the Gulag Archipelago—what was the difference?

Natasha's mother, Ksenya, wasn't involved in the political-dissident area of the mental institution. Like most Soviet-trained psychiatrists, however, she saw no contradiction in treating political deviance as mental illness. Psychiatrists are only products of the societies in which they live, just like the rest of us, and many of them found it easy to rationalize. What in the West is viewed as a terror tactic is seen in the Soviet Union as a curative effort to help a sociopath adjust to reality. Natasha's mother never even used the term "dissident." Once a patient reaches Serbsky, he has already been labeled as socially dangerous and aberrant.

Natasha's mother was in charge of taking care of armed forces officers and high party personnel who needed detoxification and treatment for heavy alcoholism. She never lacked a full caseload.

She didn't talk much about her work, but when she did I understood the reason for her reticence. She knew too many skeletons in Kremlin closets. She wouldn't mention names, but she told me once about Comrade Novikov, deputy minister of foreign affairs, whom she was called to cart off. She found him in his MFA building office having a bout of the d.t.'s induced by having drunk a water pitcher full of vodka. She also treated several members of the Central Committee for alcoholism and drug abuse.

Unlike Natasha, she was fairly knowledgeable about U.S. music and literature. I spied her Charlie Byrd and Stan Getz records the first time I visited and borrowed them immediately, despite Natasha's uneasiness about letting me go off with so valuable a possession.

I began to bring my jazz records over to Natasha's place to fill what I felt was a great gap in her cultural education. If we were going to go together, she should share my passion for jazz and other things

American. I played Professor Henry Higgins to her Eliza Doolittle and felt obligated to make her ready for her introduction to the rest of my crowd, whom she didn't know despite her former friendship with Vera.

I steered our dates to American movies. Some good, current U.S. films were making their appearances in Moscow theaters then. We went to see *It's a Mad, Mad, Mad, Mad World* one Friday, sparing me from sitting through a Tchaikovsky concert. Now there was real culture—Sid Caesar, Ethel Merman, Jonathan Winters, Mickey Rooney, Spencer Tracy, Dick Shawn, and Jimmy Durante in three hours of California car chases.

Natasha didn't take to jazz right away, but she fell in love with Dean Martin and I figured that was a start anyway. At least he wasn't German. I would translate all the Dean Martin lyrics and she would smile quizzically as I uttered some profound lines about the moon, allegorically compared to a large pizza pie hitting someone in the eye, thus inducing the state of *amore*, adding that "it loses in the translation, you have to understand."

Remembering the negative reaction Vera had received when I had taken her to my family's party the previous New Year's Eve, I had been keeping my love life hidden from my parents, but I figured Natasha would meet my parents' standards just fine and thought about introducing her to them. It was getting close to the New Year and a big round of family gatherings and parties. Still I hesitated. I didn't know for sure they'd like her and if they did it could be worse. Instead of nagging me to drop her, they would be nagging me to marry her, I suspected. I didn't know which would be worse.

My decision once more was made by Natasha herself. One night when I got home, a little tired from a long day at the Institute, I found my father waiting for me. He was seated at the dining table, watching a hockey game on television and had a bottle of Erevan, an Armenian brandy, and two espresso cups in front of him.

"C'mon sit down." He pointed to the chair opposite him and poured the brandy.

"What's up, Papa?" I asked, pulling up my chair.

"Here's to my man," he said, smiling as he toasted me.

I didn't know what I had done to deserve this unexpected honor. I raised my glass and drank the brandy as if it were vodka, downing it in one gulp. My father continued to beam.

"You know what just happened?"

"No," I said, thinking that he might have talked to Brezhnev himself by the way he looked.

"Natasha called. And we talked very long," he said, handing me one of his Viceroys.

"Uhm," was all I could muster.

"She is a great girl. How come you've never invited her, never talked about her?"

"I don't know, I guess I'm waiting to see what happens."

"Don't wait! I want to see her. If she looks the way she talks you are a lucky motherfucker." He shifted, as he did frequently, into the Russian *mat,* or obscene slang language in which obscenities punctuate every sentence, in much the same way as American ghetto dialect.

"What did you talk about?" I asked.

"She wanted to talk to you, but I thought what the hell. We talked about everything. I like what she says. Very bright girl. Not like your . . ."

"Don't bring that up again. It's over." I interrupted.

"Yeah, I know. Good for you." I shrugged my shoulders.

"Is it true Natasha's father is minister of oil or something like that?"

"Yeah, it's true, Papa," I said.

"Why don't you invite her to the New Year's Eve party. I'd like to see her."

"Okay," I sighed, and called Natasha, who gladly accepted the invitation.

Our place was filled up with people by 10:00 P.M. when I excused myself and left to pick up Natasha. She was waiting downstairs when I arrived. "You're fifteen minutes late," she said, giving me a perfunctory hug and climbing into the cab.

Natasha was an instant hit with everyone. My father took one look and embraced her as if she were a member of the family.

"Come in, daughter!" he exclaimed. "Here's Natasha," he announced to everyone as I helped her off with her coat.

She didn't act embarrassed or shy but rather like a prima ballerina all aglow, walking out to take her bows at the Bolshoi Theater. As midnight 1965 approached she had made herself the star of the show, holding court all around. Lev Skryabin was talking to her at the moment and he excitedly hung on her every word and gesture.

129

"Next step is you take her to one of your Institute parties," my father said to me conspiratorially in the kitchen when everyone was reasonably drunk. "You gotta be proud. Congratulations."

I glanced through the door into the living room and saw Natasha sitting on the couch conversing with my mother. I got myself another drink.

The party got more and more lively as we drank champagne, played music, danced and talked. As the guests began to leave one by one, Natasha and I began to pay more attention to each other. She became quite amorous as we sat on the couch together in alcohol-blurred rapture and I barely noticed my parents going off to their bedroom. The couch made into a bed and the next morning I awoke in it with Natasha draped around me. Barely getting my swollen eyes open, my tongue like a bear's paw with a will of its own, I noticed my father standing there in the kitchen doorway in his bathrobe, grinning, saying "Happy New Year, my children," and toasting us with a little hair of the dog.

The show continued. The second act took place at my friend Aleksander Kalugin's gathering. Aleksander or "Sasha" Kalugin's parents were abroad in Africa. His father worked as Soviet Charge d'Affairs either in Urundi or Burundi or Ruanda or Ruanda-Burundi—I could never get that straight. The apartment was on a second floor of one of those new look-alike buildings on the outskirts of Moscow.

We came late. The food was gone and only three or four half-empty bottles of vodka and a bottle of champagne could be seen on top of a bar. I figured Sasha was low on money with his parents away.

I counted twenty people in the smoke-filled room, mostly the guys from my class and a few young women whom I knew from previous parties. There was no point of introducing Natasha to everybody since I assumed she'd blend in naturally. And she did. Anatoly Kuznetsov was the first. He glided to us as soon as a dance was over.

"This is Natasha," I nodded, and he took her hand and raised it to his lips in an elegant gesture of "I'm thrilled to meet you."

"Not nice of you," he smiled, "you've kept this beautiful lady away from us." I shrugged my shoulder and noticed Natasha's eyes wandering around the room.

Soon other guys came up and all of a sudden I found myself in a corner with a glass of vodka talking to my old buddy Kolya Kryuchkov.

"Look at that pederast," Kolya pointed toward Anatoly, who was already rock-and-rolling with Natasha. "Can't he do anything else?"

"You know it and I know it," I nodded, "he sure does." I was referring to Anatoly's prime *stukach* duty. Kolya smiled and emptied a glassful of vodka, "Cheers," he said. "Cheers to your woman, the best I've seen in years."

"Yeah, she's okay," I replied, satisfied she'd been accepted.

Kolya Kryuchkov was a streetwise, or rather systemwise, young man. He learned through his father's experience not to trust anyone. His father, a KGB colonel, was once counselor of the Soviet Embassy in Peking. As a result of the post-Stalin KGB cleanup, he was transferred from the prestigious First (Foreign) Directorate into the Second (internal) Directorate, i.e. he was grounded. Although Kolya never mentioned his father's change, I knew he carried a tremendous chip on his shoulders. There seemed to exist between us a silent bond of condemnation of the *stukach* system, although we didn't dare to express it. Six foot three, blond, blue-eyed, always with an arrogant look in his eyes, Kolya Kryuchkov was one of the brightest students in our class. He was aware of things and adjusted accordingly.

We talked some more. Natasha finally came over, accompanied by Anatoly. The stereo began to play "Autumn in New York" by Sinatra. I intercepted Natasha and we began to slowly dance.

"Tell me about these people," she whispered in my ears and put her arms around my shoulders.

"I told you already."

"No, I mean . . . I don't mean in general," she paused, "one by one . . . who's that guy at the door?"

I decided I'd give her brief personality profiles of these people. "That is Mikhail Tsvigun. He's from our group in the Institute. He'll probably go to Tunisia or Lebanon. His father's going to be deputy chairman of the KGB." I caught Mikhail's glance at Natasha.

"Continue," Natasha demanded.

"Okay. That tall red-haired guy is Gosha Martirosov. And his father is a big shot in the Council of Ministers. Also from an Arabic group." "Autumn in New York" changed to "I Bought You Violets for Your Furs." I thought furs would fit Natasha well, and went on.

"And that person is Victor Kudryavtsev," and told her about him.

"How fascinating," she whispered and bit my ear slightly. "That one is Igor Andropov."

"I heard about his father," she exclaimed.

131

My descriptions continued as we danced all the way until "For Only the Lonely" started. Then I decided it was time for me to have a drink and left Natasha to Anatoly who was waiting impatiently.

In the months that followed, Natasha and I frequently went to parties and other social functions together. I opened her up somewhat too, though we didn't become as close as I'd been with Vera. There was always some distance in the relationship. For example, I felt free to voice the usual complaints about officialdom that were heard in our crowd. But I did not let her in on my darkest hatred of the system. I played jazz for her, taught her about American lore. But I did not let her in on my fantasies about living as an American. She knew I wanted to travel and be a diplomat, but I never told her that I would not consider the idea of living permanently in the Soviet Union, even under the best of conditions.

Nevertheless, I was beginning to feel something akin to—if not exactly—personal contentment. I had decided to let things take their own course. On the one hand I wasn't sure about my commitment to Natasha, but I began to feel that I was putting together the ingredients of success now. The uneasiness that had followed the months picking potatoes diminished.

This was a quiet year in the Soviet Union. The ouster of Nikita Khrushchev and his replacement by Leonid I. Brezhnev in October 1964 hardly caused a public ripple. The people with whom I associated looked upon it as a routine changing of the guard and the only comments I heard were in voicing the hope that the new leadership would be a bit more steady at the helm than the mercurial Nikita. The world scene likewise looked calmer from the vantage point of Moscow. Everyone breathed a sigh of relief that Lyndon Johnson had defeated Barry Goldwater in the U.S. presidential election.

In May of 1965 I was jolted from this lullaby. The purges and threats against my classmates at the Institute had begun to gain momentum. In addition, my grandmother Maria was near death. Her heart troubles had grown worse and I was summoned to her bedside. I took a train to Kaliningrad and thought about my boyhood days during the twenty-five–minute ride. The walks in the woods, the stories of old Russia, the closeness during our vacations at the reservoir, the mad crush I had on the girl from across the lake, the mushroom hunts, the Easter meals—all those seemed far away.

When I arrived, my grandfather met me in the reception room, touching his mouth with his index finger. "She's resting." He hugged me and we walked into the living room which hadn't changed since I'd been a boy.

"Where's the nurse?" I asked.

"She went down to the store."

I heard a moan from the other room. "Alyosha, who is there?" My grandmother always called my grandfather by his diminutive name, Alyosha, not Alexei.

"Volodya is here." My grandfather led me back to the bedroom.

At first I had to restrain a gasp at seeing her bluish pallor; her soft features and vitality had given way to a gaunt visage of resignation. She smiled and her wrinkled hands moved over the blanket. "Come here, darling," she said with effort and I sat on the bed. "Alyosha, why don't you leave us alone for a while." My grandfather retreated, softly closing the door as he went.

I began to tell her that she was going to get better and that we'd all go to the *dacha* by summer and have a good time.

"Wait a minute, Volodya," she put her hand on my knee. "I want to believe all of this and I'm sure I'll be all right, but just in case listen to me. . . ."

I wanted to give her more reassurance.

"Don't interrupt. This is just in case. You never called me Grandmother, only Mama, ever since you were a boy."

I nodded.

"You listen to me more than anyone else. So whatever I told you, I know you carry with you, even if it may not always have been right. I have a responsibility toward you, which I have to live up to now."

I lit a cigarette, and she reached over and took a drag off it.

"Remember how you used to steal cigarettes from me and you thought I didn't know it?" She smiled. "Well, Volodya, don't marry Natasha. You'll be sorry if you do. Believe me." She met Natasha once, when we had visited before her illness took this turn for the worse.

"I know you, Volodya, better than anyone else. I know your mother and father think she is a good catch. But Natasha is not the sort of girl who can give you what you need. She is ambitious."

"Don't worry, Mama, I haven't asked her," I said, avoiding her eyes. She was tiring and I didn't want to prolong the discussion.

"There's something else I want to tell you. You've chosen your way to carry on your family's status. But remember, when you are abroad and you have a problem, there will be no one to help you. There will be more powerful, more cunning, even more intelligent people wanting higher ranks and prestige. Even your friends won't hesitate to betray you. This is how the world is set up. The only way you will succeed is to have courage not to sell out your beliefs. You will have to play many roles. This ordeal is going to take a lot of strength, but many years from now, you can look back and tell yourself, 'Hey, I didn't change, I feel, I breathe like I did when I was twenty years old.' Then you'll make your own measure in that screwy, corrupt, cutthroat world you'll be in. You'll be okay, and I'll be proud of you."

I noticed it was getting more difficult for her to talk and the last words came in a whisper.

"Volodya, don't be afraid of anything. Fear is for idiots who don't understand. And don't be fooled by promises people will give you because ninety percent of them don't amount to anything. Be tough, but remain soft inside. I know you are that way." Now her whisper turned to a murmur I could barely understand.

"Do me a favor, tell your mother to watch out for . . ." and she fell asleep. I stood up, slowly walked out, and closed the door behind me. I'd ask her later what I was supposed to tell my mother.

I got the news of her death in the morning of May 13. Fortunately, my father was in town and funeral arrangements were made immediately.

The night after the funeral about fifty friends and relatives gathered for the traditional Russian funeral feast in my grandparents' Kaliningrad apartment. My grandfather, as custom dictated, filled my grandmother's crystal glass full of port and put it at her place. The glass was to remain untouched until all the wine in the glass evaporated, then the mourning period would be over. Then toast after toast was raised in eulogy. When it was my turn to raise my glass I was quite drunk and couldn't say much. I just stood there crying.

The next morning I found myself alone in our Moscow apartment. The phone rang. It was my father.

134

"Sonny, why don't you get out and do something." His voice sounded far. He was still in Kaliningrad I remembered.

"You go to that party tonight. Get drunk or something." He was trying to cheer me up.

"Sonny, you can't mourn forever, you motherfucker, get out there." He hung up.

Suddenly I remembered I had been invited to two parties, Natasha's birthday and a regular get-together at Lyuda Boltina's place. Not knowing why, I decided to go to Lyuda's. I was still depressed and out of touch from the night before. I didn't call Natasha.

The Boltinas lived in splendor befitting her father's position as a member of the Central Committee. Their flat was on the ninth floor of a massive high rise, built in the overbearing style of Moscow University. It had thick stone walls decorated in high relief with scenes from the Soviet conquest of nature and Soviet achievements in agriculture, industry, and science. The Boltina flat resembled the interior of a castle, with ceilings twenty feet high, luxuriously decorated. The party was in a spacious dining room, brightly lit by an enormous Italian crystal chandelier. French doors opened from it onto a large terrace from which we could see the Moscow cityscape. The Steinway grand piano I played often on other visits was in one corner.

In addition to Lyuda's family and some of their friends, there were several of my classmates and our Arabist teacher, Vladimir Segal. Twenty of us consumed a feast consisting of Italian and Russian dishes cooked by Lyuda's mother and her maid. We consumed apéritifs, imported wines, after-dinner cordials, and more drinks. Most of my crowd was well on its way toward alcoholism, which afflicts sixty percent of Soviet foreign service employees.

After eating we migrated to the living room. I put on a Frank Sinatra record, "Just One of Those Things," that was brought by Victor Kudryavtsev, and followed that with an Ella Fitzgerald disc. I could hear her singing "Blues in the Night" as Victor, Nikolai and a couple of other friends, including Kolya Kryuchkov, sipped Beefeater and Cinzano, smoked Lucky Strikes, and talked. I mused over what my grandmother had said.

This American intermezzo was interrupted by someone playing a stirring Russian folk rhythm on a guitar. Lyuda turned up the lights and Anatoly Kuznetsov danced into the room wearing a Russian gypsy outfit. He danced up to the phonograph player, turned it off with a flourish, and whirled about in a furious folk dance. Anatoly loved to show off his dancing abilities at parties. Lyuda began to sing. Things were suddenly very Russian. I eyed Lyuda. She was pretty, but I knew better than to ever to make a pass at her. My instincts told me to avoid complicating my life with a romance that would cross status lines. Among Moscow's New Elite, hers was like a royal family, while mine ranked among the courtiers.

The Boltinas were of a select group whose members belonged to the Central Committee or filled other positions of high government influence. This group was second only to the highest social circle, the inner sanctum that was comprised of Brezhnev, Kosygin, and the other Politburo members.

Lyuda seemed in good spirits, and well recovered from her friend Klyushin's demise. After her song, someone asked me to play the piano, but I said I wasn't up to it. I knew this crowd wasn't hip to jazz. Their style was to act as if they were guardians of Russian culture and I wasn't about to play Russian songs. The trouble is, I thought, they preserve only the worst of Russian culture, and in a contrived, rigid manner that deprives it of its meaning.

Vladimir Solomonovich Segal rescued me by volunteering to perform himself. In a hoarse, melodic voice he sang several songs by the Russian romantic dissident composer Okudzhava, who had been banned under Stalin and who still didn't have state endorsement but was tolerated, having become fashionable for "in" circle members. In Segal's interpretation of the lyrics I discerned the hint of a jeer at the "in" circles themselves. His sharp eyes flashed a jibe as he looked at these spoiled, powerful kids.

I knew it was time to leave when Tsvigun went on the terrace and did a balance beam act along its railing. We watched as he walked, stopped, holding his glass of vodka, turned his back on Moscow nine stories below, and downed his drink. He jumped down to everyone's hoots and cheers, and mine too. And why not—he couldn't have made a more incisive comment on my life. I wanted to see Natasha.

I took a cab across town to her place and somehow made it to the elevator and up to her eighth floor apartment. She opened the door in a nightgown and gave me a push that sent me staggering back as I tried to walk inside. "Get out, Vladimir. I called you ten times tonight."

136

"Look, I can explain. . . ."

"I don't want to see you anymore . . . I waited for you . . . alone . . . you screwed up my birthday . . . I didn't even invite anyone . . . to surprise you . . . you bastard!" She slammed the door in my face.

I didn't see Natasha again for several months. That summer of 1965 I went on vacation to the Crimea, at a special resort camp for IIR people, a nice place that overlooked Yalta and the Black Sea. I went water skiing, played water polo, soccer, and took up with a local girl, but I kept thinking of Natasha.

When I got back to Moscow I telephoned her, and I proposed—in German. She always liked German.

"Vladimir, is this some kind of joke?"

"I'm serious. What's your answer?" I said, switching back to Russian.

"Vladimir, you've never said you loved me."

I answered by crooning one of her favorite Dean Martin lyrics in English that said I'd cry for her, die for her, snatch a star from the sky for her and if that's not love, it would have to do "Until the Real Thing Comes Along." "Do you want me to translate?" I asked, switching back to Russian. "It loses in the translation."

Our wedding, on November 9, 1965, was held in the *Dvorets Brakosochetaniye*, or "Castle of Matrimonial Contracts," which was not a castle but a large hall which the government recently had built just off the Prospect Mira. Only those getting married for the first time were allowed to use it, and it was very popular with young couples. It was of neoclassical design, with marble stairs and a facade of Greco-Roman columns. Bride and groom came out from their respective dressing rooms and into a large room decorated with kitschy romantic frescos; some music by Bach was piped in. Natasha wore a handmade ornate organdy white dress and I was in a new black tailored suit. My best man, Nikolai Kryuchkov, was holding the flowers. A dozen friends and relatives looked on; a woman civil servant who would perform the ceremony stepped from behind a desk and asked us if we were prepared to marry, then asked if we would promise to be husband and wife, to which each of us said our "I do's." She then pronounced us man and wife and a staff member brought out champagne for everyone to toast the new couple. From there we all went off to the reception.

For the wedding reception, my family had rented a two-story

restaurant in Moscow and invited 100 people. My father footed the bill. Her father didn't come, and I never saw him again. We consumed mounds of caviar, chicken Kiev, steaks, vodka, cognac, whisky, and champagne. We danced. A couple of fist fights broke out. They say in Russia that if there isn't a fight at your wedding, the marriage will not be a success. We also had a general at the wedding, for they say in Russia, "If there's no general at the wedding there won't be wealth in the house." I didn't drink at the wedding because I knew we'd have to stay until the last guest left and then carry a mountain of presents to the Chaika limousine, which my parents hired for the occasion. Everybody was getting drunker and drunker; the cooks and waitresses were getting smashed. Finally Victor Kudryavtsev and Kolya Kryuchkov ganged up against some man, whom I didn't even know. The fist fight and a bloody nose indicated that the party was over. Ivan Baikov took me and Natasha by the hands and said, "Just be good to each other. Don't give up your love." I knew he meant well. We dropped off our presents at home and went up in the Chaika to the *dacha* on Pirogovo Reservoir for the honeymoon. It was a road I'd traveled so often, I knew every tree alongside it. The passing scenery, now resplendent in fall colors, reminded me of carefree vacations and of going with my grandfather to cut a Christmas *yolka*. As we drove, I glanced over and caught Natasha looking wistfully at me. We really didn't know each other very well, I reflected. But that would work out. We had to be the luckiest couple in Moscow. Soon I'd start my career and we'd get to travel. Natasha would get the prestige and prosperity she'd craved since her childhood in southern Russia. I got a beautiful wife. My parents are happy. We make a handsome couple, with every appearance of upright Soviet respectability.

I could feel an autumn breeze on my cheeks and smell the fall leaves through my half-open window as we drove. "Ah," I said, "this is so beautiful. When we get there I'll show you a special place where I used to go to find mushrooms in the forest when I was a boy. It's really a magical spot. Are you happy?"

"Could you roll up your window, Vladimir, I'm cold," she said.

We moved into the Skryabins' spacious Moscow apartment upon our return to Moscow. Lev Skryabin's uncle, Molotov, was back in good favor with the Politburo. They were off to Indonesia on a two-year diplomatic assignment and gave the place to us. Natasha quit her ballet lessons. She had never planned a dancing career, she just wanted to dance as a hobby. For now, she was anxious to complete her linguistic studies, she said, and took a heavy schedule of classes. Meantime she kept her job in the foreign languages department of the High Party School. We didn't need the money. Like most Russian families, we shared funds, freely, so, without obligation, we had the backing both of my parents and Natasha's mother. Plus, when we married, it entitled me to a stipend from the school, since we now qualified as a separate family. I only drew the stipend for a year, however, then turned it down because we didn't really need it and I found that taking it offended my pride. We needed little money anyway, what with not having to pay any rent at the Skryabin apartment and our parents buying most of our clothes. In a system where basic needs—health care, for example—are provided by the state and where there are few consumer goods to buy, money doesn't mean much at any rate, and on top of that we were an upper class family, and like well-off families anywhere, we didn't worry about money.

Natasha kept her job because she found it interesting and she needed the experience to build a career in linguistics. With this schedule, she was gone much of the time—daytimes for her job and four nights a week for her classes. Meantime, I became very busy with my own studies. My last year was coming up and I was informed that I'd be doing an internship at the Soviet Embassy in Yemen. Between our two schedules we spent little time together. But that isn't what bothered me. We seemed less intimate now than when we had been dating. We didn't talk much and we made love even less. It seemed she would liven up only when we went out. Natasha had no interest in attending the private gatherings or jam sessions, or seeing films together the way we had done before the marriage. What little time we had for social engagements was cut back to only those gatherings that could benefit our careers.

That meant parties at Lyuda's place. Natasha loved those gatherings, especially dancing with Anatoly Kuznetsov. To my irritation, she and my ever social-climbing *stukach* classmate continued to hit it off. Anatoly was a good conversationalist and a terrific dancer, which I was not, and that part of it was okay. The two of them could gyrate on the dance floor because then I could sit around and talk to Victor and a few other acquaintances I'd been seeing so little of these days. There was nothing romantic about the attachment between my wife and Anatoly. It was just a chance for Anatoly to be part of our crowd and circumvent my aloofness toward him. I had a strong suspicion by this time anyway that Anatoly didn't prefer women, but I kept my opinions to myself. I couldn't even tell Natasha, for something in our relationship prevented that openness.

As the months wore on, I all but abandoned my campaign to acculturate Natasha into my ways.

"Please, I have to study," she'd say, for example, when I'd sit down at the piano. Later she might say, "I can't concentrate here, I have to go over to the school," and leave. But one day it dawned on me that she used only one book and she didn't have any writing pads. I asked her why she didn't have any writing pads. I asked her why she didn't take any notes at the lectures. The answer didn't make much sense and she seemed irritated by my asking her.

One night in May, shortly before her birthday, I went to Moscow University to pick her up from her classes. I wanted to talk to her. She wasn't there. I checked at the office and found out she wasn't even enrolled. I wandered around Moscow for several hours.

By midnight I was standing in the shadows in front of our apartment building. The traffic died down and only an occasional empty trolley car would thunder down the street. The street was empty. A pair of headlights pulled around the corner and a black foreign-made sedan pulled to the curb several doors down from me. I saw that it was a Mercedes Benz, an exceedingly rare sight in Moscow those days. I thought that it must be a foreigner or some bigshot, probably no less than Central Committee rank. A tall, elegantly dressed man got out and went around to the right side of the car to open the door. Another figure stepped from it and the two of them stood together for a moment. I started walking toward them. As I got closer I broke into a sprint. The woman shrieked and the elegantly dressed man was trying to scramble back into the car when I reached him. I yanked him around and slammed him back against the side of the car and in one motion smashed my fist into his face. "My God, Vladimir," the woman was screaming.

I'll kill him! The phrase kept repeating itself in my head as I held him for a long moment against his imperial German chariot. Blood streamed from his nose and bubbled from his mouth as he gasped for air. Then I let him go, dropping my arms and turning away as he retreated sideways like a crab.

Natasha followed me silently to our building. I heard the Mercedes drive off as we went inside.

We talked until dawn. Natasha's boyfriend turned out to be a member of a very select group of Soviet journalists called *pyatitysyachniki,* or literally translated, "five-thousand-niks." This was because they received a yearly stipend of 5000 rubles in addition to all living expenses, luxury living quarters, *dachas,* and a Mercedes Benz apiece. There were only five Mercedes Benzes in Moscow at the time. I knew, being a foreign car buff. This elite had been created by Khrushchev to supervise the Soviet Union's international journalism. Their duties included regulating all public information going to and from the country via newspapers, wire services, magazines, and other print propaganda sources. The Big Five to which Natasha's paramour belonged were not strictly journalists in the American sense; they were high-level KGB and party officials who reported directly to the party Central Committee. The Central Committee directs, selects, and channels the input and output of information and propaganda both domestically and abroad. The "five-thousand-niks" work as counselors responsible directly to the CC.[1] Down the journalistic ladder the party, KGB, and GRU place their agents, who work under the guise of correspondents for TASS, APN (Agency for Press and News), *Pravda, Izvestia,* or *Soviet Sport.* Local Soviet journalists are at the bottom of the ladder. They simply report what they're told to report by the party.

Natasha confessed to seeing him since before the marriage. "He taught me a lot; I wanted to further my education, get ahead. In addition to journalism, he is director of the Russian Language Institute at the university and we started going out before you came back into the picture last year."

I was trying to convince Natasha that, no matter how valuable a man he was for her general artistic development and intellectual

[1] Among them were the notorious KGB operator, Victor Luis; Melor Sturua, Soviet "UN correspondent" who got in trouble in 1978 with U.S. authorities for allegedly acting as a liaison with Soviet intelligence operatives in the U.S.; Yuri Zhukov, *Pravda* editor and my Natasha's paramour, whom the Party later sent to work for UNESCO.

betterment, she was my wife. We talked more. She cried a lot. I was surprised by her reaction—a complete turnabout from her usual cool self-assurance. I wanted to feel compassion. Her sudden display of vulnerability begat a desire to forgive which my anger quickly chilled. My anger said make her pay. Compassion would have to wait until later—and guilt. She begged me for pardon, promised to abandon work, school, all except devotion of her existence to me. And she could afford to do nothing else, for while divorces are easy to get in the Soviet Union, it was frowned upon in our circles as a mark of poor or untrustworthy character. But it was me she loved, she kept saying, she had been going to break it off with him, he was leaving for Paris anyway. I let her go on. I didn't care that her emotions seemed genuine. I wasn't going to trust my own feelings toward her any more than I could trust her words.

If it wasn't love, however, then necessity would do. I could afford a breakup even less than she. Divorce, especially so soon after the wedding, would be viewed by the KGB as a sign of instability that would certainly damage my career and probably result in a delay of several years before I was assigned any post outside the country. I would have to prove myself all over again. I'd be penned up and chained to a Moscow desk job. No London, no Paris, no New York, and no Bahrein.

We decided to go onward in public as if nothing had happened. And we promised to try to mend things between ourselves in private. In the end, I said bitterly, she could do as she wanted for all I cared as long as she played her role in public.

When morning came we made love.

The following day I discovered I had contracted a case of the crabs—a gift from him to her to me. Lousy fucking party, I thought. The pun loses nothing in translation from Russian to English.

Our lives went on in orderly fashion into the summer. I made the mistake of confiding in my father about Natasha's infidelity. "Whore, bitch, pig . . ." he ranted and raved. It only strained family relations from then onward so that I had to act as a buffer between my wife and my parents.

By July, Natasha announced she was pregnant. I greeted the news happily. This would change things. I looked forward to being a papa. My parents would be happy too, I thought. But Natasha said not to tell anyone because she didn't want to have the child. We weren't ready. I had to graduate. She wanted to get her career started before settling down to motherhood. She had already enrolled at the university, this time for real. No, I objected; let's have the baby.

I came back to our apartment from classes one day and she was gone. She returned two mornings later and announced that she'd had an abortion. Perhaps the child hadn't been mine, it dawned on me. Or perhaps she didn't know for sure. Or perhaps she understood better than me that we would never have known and always wondered.

I didn't fight with her. I walked out. I had to get away—from her, from the Institute, from my parents, from Moscow.

By nightfall I had consumed a bottle of vodka. I staggered out of the *dacha* where I'd spent the afternoon. I had another bottle under my arm as I made my way through a summer downpour to the boat landing on the Pirogovo reservoir.

I took the boat at full speed out into the blackness of the lake. I wanted to see the girl who lived across the lake, the one for whom I had my big crush at age thirteen. Her name, by coincidence, had also been Natasha.

After many hours careening through the wet void, I managed to dock the speedboat at which I thought was her landing—though in fact she'd long since moved from the vicinity. I climbed out and lurched through the mud and pounded on the door of a little house.

The early morning sunlight angled through the window and awakened me. I was in a strange bed in a room I didn't recognize. I sat up and looked outside and saw the lake. The family who was staying in this little *dacha* gave me black coffee. There were a couple and their daughters.

I thought of my grandmother. I thought of Natasha's lover. I had wanted to kill him, but why do that? He was not the enemy. I thought of going back to Moscow, but what was there for me to go back to? Yet I knew that I had to go back and resume my zombie role. That was the only way I could get out of the Soviet pen. Then maybe I could defect. No, I didn't want to do that either. That, from my viewpoint—a perspective no doubt skewed by official indoctrination denigrating defectors—was a coward's way out. That was for KGB bigshots who, after a career of being parasites in the Soviet

Union, went to America to sponge some more. Those were my feelings at the time, and this attitude stopped me from even considering an outright defection.

I looked out of the window at the panorama of blue water and forest. Russia was a beautiful place—for the squirrels, the deer, the birds, and even for the wolves out there. For them there was no KGB, nor was Natasha's lover their enemy. At least not the only one, I thought.

PART FOUR

Man in the Middle

10: Soviet Nose Under the Arab Tent

At the end of their fifth year at the IIR, students were assigned to six-month internships with Soviet diplomatic missions abroad. This would familiarize them with the day-to-day workings of the Soviet foreign service and with the politics, economics, and cultures of the countries to which they were posted. The student would be expected to complete his graduate thesis upon his return and include in it what he'd learned during the internship. Otherwise there were no instructions except to work hard under embassy or consulate supervision in our destination countries and to cultivate good relations with local citizens. Once we got there we'd be given further instructions, and the ambassador or other senior diplomat would assign us a job and an immediate supervisor.

Each internship post was selected according to a student's specialization. Among those in my circle, for example, Victor Kudryavtsev specialized in Algeria, and thus was sent there; Nikolai Kryuchkov, who'd been best man at my wedding, was going to Iraq. I was assigned North Yemen, This was because I'd selected the Arabian peninsula and the economics of oil as my thesis subject, and Yemen, at the southwest corner of the Arabian peninsula guarding the entrance to the Red Sea, was where the Soviet Union was most involved in that area at the moment. Moscow had no diplomatic relations with Saudi Arabia, nor with the other Arabian sheikdoms.

I was excited about my first assignment outside the Soviet Union but my enthusiasm was dampened when I learned that I would be accompanied by my *stukach* classmate Anatoly Kuznetsov. All of us were sent on our internships in pairs and I knew Anatoly would be doing double-duty as an informant the whole trip.

Even before I left for my assignment in March of 1967, I knew from my briefings that the remoteness of North Yemen—or the Yemen Arab Republic—belied its importance in the Soviet geopolitical schemes. North Yemen was vital on three counts. The first concerned the political situation which presented a special opportunity for the Soviet Union to improve its position in the Middle East and to demonstrate its solidarity with the United Arab Republic's President Gamal Abdel Nasser, who was at his zenith as the revolutionary leader of pan-Arabism. A Soviet-approved coup had recently deposed North Yemen's feudal leadership and replaced it with a military government headed by Abdulla As-Sallal. Sallal, backed by 20,000 Soviet-armed Egyptian troops, was trying to wipe out the remaining resistance by mountain tribes and establish a Soviet-model government.

North Yemen's tribal conflicts always interested the Soviets, for through those conflicts it was possible to manipulate each side. In the late fifties, the North Yemen heir-apparent, Ahmad Al-Badr, was made an offer: if he would terminate Yemeni ties with the United States, the Soviet Union would provide the country with all necessary aid, technical assistance, military help, etc. However Al-Badr chose to remain partial to the U.S. and stay even more loyal to the Saudi regime with which the Soviets had no close relationship. Thus, the situation was unsatisfactory for further Soviet advances.

But suddenly an opportunity presented itself. Al-Badr had a falling out with Nasser, with whom he'd allied North Yemen in the United Arab Republic. Nasser was getting irritated with Al-Badr and was thinking of disposing of him. The Soviets came to help immediately. Their overtures to Al-Badr stopped and they stretched their support to Nasser's protégé, Abdulla As-Sallal. The coup against Al-Badr in 1962 was successful, the royalists were pushed inland to desolate mountains, and the Soviets were welcomed as true friends and brothers of the developing republic.

By 1966 the Soviets were very active in the internal affairs of North Yemen. To insure the victorious advance, a fifth column had to be established, supported by the Soviets, Egyptians, and As-Sallal. Thus, one of the first of a succession of Soviet-dominated liberation fronts in Arabia was the Front of Liberation of South Yemen, with its leader, Abdel Qawi Magawi. The front, trained and structured to conduct clandestine operations in the oil-rich Arab Emirates, became the nucleus for new liberation fronts in the area which would eventually spread to Bahrein, Oman, Qatar, Saudi Arabia, and Kuwait.

The second reason for North Yemen's importance involved long-term Soviet economic strategy. What had happened in North Yemen made a good dress rehearsal for a bigger show someday in neighboring Saudi Arabia—infiltration of the government, armed forces, and business, followed by a Soviet-instigated coup resulting in an open, Arab-socialist–Soviet takeover. North Yemen was the first socialist beachhead on the oil-rich Arabian peninsula and provided a back door to the Saudi kingdom, Aden, Oman, and the Emirates of the Arabian Gulf. It was also the first Soviet chess piece at the gateway between the Gulf of Aden and the Red Sea and provided a foothold for Soviet efforts to control Aden—now called South Yemen—and Somalia and Ethiopia across the straits in Africa.

The third reason concerned the golden opportunity provided by the collapse of Western influence in the region. Traditionally the area had been ruled by the British, with some American participation. But the British were abandoning their naval base and colony of Aden and their patronage of feudal leaders in the Yemeni hinterlands. For the first time in history the Soviet Union was put in a position to implement its standing policy of establishing strategic naval control over the Indian Ocean.

The party and the KGB found, however, that they weren't moving into a total vacuum. Washington and London may have failed to see the significance of what was happening in North Yemen, but the events had not gone unnoticed in Peking. Like the Soviets, the Chinese understood that whoever could seize control of the resource-rich Asian and African nations would have world hegemony.

Therefore, chanting the rhetoric of anti-colonialism every step of the way, the two Communist superpowers were locked in a struggle to recolonize the Third World for themselves. North Yemen, in 1967, was a key battleground in the struggle. China and the U.S.S.R. were pouring military and economic aid into the region and had sent in large contingents of technicians, military advisors, and trouble-makers. When I arrived in North Yemen the Soviets, because of their patronage of Nasser, were pretty much in control.

The Yemenis, meantime, had been distracted from the main event by Sallal's Soviet-inspired exhortations against the United States. By the time I got to the new capital of Taizz, what little U.S. representation that had been there had been run out and the U.S. mission had been razed by a bazooka-firing Yemeni mob. Sallal had recently moved the Yemeni capital from Sana, deep in the moun-tains, to the more modern—by Yemeni standards—town of Taizz, 350 miles to the south of Sana.

The dust was still settling. The main Soviet Embassy was in Taizz with consulates in Sana and Hodeida, the port on the Red Sea. No one was entirely sure where the real capital would end up, but for now Anatoly and I were sent to Taizz to get our briefings and work orders.

We changed planes in Asmara, Ethiopia, and arrived on a Yemeni Airlines DC-3 in Taizz. The dusty runway was empty and a shack at the end of it was guarded by an Egyptian soldier. Mountains on both sides of the airport looked unfriendly. The embassy sent a car for us and, without formalities, customs, or greetings, we were taken to the embassy.

Taizz was just about what I expected, a small ancient town with narrow streets and a few one- and two-story buildings cropping up along the steep landscape. Even by the standards of the potato farm and Soviet south where I'd often vacationed, I found Yemen's squalor hard to take. One could see little to indicate that this land, according to legend, had once been the domain of the Queen of Sheba and the site of King Solomon's mines.

People crowded the narrow streets. Traditionally dressed in skirts, Yemenis carried *janbiya*, decorative tribal knives, and rifles; they mingled with the khaki-clad soldiers of the New Order. I felt conspicuous, a blond Slav in my Saville Row suit, towering above the natives. But I soon found the common people—as opposed to their new masters—to be very friendly.

Anatoly and I were given an office to share at the embassy. Soon, my first priority was to get away from him, and I took to walking about the streets to avoid him after work.

The stores in Taizz were centered around a small block of buildings surrounded by narrow winding streets. Foreign goods were plentiful, and one day I bought a gold Parker pen for my father and several bottles of French perfume for my mother. As I started back toward the embassy, I heard something that contrasted sharply to the Arabic music that constantly blared from Japanese transistor radios along the street.

I followed the unusual sound to a store where I saw an Arab sitting on an ottoman chewing *gat*. (Many Yemenis chew *gat*, a narcotic shrub of mildly hallucinogenic character cultivated on fertile plantations of Al-Jebel Plateau.) Two dozen or so records were lying on a dusty counter. There were Grundig stereos on display and one was playing a Brazilian bossa nova.

"Ahlan, salam alaykum," the Arab greeted me in a thin boyish voice.

I said "Hello, *alaykum bī salam."*

The Arab poured tea in a tiny cup and offered it to me.

"Shukran," I said, taking a cup. Within five minutes I bought all his records. Two were by Astrud Gilberto, whom I'd never heard, and I soon became a lifetime fan.

I checked in at the embassy after my stroll. The ambassador, Mirzo Rakhmatov, greeted me with a heavy Tadzhik accent. "How are you doing my friend?" he asked. Before being appointed as the Extraordinary and Plenipotentiary Ambassador (the usual formal title of Soviet chief envoys) of the U.S.S.R. to the Yemen Arab Repubic, Rakhmatov had enjoyed a comparatively easy job as minister of culture of the Soviet Republic of Tadzhikistan in Soviet Asia. As a Tadzhik, he came from a Moslem cultural background and was familiar with Middle Eastern sensibilities. His appointment was good public relations.

"Good," I said, and added patronizingly, "trying to be more instrumental in the embassy's activities."

I noticed a middle-aged man sitting on a couch. The glare from the window obscured his features, but he looked familiar.

"Comrade Sakharov, let me introduce you to the consul from Hodeida, Ivan Skarbovenko. He knows your father." When he rose to shake hands I vaguely remembered having seen him in Moscow. Thank God, I thought, he's my ticket out of here.

Skarbovenko was a gray-haired, chunky man with the thunderous voice of a football coach. Like any good coach, he was in town to scout help to take back to his consulate. He didn't need reminding that as an IIR Arabist, with fluency in Arabic, I could be of service to him. "My staff is small," he complained. "My vice-consul was pirated by *him*," he laughed and pointed to Rakhmatov. "My translator is worthless! My chauffeur is a drunk. Only the 'neighbors' are left. What do you say?"

I looked at Rakhmatov like a loyal dog would look at its owner. The ambassador waved royally. "Go ahead, Vladimir, help him out. He will do you some good."

I went back to my apartment which the embassy had rented for me and packed a light bag for my trip to Hodeida. I knew the weather would be even hotter and more humid there on the coast than in Taizz, but at least I would have some freedom, away from Anatoly and the large embassy staff. The month I'd been there was enough. I had a little time before our departure and took one last walk around Taizz.

I noted with disappointment that what was left of the American mission was deserted. So was the West German Embassy across the alley from ours.

I went past a volleyball court and the Soviet Embassy building through a backyard gate that led to the garage so I could put my bag in Skarbovenko's car. As I went through the gate, I could see Ambassador Rakhmatov watering his tomatoes in the garden behind the embassy. I nodded in his direction, but he didn't notice me. Just recently he had issued directives to cut down on embassy spending. The garden was the ambassador's prize project, a pioneering effort toward self-sufficiency. He had imported a full-time gardener from the Soviet Union, and had hired the wife of another diplomat to tend the vegetables and look after the chickens, a goat, and a cow. The vegetables were served at diplomatic receptions, the goat's milk was reserved for his personal consumption, and the cow's milk was used to make yogurt that was consumed with whisky.

I opened the door to Skarbovenko's dusty jeep and, as I was putting my bag inside, I noticed a book on the back seat entitled *A Guide to Germany*. I thought it belonged to Skarbovenko, or to his chauffeur. I slipped my newly purchased phonograph records behind the back seat.

It turned out there would be four of us going to Hodeida: myself, Skarbovenko, his chauffeur, and Vladimir Ivchenkov, who was introduced to me as an engineer of the Soviet economic counselor mission. As we walked toward the car I asked Skarbovenko, "Are you interested in Germany or will you travel there on your way home for the holidays?"

"No" he answered, "Why do you ask? I bake lousy pretzels. I fought the war against them. I even lost hearing in my left ear as a result of a contusion suffered when my tank was hit by a German shell."

I answered quickly, "I found a guidebook to Germany in your car. But I guess someone must have dropped it. Maybe embassy, whoever . . ." Suddenly I realized no one from the embassy had dropped it, but that it was a message for me. I felt a surge of excitement, remembering George, Rita, and the subway meeting with the "German." But who would now be contacting me in this place? How was it possible?

We drove 200 miles through the Yemeni desert to Hodeida, and stopped only for a sip of warm Scotch. "You gotta drink here, or you'll get sick," Skarbovenko declared.

Ivchenkov did most of the talking, describing local tribes, their customs, political profiles, dropping Arab names, and describing settlements. I couldn't understand how an engineer would have such a thorough knowledge of this place. I concluded that Ivchenkov must be the KGB resident in Hodeida. Every Soviet mission has one.

Hodeida itself was open to the sea and the dessert. In fact, one could hardly call it a city, for there were only three main streets covered with desert sand. There were several new, rashly erected buildings, mostly for Soviets, Egyptians, and Yemeni administrators to live in.

The morning after our arrival I went down to the local beach to cool off in the Red Sea. Before I had a chance to go in, however, I heard Ivchenkov's voice behind me. "Forget it, this isn't the Crimea," he said. He was wearing a shortsleeved shirt and gray pants. I noticed he wore a towel around his neck. "It's handy. Helps you wipe off this sweat."

Ivchenkov talked nervously and abruptly which fit with the way he looked: quite short and wiry. Ivchenkov's long face took on a fatherly expression when he advised me not to bother going into the water. But the heat was so unbearable that I went in anyway. The water was hot and extremely salty and I emerged quickly.

Ivchenkov invited me to his office for a chat. His two-story office and living quarters faced the beach. Westinghouse air conditioners kept the spacious interiors cool, as they did for the rest of the Soviet mission offices. The KGB was preaching Soviet ideology as the materialist wave of the future, but when it came to keeping one's backside comfortable, American technology, as always, carried the day. Ivchenkov smiled broadly as I glanced around the room. "This is where I work, live, and receive guests. Do you like it? What would you like to drink?"

"I'd love some espresso," I said, spotting an Italian six-cup coffeemaker behind his desk.

"How about some Scotch instead?" he pressed, "I don't have coffee. I have ulcers and Scotch is the only medicine, with mineral water, naturally." He poured some King George Scotch into a tall glass and looked at me questioningly. I knew he was testing me. "I'll have some mineral water."

We sat down, and he took a long sip of his drink. Shifting from easy hospitality to a more official tone, he said, "Vladimir, I'm supposed to brief you. What I'm going to say is not advice, it is direct instructions."

I looked at him the way I thought I was supposed to look at a KGB resident: seriously, understandingly, honestly.

"I'm ready," I said, lighting up a cigarette, and keeping that honest look of mine.

"Vladimir, you know why I am really here, but to the outside, I am an engineer at the economic counselor mission. My people in Moscow think you are a very capable person. Your family's credentials are spotless. Your father has a very special position with us. A very good man your father is."

I nodded my head.

"You've come here at the right time. The consul is just about to leave. You'll take his place."

At first I couldn't believe what I had just heard, for no one in his right senses would have an unexperienced young guy like me run the consular affairs. They could have called some seasoned diplomat from Moscow or someone from the embassy. Then I thought, the embassy's KGB *residentura* must have its hands full.

"Why me?" I asked.

"For the reasons I mentioned, and besides, Skarbovenko's replacement won't be ready until five or six months from now. He paused, smiled, and added, "So, I thought, I'd promote you. Mirzo Rakhmatov knows already. He's okay . . . You know, we'll work together . . . good experience for you . . . great for the record."

"I understand. Fine with me." I smiled back at Ivchenkov.

"Listen, along with the position, you'll get all those boring duties. But don't treat them as such," Ivchenkov went on. "Our Soviet idiots will come to you with their squabbles and complaints," he said, meaning the sizeable colony of Soviet technicians and advisors and their families. "And Egyptian military officers will court you, and the Yemenis will be on your back.

"But don't get too involved," he added, pausing for emphasis. "Do what I tell you. We would like to have you working for us after you complete your training period here in August," he said slowly and deliberately. "Is that when you are scheduled to go back to Moscow?"

I nodded.

"Well, maybe I'll keep you longer," he added. I immediately put myself on guard. No one was going to keep me here. I had to graduate.

He paused again to let it sink in, then went on, speaking more rapidly now. "Okay, I will need the following. Single out all the imbeciles in the Soviet colony. Give me names of Soviet specialists who, more often than others, get drunk and beat up their wives. We must clean up this multinational gathering of degenerates we call Soviet road builders. These people do everything to make us look bad, not only here but every country we bring them in."

He was referring to the Soviet colony which consisted of six or seven hundred specialists who worked on civil construction projects, road building, and agricultural developments. While military advisors were no problem, the construction and agricultural workers were not easy to control. For the first time in their lives they were taken out of their Tadzhikian, Turkmenian, Russian, Georgian, and Ukrainian villages and forced into a multinational whole. Their centuries-old nationalistic animosities suddenly exploded here in Yemen, resulting in fist fights, broken ribs, bloody faces, and beat-up wives. Later on, the Central Committee of the Communist party, having considered the Yemeni experience, would more carefully select and match groups of Soviet specialists for contracts abroad.

155

Ivchenkov then went on to the more important matter of recruiting Egyptians for the KGB. "They'll go home one day and work for us," he said matter-of-factly. The KGB, I knew from my Moscow briefings, was concentrating on long-range infiltration of the armed forces in the Middle East. "It is very important to get closer to the Egyptian military personnel. They will be withdrawing from Yemen shortly. Try to develop some important people here, and we'll take them over once they are back home in Cairo or Alexandria. And please, let me know anything you find out about Saudi Arabia, anything at all—people talking in the marketplace, radio broadcasts, whatever. Make it your business to keep those musical ears open."

Soviet propaganda in the Middle East emphasizes the common goals of the Soviet and Arab peoples. The propaganda, which all of us were required to reiterate in contacts with Arabs, made a point of advertising the fact that the U.S.S.R. had sizeable Moslem populations in Turkmenistan, Uzbekistan, and elsewhere. Thousands of technicians were selected from these minorities to go to Arab countries, and their passports were stamped "Moslem" where possible, even though the practice of Islam, like other religions, is severely restricted back home. The Arabs were our "brothers" too, because we shared the same revolutionary aspirations. And in practice, I have to admit, the KGB did act as if Arabs and Russians were brothers—the KGB was ready to treat Arabs with the same contempt and brutality it has always shown toward its own people.

"Use booze as your weapon," Ivchenkov went on, draining his glass. "Get them drunk; get them to talk. Then talk to me. I'll say a good word for you in the Center. You understand."

Hesitantly, I asked, "I've seen Arabs get drunk in Moscow, but don't you think it might hurt the development of a contact here if I got him drunk here where Islamic dogma is so strong?"

"Don't worry about that," he said. "You get him drunk, first, and once he's sinned in the eyes of Allah, that's it. Since there's nothing to lose, he'll go for the forbidden pleasure again and again. Plus most of them are high all the time on *kutt*. Just do what I say." Ivchenkov smiled approvingly at my pertinent comment.

Ivchenkov's predecessor, Colonel Shelenkov, had made a big score with the inebriation tactic not too long ago, I learned. He'd taken the Yemeni deputy minister of foreign affairs to his apartment and gotten him so drunk he passed out for a couple of hours. In the meantime, the minister's briefcase was opened, sensitive documents concerning Egyptian-Yemeni military agreements and plans were removed, photographed, and put back. Then the minister himself was photographed, sprawled on the couch, half-undressed, and surrounded by empty bottles.

Later the KGB "persuaded" the minister to cooperate. He was told that if he didn't the photos would fall into the hands of the press and the sensitive materials in the documents—which could have compromised Sallal with the Yemeni populace—would be leaked. The official capitulated and the KGB thus received valuable information about such matters as closed-door decisions of the Arab League—and activities of anti-Saudi tribal groups on the border.

Our conversation seemed to have exhausted itself and we fell silent for a moment. Then Ivchenkov looked right into my eyes and made it clear by his expression—as if I didn't know already—that he was boss. There was no question I'd been drafted into the service of the KGB. "There will be special assignments for you. I'll tell you about it every time there's need."

He poured himself another Scotch. "I know your training will make you a good Arab interrogator. One thing you must learn, though, is to drive the desert well."

"I'd love to. I mean driving and all," I said, looking for any chance to get off on my own.

Ivchenkov continued, his voice darkening, "Vladimir, don't miss anything. If you do, you'll live for the rest of your life like a poor Jew. How's that?" He put his legs on the table, leaned back and laughed. "Like a shit-fly trying to get out of a sealed jar."

Back at my office in the consulate, a hundred yards up the road from Ivchenkov's quarters, I turned up the air conditioner and shuffled through some papers, all the while thinking about my predicament. I looked out the window behind me which was sealed with Scotch tape to keep out the heat. All I could see was a hotel for Egyptian officers and, beyond it, the Red Sea. There was nothing else, except dust everywhere, even on the horizon. Looking out at this, I already felt like a fly in a bottle.

After a while, I heard the gurgling sounds of a loudspeaker coming down the street. A Soviet-made, Jeep-type vehicle with two Arabs inside drove by. Loudspeakers mounted on top blared slogans in

Russian and Arabic. "Down with Soviet imperialists," they said at deafening volume. "Soviets betray Arabs—Soviets go home."

Doing my duty, I rushed outside. Seeing me, the driver speeded up, but I managed to jot down his license number as the jeep careened away. The sound truck was a familiar annoyance to Soviets and their families. It would show up at all hours, driven by Chinese or Arabs who worked for the Chinese, honking in the wee hours and waking everyone with Maoist and Anti-Soviet slogans. The whole colony was in a rage about it and everyone wanted to find the center of these subversive operations.

Getting something on the Chinese, I realized, would solve a lot of my problems. It would score points with Ivchenkov and keep him at bay, and it would enable me to move about more freely. I set to work finding out more about the Chinese presence, and within a week I learned that there were about a hundred Chinese specialists in the vicinity, most of them working on two projects—building a new road from Hodeida to Sana, and collecting scrap metal (mainly old barrels) that they trucked to ships docked in Hodeida to be ferried back to China.

I didn't doubt the legitimacy of the road-building project, but the scrap metal operation aroused my suspicions. I couldn't see any profit in hauling the old barrels. It was taking the Chinese about two months to load each ship and even then the holds would be half empty when the ships sailed. I decided to investigate this operation.

My starting point was the headquarters for the scrap metal operation, an army shack with a small generator, a tall radio antenna, and a garage on the outskirts of Hodeida. I drove one of the consulate's Volga sedans to a side street nearby and walked to where I had a good view of the place. I hid behind what remained of an old stone wall. The stones radiated unbearable heat and as I stood on the sand, I felt the soles of my sandals burning. Fearing I would be spotted, I didn't move.

A few Chinese appeared to be living in the shack, but there was little activity. I kept up this surveillance for several days with little results, except becoming acclimated to the heat and humidity. Finally something interesting happened. A car, which I knew belonged to the deputy governor of Hodeida, drove up and pulled into the garage. I couldn't see what went on in the garage, but after a while the car pulled out and drove off. Later it came back again,

158

going into the garage, then driving off once more, taking a road that led away from town and which I knew led to an abandoned airport on a peninsula that jutted into the Red Sea. This happened on a Tuesday, and again on the following Thursday.

At dusk the next Tuesday, I drove to the airstrip. It was only about two miles from the consulate. The sunset didn't bring much relief from the heat. The hot moisture hung suspended in the air and the jellylike sea reflected smudged yellow and gray colors of unblinking stars. When I made sure I was on the right track I stopped the car. An intense darkness surrounded me. Somewhere far away in the sea I could see two ships' lights. The city behind me was dark and only a few road lights punctured the darkness. The lights didn't move. No one followed. I sat still for awhile, listening and looking. Then I started the engine and proceeded slowly with the lights out. I knew the rest of the road very well.

When I arrived at the airstrip, it was pitch black; there were no people or cars in sight. I parked my Volga behind a rusty hangar. An old, rotting stairway led to an observation platform atop the hangar and I climbed up to get a better view.

Just as I stepped out on the platform, I saw a pair of headlights come up the road, pull to a stop at the end of the runway, and blink off. Ten minutes passed and by now it was too dark to see much of what was happening, but I could make out some people moving about. Then the headlights blinked back on and the car pulled away. I went back to my car and drove slowly to the spot where the other car had stopped. I got out and shined a flashlight around.

I noticed a spot where the fine layer of sand that covered the pavement seemed thinner, and I caught a glint of metal. Walking over to it, I discovered a manhole-size concrete plate. I got a tire wrench from the car and opened a hatch to a cement-lined hole. A metal ladder bolted to the side led downward as far as I could see with the flashlight. I climbed down carefully.

When I reached bottom it was so wonderfully cool that I stopped for a moment. I was in a large room that reminded me of one of those bomb shelters back in Moscow. Two commercial refrigerators stood against one wall. The other walls were lined with unmarked, wooden packing cases.

I noticed one partially opened crate and peered inside. It was filled with Soviet-made Kalashnikov machine guns. I checked a few other

159

cases. There were grenades, bazookas, and all types of small arms, enough to start a small guerilla war.

I quietly climbed up the ladder and was relieved to find the strip still deserted when I poked my head above ground. I replaced the hatch and drove back to the consulate.

11: Dues in the Desert

I immediately went to Ivchenkov when I got back. But before I could tell him about my find, he waved a cable in front of me. "Dance, dance for us," he shouted, "I've got something you might want." When a Russian receives a telegram, it's a custom to ask him to dance if the news is good. I tore open the cable, thinking that it might be news about Natasha. She had been six months pregnant when I left Moscow and I figured the baby had come. Instead the cable read: "Our baby will come soon. I wish you were with me. I will wait for you. Love, Natasha." I wished I was back in Moscow.

"Have a drink, let's celebrate," Ivchenkov said. "I will be your baby's godfather." *So it can grow up and work for the KGB,* I thought.

Only now I noticed three attractive women sitting in the room.

"Let me introduce Lena, Irina, and Rita," Ivchenkov said. "They are Aeroflot stewardesses. This is their first trip here."

"Wonderful," I said sourly, and went over to make myself a drink.

"Are you upset?"

"You're damn right. You'd be too if you'd seen what I did."

Ivchenkov turned down the Ray Connif tape on his Phillips. He quickly dismissed the three stewardesses and I proceeded to relate my news.

161

"Do I do anything now?" I asked.

"No, just look around."

"Look around for whom? At least tell me what you think is happening. You know, it might be our lives," I continued.

"No, don't worry," Ivchenkov waved his hand, "let me tell you what's going on."

I walked up to the air conditioner and turned it up. Then I moved my chair a little so the cold air would be coming at my face.

"Those yellow parasites," Ivchenkov continued, "have been trying to develop their own resistance against the Republicans. Not against the Al-Badr's royalists, mind you, but against As-Sallal. So, they managed to get a pro-Chinese movement going. And, again, it's not against Saudis, but *against us!*" Ivchenkov moved impatiently in the chair and made a crushing gesture with his hand. "We must cut them off. We know who their Yemeni supporters are. We'll start from there—turn them over to our friendly Egyptian army, along with their arms."

But what Ivchenkov was saying didn't give me much confidence. He wants to think the Egyptians would help, I thought. Let him. But I wouldn't bet my life on it. The situation was much more complicated. As-Sallal's government was receiving help from the Chinese and it wasn't about to give it up instantly. In the meantime, local pro-Chinese elements could kill one or two Soviets, or even more. Then, knowing the ambassador's temper, there would be a heated protest to As-Sallal. In turn, some of As-Sallal's cabinet members would surely get insulted by the Soviets pushing As-Sallal around as they please. And the Chinese would not overlook the opportunity to get their supporters together and quickly organize a coup, which would install a pro-Chinese government and end the Soviet rule of Yemen.

Keeping my thoughts to myself, I decided the whole thing was too close for comfort and hoped I wouldn't be the one to get hurt.

When I got to the consulate, the lights were all out. That drunken chauffeur Boris must have forgotten to turn on the lights, I thought. I opened the front door, using my key to turn the bolt seven times as the lock required, and cautiously stepped into the darkness. When I turned on the lights, I saw a piece of paper on the floor that someone must have slid under the door while I was gone. It read, "Admired your climbing that rusty old hangar structure. I hope we'll get together soon. You'll recognize me. Your friend."

At first, my professional pride was hurt. But then I felt a new surge of confidence. I'd almost given up hope that any contact could be made here in Yemen.

Something happened the following week that redoubled my determination to make that contact.

As promised, Ivchenkov summoned me. I went to meet him in a utility room of one of the six buildings used as living quarters for Soviet dockworkers. The building was deserted during daytime working hours.

Inside one small window facing th Red Sea, several air conditioners were stacked against a wall, a diesel motor and some broken fans littered the room. Ivchenkov sat in a wooden chair facing the wall. A diminutive Yemeni, dressed in European-style clothes, squatted on the floor in front of him. The Yemeni looked pleadingly at me when I came in, his eyes full of fear.

"Look what I've got here," Ivchenkov smiled. "This is the guy who drives the car with the loudspeakers. He works for the Chinese. And he's the same man you saw on that strip, isn't he?"

I said he might have been. I wasn't sure. "That's him. No doubt. Fucking Yemeni spy pederast. Let's talk to him. You translate."

I remained near the door. The Yemeni looked at me.

"Ask Mr. Ismail what he's doing for the cross-eyed."

I translated but the Yemeni began to shake so much that he was hardly capable of speech. He just kept stammering, *"Allahu Akbar . . . wallahi, walla shi."* ("Nothing, in the name of great God.")

"Come on. Get cracking." Ivchenkov snapped. "Tell us what's going on. Airstrip. Your relationship with Mr. Dobi." (Dobi was governor of Hodeida. I met him several times. A polite man, he was mostly concerned with local tribal conflicts and once asked if I'd travel with him to some remote tribe. I didn't go do the PR but maybe one of the Chinese went.)

Ivchenkov went on: "Tell us about the Chinese specialists. I want to know which tribes you supply with arms. Who are the pro-Chinese people in the government? Where do the Chinese military advisors work? Vladimir, go ahead, get it out of him." Ivchenkov made a kicking motion.

I kept translating, but the Yemeni didn't answer. Ivchenkov got up and kicked him hard in the stomach. "You're going to talk, or you're not going to see your employers again!"

I translated. The Yemeni sobbed. "I can't tell you anything. My people will kill me. I don't know much. Let me go." I translated to Ivchenkov, but couldn't stop looking at the Yemeni's agonized face.

"What do you mean, he says he doesn't know much? I know the bastard knows a lot!" With that Ivchenkov picked up a three-foot steel rod and played it around the Yemeni's face.

I wanted to grab it from Ivchenkov, smash him, and send the Yemeni home, but I stood rooted to the spot. We interrogated him for another hour but got no information.

Then, without warning, Ivchenkov smashed the steel rod across the Yemeni's face. It hit crosswise and squashed his left eye, half of the nose, and cut into the right part of his mouth. As if in slow motion, I could see his eye leak out of its socket and the white cartilage of his opened nose fill with blood.

"Please translate to him. This is my final question. Arms, Chinese, tribes, and government officials!" Ivchenkov grinned, his eyes glowing in lunatic fashion. I translated. The Yemeni groaned, blood dripping onto his white shirt.

"Okay, that's it, Vladimir. You can go. I'll take care of him." Ivchenkov barked and I retreated. As I went out the door, I saw him jam the rod into the Yemeni's stomach.

It would be a slow death. Ivchenkov needed practice for when he might one day be transferred to "Moscow Center."

I went back to the consulate and found Comrade Maslov, chief civil engineer from a Soviet specialists' group, awaiting me.

"Hi, boss. Got news for you. Just came off our merchant ship out at berth. They've got a cable for you." He handed it to me: "Ekaterina was born on May 28, three kilograms, seven hundred grams. Healthy. Beautiful. Waiting."

I opened the bottom of my huge, authoritative desk and pulled out a case of Teacher's Scotch. I bought this case from the free port of Djibouti on the Ethiopian side of the Red Sea for this occasion realizing that the good news would be a reason for many engineers and trade mission employees to come and congratulate me. It would be absolutely necessary to offer drinks. I tore open the case and handed a bottle to Maslov, then opened another one and filled two glasses. We sat for awhile at the long conference table, Maslov nourishing the glass and I looking out the window toward the Red Sea.

"Is everything smooth with your contract now?" I asked Maslov after awhile.

"The usual things, you know, some squabble among the road builders, but as far as locals are concerned . . . Well, it's better now," Maslov said and emptied the glass.

He was referring to a problem that Ivchenkov and I had resolved two weeks before. The desert road building contract from Hodeida to Taizz had been delayed, because one of the local tribes didn't want any palefaces to build on territory they controlled. Having learned the local dialect, I had gone to see the tribe's chief. Ivchenkov had driven the car and we had been stopped by several vicious-looking Yemenis just as we approached the tribe's compound. They searched us and I convinced them we were not Americans. *"Russi, Russi, Tamam,"* one of them, obviously of authority, nodded and showed us into the compound. The *janbiyas* were put back under the belt and we were given an audience with the sheik. He was a young man of about twenty-five. As we walked into his Spartan quarters, he greeted us in perfect English.

"I went to England, studied economics," he mentioned later as we were drinking strong jelly-textured coffee. That coffee kept me up for a couple of days.

I stated the reason for our visit. "Don't worry, I'll take care of it. *"Insha'alla"* (God willing), he said, "just let me know in advance when you'll be building here so I can have my people guard your specialists." I was curious about his young age and indirectly asked him about it. The story he told me was unusual.

A short time before I arrived in Hodeida, his tribe ended a war with an Hodeida tribe which had been going on for centuries. One night, his tribesmen quietly surrounded their rivals' compound and slit all their throats. The operation took a couple of hours. Only one from my new friend's tribe got killed. It was his father. *"Allahu Akbar"* (God is great), the young sheik shook his head. I agreed. Ivchenkov kept silence. We were accompanied out of the compound by the sheik himself and his bodyguards. "Please, take this," he handed me his *janbiya* knife, "We will be friends." I took the ornamented present and invited him to visit me in the consulate. It was safer to have a man like that on my side.

During the following weeks I was busy managing the problems of hundreds of Soviet specialists. Their nationalistic rivalries flared, exacerbated by the harsh conditions.

Meantime, Ivchenkov kept me sleuthing for more on the Chinese who continued their loudspeaking exercises with even more gusto.

One day Ambassador Rakhmatov came down from Taizz. He was accompanied by Aleksander Zaitsev, first secretary of the embassy and Ivchenkov's boss. Zaitsev had been working in Yemen for three years. His main responsibility was to organize and direct guerilla operations in Aden and the east coast of Ethiopia, control the embryonic liberation movement in Oman and Saudi Arabia, and interface with Abdel Kawi Makkawi of the Front of Liberation of South Yemen. He also had responsibility for all KGB operations in the area. Bulky and energetic, with receding hair and a round face, Zaitsev could have been taken for a secretary of a remote regional party committee back home. But in Yemen there was something about Zaitsev which made everyone, even Rakhmatov, stiffen up. I found out later that he had come out of KGB Internal Security and naturally suspected everyone of being a foreign spy—guilty until proven innocent.

I ushered Rakhmatov and Zaitsev into my office, where Boris served Borjomi, Soviet mineral water, as we talked about the weather and their long trip. As soon as Boris left, Rakhmatov looked at Zaitsev and said, "We need you for two days."

I looked at Zaitsev, who stared at me as if measuring the degree of my trustworthiness, and said, "Always at your service, Comrade Ambassador."

Rakhmatov looked at Zaitsev again, then turned to me and continued. "We are taking you with us. Not far."

"What about the consulate?" I thought it looked good to show my concern. I noticed Zaitsev's stare become somewhat less penetrating.

"Ivchenkov will take care of it. Right?" The ambassador turned to Zaitsev again. Zaitsev nodded and took over the conversation.

"Turn on the radio, please." I noticed he had a pleasant voice. "You know the procedures."

I got up and turned on the Phillips. Arabic music filled the room.

"We want you to translate," Zaitsev continued, "I heard your Arabic is not bad. You'll follow us now."

I assumed the meeting was over and was ready to get up.

"Just a second," Zaitsev waved at me. "By the way, what do you think about that classmate of yours, Kuznetsov?"

"I suppose the guy is trying. You know, he's older than I am . . . must try harder." I smiled and gave Zaitsev a what-can-you-do look. He sighed, "I want to talk to you about him later." I figured if everything was okay with Anatoly Kuznetsov, Zaitsev wouldn't bring it up, especially in the presence of the ambassador.

Finally we got underway and headed toward a peninsula outside Hodeida. The car stopped at a beach house that I knew belonged to the minister of internal affairs of Yemen. There we had an elaborate nine-course dinner. We had roasted pigeons, pilaf with large chunks of lamb, cucumbers in yogurt, marinated shredded beef with red peppers, boiled shrimp on ice, eggs stuffed with caviar, lobio, sherbet, bakhlava, and ice cream. That was accompanied by Armenian cognacs and Georgian wines from the embassy's reserves.

This stomach-expanding exercise lasted two days. However, the main reason for us all staying in the house was not the ambassador's culinary escapades. Rakhmatov's presence was a PR move to give Zaitsev's negotiations more authority and diplomatic weight.

The meetings were attended by As-Sallal, Abdel Kawi Makkawi, and some people from Aden, Saudi Arabia, and Oman. I learned that Makkawi had agreed to serve as a Soviet intermediary to establish relations with liberation organizations in the south, including tribes which were engaged in the guerilla war against the British. He would be responsible for the identification of the various liberation movement members, who could be very reliable individuals, i.e. Soviet agents.

One of Zaitsev's responsibilities was to establish the Front of Liberation of the Southern Arabian Peninsula and the Front of Liberation of Saudi Arabia. Abdulla As-Sallal assured him he definitely would help with such an honorable task in any way.

With a functional front of liberation in Saudi Arabia he would be able to destroy Al-Badr royalists' resistance and become a leading figure in the Arabian liberation movements against American and British imperialism. All parties agreed the emphasis must be made on attracting and recruiting new members for the liberation movement. Makkawi and a young man from Aden who represented some other—at the time, obscure—guerilla organization, rose and shook hands when Sallal offered Zaitsev the use of Yemen's airports as the Soviets pleased. Zaitsev immediately replied that "we might, fairly soon." At that the meeting ended and I returned to the consulate.

Privately the Soviets were not interested in Sallal or Makkawi as future Arab leaders. They were considered only two temporarily useful characters in the ever-changing drama that was unfolding in Yemen. The main objective, as Zaitsev and Ivchenkov would remind me—echoing the lectures about Third World strategy I'd heard at the IIR—was to establish long-term Soviet influence by whatever means necessary, be it through above-board diplomatic approaches or underground armed struggle. Moscow was interested in controlling the Arabian peninsula and its oil, directly or indirectly, so as to have the Western capitalist nations eventually at its mercy.

It was a busy time, but it couldn't tire me enough. Each night, when I went to bed, I saw the face of the Yemeni that Ivchenkov had tortured.

I waited.

One day I received another message. I took the consulate's Volga on the pretext of one of my scouting missions. I headed inland into the hills. After fifty kilometers, I came to an abandoned nomad trading station and took a dirt road that forked to the right. Up ahead was an Opel coupe. I parked behind it and a man got out. We shook hands.

"Hello, George."

"Glad you came," he answered in Russian.

I continued in English. "How are you?"

"I'd rather be home in my swimming pool. How's by you?" He switched to English.

"Except for the heat, the KGB, those ignorant specialists, the ambassador, his goat and his cow, all right."

"That bad, huh?"

"You're a godsend. How did you know I've been looking for you?"

"Just lucky, I guess . . . Well, is it now or later?" George smiled.

"What's that?" I didn't understand right away and hesitated. Then it dawned on me he was asking if I was going to defect now.

"What do you say?" George repeated.

"Oh, not now." I answered, "I want to earn my ticket, so to say."

"That's very good," George said seriously.

Just as at our first meeting many years earlier, there was an immediate rapport that required few words.

We switched to Russian and got down to particulars. "I have to return to Russia soon," I told him. "It's going to be hard work once

168

I'm back. You know, tapped phones, bugged rooms—there is no way to escape their surveillance—especially for people like me who do most of their work abroad and come back to Moscow for reassignment and a short stay."

"Don't worry," he said. "We understand and give you our assurance that you will be utilized only during the time when you are abroad. We don't want to lose you. Since we try to take good care of our people, we won't bother you in Moscow and will protect you abroad as much as we can."

I wondered how they could possibly manage to protect me abroad. I insisted that no more than three people on the U.S. side know about my identity and relationship—four or five at the most. We talked for a while more, setting up procedures and arrangements for future contact.

"How's Rita?" I asked when we'd finished. "She's quite a woman."

"Fine. Would you like to see her again?"

"Just give her my best."

Driving back to Hodeida, I felt no fear, no doubts, no alienation. I had a heightened awareness of everything around me and everything in myself. I wasn't playing a role; I was myself at last. That night, for the first time in weeks, I fell asleep without seeing the Yemeni.

The June 1967 Six-Day War caught the Soviet mission by surprise, although I learned much later it did not have that effect on the KGB in Moscow. On the morning of the Israeli attack I was working at the consulate. I asked my secretary to tune the radio to the "Voice of the Arabs" from Cairo. The station was playing "Biladi, Biladi, Biladi" ("My country, my country, my country"), an Arab patriotic song. Then the commentator said the Egyptian forces had pushed the Zionists deep into the territory which they occupied, and the war was being won by the Arabs. I wasn't surprised because of my confidence in the Soviet backup. But, just in case, I thought I'd check it through the BBC. I knew that Moscow radio wouldn't broadcast anything about the clash until the situation had stabilized. The British said Arabs were suffering a tremendous defeat; their air force and army were totally wiped out. We had anticipated some sort of conflict, but the Arab debacle was unexpected.

That conflict caused a sudden change in the Yemen situation.

Nasser began sending his troops back to Egypt. As-Sallal seemed to have stabilized his situation anyway. The Egyptians in Yemen remained as cordial as ever towards us. But we knew that in the Arab world there was backlash against the Soviet Union because of what some Arabs perceived as Soviet failure to fully back its Middle Eastern friends. Moscow tried to scotch this by issuing statements of undying solidarity with Nasser and promises of unlimited aid in rebuilding and rearming his and other Arab armed forces. Since the Americans remained unorganized, this was a perfect opportunity to bring the Arabs even closer to the Soviet camp. For a while, however, Arab anger simmered—an opportunity our Chinese comrades in Yemen couldn't pass up.

A week after the war began, I got word there was trouble in the center of town. I told Boris to display the Soviet flag on one of the consulate cars and check out the problem. I figured the flag would signal diplomatic immunity and keep him safe, but he drove back shortly with a window smashed and the flag missing.

It turned out there was a mob shouting anti-Soviet slogans marching toward the consulate. It was apparent that the Yemenis now had been caught up in the anti-Soviet backlash—a situation, no doubt, precipitated by the Chinese.

"Vladimir, you better get the hell out. There are thousands of them and they are moving in this direction like a bunch of angry ants. The bastards have burned two cars that belonged to our road builders. One of our guys was inside his car when they burned it and they wouldn't let him out."

I thought a moment. A wrong decision now could cost lives. "All right, go to Ivchenkov and give him this note." There were no telephones in Hodeida and Ivchenkov was in the desert with our group of 500 specialists. They had been housed in temporary buildings while building a road, and they'd be easy targets. Luckily, this meant that their regular quarters, across from the consulate, were empty.

I told Boris to try to get to Egyptian military headquarters. "Tell the commander I need help. Tell him to bring his tanks and fire over their heads if they come too close. Then go to our port specialists' compound on the seashore and warn as many people as you can. No one must go out or show any movement."

Boris left and I was alone in the consulate. I could have left, but I figured it would look bad back in Moscow if I did.

170

I barricaded the front door with a stereo console, went upstairs and barricaded the door to the second floor with a stove I'd disconnected and shoved into the corridor. Then I went up to the flat roof.

Below, I could see a crowd of 5000 Yemenis surging towards the building, raising a cloud of dust as they came. Some of them carried old Winfield rifles and all of them carried *janbiyas*, which they waved over their heads. I heard the familiar Chinese loudspeakers blasting, "Soviets go home! Soviets betrayed Arabs! Down with the murderers!" The crowd repeated each loudspeaker slogan, over and over.

First one stone, then a hail of them, hit the front door of the consulate. Several Yemenis scaled the wall around the consulate and moved toward a broken window. A larger group stopped within sixty feet of the building and began firing their rifles. I heard more windows breaking. The downstairs door gave a mighty crack. Staying low, I crawled to the roof's edge. I could see them breaking into the building. My heart pounded. I stood up, expecting they'd shoot me. One shot rang past me, but then I heard machine gun fire. Two truckloads of Egyptian soldiers pulled up and the crowd began to scatter.

I went downstairs and put out a small fire. The stereo was smashed, but otherwise there was no damage.

I sent a brief report to Rakhmatov in Taizz. Following his penchant for royal flair, he sent a car and I was given an audience to describe my reluctantly heroic exploit.

"You are certainly fit to occupy key posts abroad," he said, putting an arm around my shoulders. "Let me look at you. Let me commend you for your most dignified behavior in protecting the interests of our motherland."

He offered to reward me by transferring me back to Taizz to work under him. I managed to get out of that with some fast footwork. Rakhmatov had the reputation of a tyrant who used his staff as personal servants, and I didn't want any part of that.

Instead my reward was another Volga sedan for the consulate. With it I could drive back to Hodeida alone, taking care of some pressing business on the way.

I didn't go straight back to Hodeida that morning. I went to Mocha, about 150 miles south of Hodeida, a seaport at the strait of Bab el Mandeb, entryway to the Red Sea. As I approached Mocha, there was an exquisite view of the sea ahead. The sea, blue, green, and silver in the bright sun of the morning, gently embraced Mocha, where it gave way to the mountains and welcomed the coastal desert. A light breeze, in which mysterious fresh scents of the Middle East blended together, caressed my face and gave me a feeling of exotic inspiration, which can only be experienced in the Middle East.

Mocha, the ancient port famous for the coffee that bears its name, shimmered like a mirage against the desert sounds. Scores of minarets spiked the deep blue sky. I drove into the dusty, twisting streets. I could hear the chanting of the Koran from the minarets above me.

Mocha was an enchanting oasis out of an ancient fairy tale, a place bypassed by time, politics, war, and modernization. There were no grandiose mosques or other tourist attractions, but the spirit of Islam and centuries-old civilization lived, preserved in untouched purity. The streets were empty except for a few women dressed in black, holding clay pots, and standing on the street corner.

I didn't stop in Mocha. I took a little-used dirt road that winds up the coast back to Hodeida. I had to time it correctly because portions of the road were passable only at low tide. This would turn to my advantage, however, once I got by the low spots and the tide rose, blocking anyone who might be following me. At times the road came so close to the surf that my tires kicked up a cloud of salty mist. The road was deserted and the countryside barren, with the sea to my left and sand dunes to my right. Occasionally I caught sight of distant mountains looming like Arabian castles against the dark blue sky beyond the dunes.

After several hours I came to an old breakwater. This was the spot George had told me about during our meeting when we'd agreed upon procedures for my passing on information. The drop point was a saksaul tree twenty meters off the road in line with the breakwater. I dug into the soil and found a metal box.

Inside it was a note, "You're doing fine. We are grateful." I put the note and my report into the box, and buried it.

My note was short, but thoroughly reported the latest development in the consulate and embassy. George had left the content of my messages up to me, but I sensed that the Americans would be judging me by the quality of information I provided and I was anxious to prove myself a valuable ally. Writing things down was risky, but less dangerous than additional face-to-face meetings with

172

George. I spread the sand to cover my tracks, got back into my car and drove north to Hodeida, feeling a sense of accomplishment.

Three aerial mapping specialists were waiting for me at the consulate when I arrived. They had just flown a specially equipped twin engine reconnaissance plane from Moscow. Their mission was to take part in the intelligence activities against Saudi Arabia that had been coordinated at the secret meeting in Hodeida. Moscow Center, the Egyptians, Sallal, and the emergent Front of Liberation of Saudi Arabia needed more precise information on the terrain and supply routes leading from their Yemeni base into the Saudi kingdom. They especially needed data on the mountain trails that might serve as overland routes for undetected infiltration and supply.

We knew at that time that Yemen was not well situated in respect to Saudi oil fields; between them was a huge and rugged desert. We knew, however, that there must be a way of land transportation because royalists in the Yemeni mountains got their supplies by land. If there was one way there had to be more.

Another reason for the overflights was to conduct photogrammetrical surveys of the geological structure of the land to determine the possibility of oil fields in the desert itself. If oil existed, the Soviets would be the first to announce it to the Yemeni government. Then more Soviet specialists would arrive to do exploration and there would be more room for them to direct and monitor the underground in Saudi Arabia.

These were perilous missions because the Yemeni royalist tribes were still active in the mountains and would try to shoot down any plane they saw. There was also the more remote but dangerous possibility of Saudi air force interception. The last thing Moscow wanted was for a Soviet spy-pilot to be downed over Saudi Arabia.

To minimize these risks, we briefed the airmen on routes that would be safest. We also arranged for the Egyptians to provide air cover if necessary.

The Egyptian command was aware of the whole operation. After meeting with the Soviet airmen, I was assigned to drive to the Hodeida military airport and discuss support plans with Colonel Sidki, Egyptian air force commander. We agreed upon a contingency plan where the Egyptians, with their Soviet-built IL-28s and MIG-17s, would stand by on red alert during our spy flights.

173

If the Soviet surveillance craft signaled trouble, the Egyptian warplanes would be there in minutes to drive off the attackers and divert attention from the mission. An air clash involving the Egyptians would cause a diplomatic brouhaha that could be written off as an inadvertent border violation by overzealous pilots. The more sinister espionage overflights would then have a good chance of going unnoticed.

The mission began the next morning and everything went smoothly. The overflights continued for two weeks, producing excellent, detailed photomaps. The photos are probably still in Moscow Center's files.

When the flights were over, Ivchenkov and I decided to give a party at the consulate for the Soviet pilots and the Egyptian air force and navy commanders who were leaving the country. Ivchenkov would not let me use the consulate's MFA account to pay for the reception. He insisted that his department would pay. I didn't mind. The KGB's funds certainly were greater than the consulate's skimpy account. But when the party began I felt sorry that I didn't. I would have ordered more food. There were a dozen bottles of Scotch, cognac, and vodka just for the ten of us. And there were only three plates of peanuts. Ivchenkov had overdone his "get them drunk" act this time, but it was too late for me to straighten out the situation. My driver got drunk again and I couldn't take the risk of sending him out for food.

As I anticipated, the reception was boring. There were no women and half of the guests got drunk very early. Soviet pilots didn't speak any language but Russian. They just laughed and drank and the Egyptians laughed back and also drank.

I ended up talking to Commander Gallal, an Egyptian, who was in charge of the navy base in Hodeida. He looked like an actor from an Italian neorealist movie, tall with an expressive face, sad eyes, thin lips, and aristocratic gestures. He explained to me he was being transferred to Alexandria to take command of a missile boat squadron, which would shortly go into action against the Israelis on the Mediterranean. More Soviet military advisors and new Soviet naval hardware were already on the way to Alexandria.

My internship was coming to an end. A week before my departure in September 1967, Ivchenkov summoned me to his office for another chat.

174

"Now what are you going to do?" he asked.

"I'll go back and finish with the Institute. Then they'll send me someplace else. I really don't want to come back here," I said.

"I understand." Ivchenkov handed me a glass of King George Scotch. "It's a rotten place. Try to be assigned to Egypt, Kuwait, or Lebanon. You'll be okay there. It's good pay, good living, and good for your little baby."

This sudden concern was touching. I knew that Ivchenkov would be filing a report on my performance and I didn't want to discourage any friendly overtures. Because of his personal approach, I assumed he was satisfied with my work. I continued the small talk. "Well, could I do anything for you when I get back to Moscow?"

"Yes, you might," he said, looking straight at me. "When you talk to your father, mention my name. I know he has some friends in the department. Just between us, before I retire, I have one more assignment abroad, and I'd like to spend it somewhere nice—in Paris, or better, London. One good word from your father wouldn't hurt."

Before I left, a mob of pro-Sallal Yemenis caught two Soviet diplomats on the Taizz-Sana road. The Yemenis mistook them for Americans and hanged them. Neither one of them was Ivchenkov. But then, neither was me, either.

The worst I got was a severe tropical rash, one of those unspecified skin infections that resisted treatment but disappeared when I returned to the more temperate climate of Moscow. It left scars on my legs, but thanks to my new sense of purpose, the scars were only skin deep.

Ivchenkov accompanied me to the Hodeida airport. He handed me a yellow folder which I looked through.

"Report on V. Sakharov's Training in Yemen," read the title, and underneath, "V. Sakharov's Characteristic is Enclosed." It depicted my service in Yemen in glowing terms. ". . . V. Sakharov was Acting Soviet Consul in Hodeida. He conducted recruitment and development of Egyptian military officials, Yemeni government employees and members of Yemen's diplomatic corps. His activities in this direction should be highly valued and regarded."

The character report described me as a devoted Marxist-Leninist whose "unshakeable standards and beliefs in the cause of international Communism and the party would make him a most fit

175

candidate for any position of importance within the Soviet international apparatus."

"I don't know how to thank you," I said, looking up from the folder. "Looks like a lot of it should be attributed to you."

"Don't worry," he laughed. "I am sending it to Moscow tomorrow with the diplomatic mail. You can't carry it yourself, it wouldn't look right." He shook my hand. "And, Vladimir, thank you, I'll always remember your help." He looked into my eyes meaningfully. "But watch out. I'll always keep an eye on you." Then he smiled.

The Ilyushin turbo prop landed roughly, bouncing on the short runway. I climbed aboard and recognized Ivchenkov's three stewardesses. I smiled, but not at them. I was thinking about the unexpected gift Ivchenkov had handed me.

12: A Neighborly Invitation

"Call this number today; use a public telephone." The IIR's deputy director of personnel handed me a slip of paper. "Ask for Vasily Ivanovich. He'll give you further instructions." The "neighbors" no doubt, but what was so important that the KGB couldn't use normal channels?

It was January 1968, and I had just passed my state examination. I was getting ready for the IIR graduation and party that would take place at the new Rossiya Hotel in three weeks. Like all IIR graduates, I was being wooed by top government and military agencies. And graduating as an Arabist I was even more in demand.

Soviet leadership didn't start to emphasize Arab studies until after the 1956 British-French-Israeli attack on the Suez Canal, and it was another three years before the IIR offered Arab studies as a formal academic specialty. There were plenty of Soviet Middle Eastern minorities who spoke Arabic and had varying degrees of Middle Eastern expertise, but in 1968 I belonged to only the third group of Soviet Arabists to graduate from the IIR. Now with the thirty from the two previous years there were only forty-five of us with the Arab specialization. The large percentage of Middle Eastern specialists—

fifteen in a graduating class of sixty—showed the emphasis the Soviet leadership was placing on the Middle East.

There were at least five jobs for each IIR graduate. The Ministry of Foreign Affairs, the military, and other government departments were in need of translators and international economic and political experts like ourselves. But the extreme difficulty of getting into the IIR—fostered not only by high academic standards, but even more by the clannishness of the Moscow elite—resulted in the IIR not completely filling the needs at this point.

In addition to being an IIR graduate, I had three other advantages that caused prospective employers to beat down my door. I had a solid academic record, including special awards like the one I got for my final thesis on Yemen. I had a clean party slate, qualifying me as a good security risk, And, thanks to the backscratching Ivchenkov's buttery report on my Yemen internship, I was regarded not only as promising, but as proven in the field.

I graduated with the title *Referent Po Stranam Vostoka,* which translates to "Expert on East Countries." Like all IIR graduates, I was commissioned into the military and automatically received an army lieutenant's I.D. with a military code number on the lower portion inside. The code classified me as a "preferential utilization" military interpreter. This meant that I was a member of the GRU, or military intelligence.

I had no desire to work actively for the GRU, a fading organization that operated in the shadows of the KGB. I knew that any other position I eventually took would entail some degree of cooperation with the KGB, that being *de rigeur* for IIR graduates or anyone else who worked for the Soviet foreign service. But I didn't want just any job. I wanted a position that would allow me the freedom and privileges I'd worked so hard to get. More importantly, I wanted to place myself in a job that would allow me the greatest access to information in order to be of maximum use to my new American allies against the very Soviet system that at this moment was falling over itself to embrace me.

I had lucrative job offers from the GRU, the State Committee for Radio and Television, the Ministry of Foreign Trade, the Ministry of Culture, the Central Committee of the Komsomol, the Council of Ministers of the U.S.S.R., Aeroflot, Soviet Export organizations, the State Committee on the Affairs of Churches—which is a KGB front—the Committee for Economic Relations with Foreign Countries—also a KGB front—the Soviet Academy of Science, and the Ministry of Foreign Affairs itself.

In any of these capacities, I would have had to perform for the KGB, just as I had to do in Yemen. But what about the KGB itself? I was waiting for them to make their move. They had first choice of everyone, and if they wanted me I would be flattered, even though I hated them so much.

As I shut the door to the personnel office, I saw Igor Novikov, *stukach,* down the corridor. He graduated lowest in our class, but I knew that would never hurt him. As with Anatoly, I was always careful to affect cordiality toward this bowlegged informant. "Well, are you going to call?" he said.

"Call whom?"

"You know, the number they gave you?"

"I don't know what you are talking about," I said and walked off. It was another of their tests, I was sure.

I went past the guarded entrance and out to the street. I saw my old friend Nikolai Khlopinsky sitting on a bench. I hadn't seen much of him in the last year.

"Hey, Vladimir, how's it going?"

"Not bad." Approaching him, I could smell alcohol on his breath. I felt sorry for him.

"What d'you say we go to a bar?"

Nikolai was broke and wanted me to treat at the Peking Restaurant bar. The Peking Restaurant, on Sadovoye Koltso near Gorki Street, was related in name only to a Chinese eating establishment. Very few Moscovites ate there and even fewer drank at the bar. Anything of Chinese origin had long ago become an atrocious vulgarity in the Soviet lexicon. I wondered when they would finally change the name of the restaurant, for the food there surely smacked of regular Russian borsht. Except for Mandarin duck and noodles, there was no Chinese food on the menu. I didn't want to go there with Nikolai, but there was a note of desperation in his voice.

"Maybe later," I said, "I have something to take care of."

"Oh, come on, I've got to talk to you."

As we walked in the snow toward a taxi stand, I noticed he was staggering. "Looks like you've been having a high time," I told him.

"Screw it, just trying to get drunk and stay drunk."

The taxi driver was a heavy-set woman in her forties with a woolen scarf around her head, just like a village woman. You couldn't get any men to drive today in the twenty degrees below zero weather. Women get all the nasty jobs, I thought; same old Moscow.

We went into the bar. It was not attractive at all. Four plastic tables, a gray bar facing an old mirror, and an old woman at the cash register created a cold and transient atmosphere. We were alone except for a man at a corner table reading a newspaper—surely KGB. We ordered two *Mayak* cocktails, cognac and champagne with the egg yolk floating on top, and drank slowly. "Vladimir," Nikolai began after a while, "you are the only one I can talk to. I've got some problems and see no help forthcoming." I got ready to listen and ordered two more *Mayaks*.

"When I got married some months ago," he went on, "—you remember, you knew her—I loved Maria. Now I hate her. We got divorced last month."

This was news to me. He went on about his marital troubles. "Maria lied to me before we were married. Her father, General Miyscek, didn't die in the war like she said. It turned out he was Beria's right arm. Remember Smersh?" I nodded. Smersh *(Smert Shpionam* or "Death to Spies") used to be one of the most gruesome of Stalin's projects. As a part of the KGB, then called GPU (State Political Department), Smersh was in charge of capturing and torturing foreign agents. The majority of those "foreign agents" never lived to find out why they were arrested. They were plain Soviet folks. Khrushchev liquidated Smersh and killed off most of its officers. "So, you see," Nikolai continued, "he was executed in fifty-four when Khrushchev ordered Stalin's and Beria's KGB cadres killed. I was too stupid to check on her background. Then I find out she's practically a socio-political leper. My wife, daughter of a top Smersh murderer."

He finished his drink and I ordered him another. I thought to myself, Nikolai was so far down the road to alcoholism he wouldn't make it anyway, marriage or no marriage. If the *stukachi* didn't zero in on him first, someone would later. With everything being equal, pull works only when one performs well, abides by the rules, and doesn't foul up too often. Nikolai had fouled up too often and lacked influential parents.

"All right, Nikolai," I said, "now what? So you are divorced. You should try to get over it." I feigned ignorance of his predicament.

"Get over what? My life? It's over. They know—the Institute, the KGB, everybody. All doors are closed to me now. There will be nothing for me. Vladimir, I was called to the personnel department. They told me to report to the army staff for my assignment to the Chinese border, somewhere around Magdagashi. I don't even know where the hell that is. That's my future—a military interpreter out in Siberia. Thank you, dear Communist party, for your high trust. Fuck you, dear Communist party, for ruining my life." Nikolai's voice rose with alcoholic stridence. I tried to calm him down, glancing over toward the KGB man at the corner table, hoping he hadn't heard us. If he had, he didn't react. I talked with Nikolai a few moments longer, but knew there was nothing I could do. Then, looking at the man in the corner again, I remembered something.

I checked my gold Omega. I was supposed to call that number given me by the personnel chief. Nikolai was downing the last of another *Mayak*.

"There, Nikolai, I hope things get better for you. I really have to go."

"Go, go. You're just like everyone else. You all act like I have cholera." I was standing up to leave.

"Just leave me some money," he said. I left some money for him and walked out without looking back. I never saw him again, but several years later I heard that he was in a mental institution.

Outside, I found a phone booth and carefully picked up the receiver, trying not to get a frost burn from it. Vasily Ivanovich, the name on the paper, brought a grin. If the stupid ass were going to use a phony name, I thought, he could have picked a less obvious one. Vasily Ivanovich Chapayev was the name of a famous Red commander who fought in the revolution. Every school child knew it. I guessed my KGB contact chose the name so he wouldn't forget his alias—rather like an American agent calling himself John Paul, after John Paul Jones.

"Vasily Ivanovich, please," I said when a voice on the other end answered.

The voice was mellow and soft. "Oh, you must be Vladimir Nikolayevich Sakharov. Glad to hear from you. I'd like you to come to Neglinaya Street tomorrow at ten. Our reception office is just opposite the old building of the Ministry of Foreign Affairs." He was talking about the original Moscow Center KGB headquarters on Dzerzhinsky Square, where I'd often gone to meet my father as a boy. There were still KGB offices there, although a new building was being completed on the outskirts of the city.

When I got home I didn't tell Natasha about my appointment. But apparently I had a concerned look. Otherwise she wouldn't have asked what was wrong.

"Nothing," I answered. "I'm just sick of all the bullshit about work."

"It'll be over soon. You know—don't bother with decisions."

"I won't," I said, but my curiosity about the next morning's meeting was growing by the minute.

"You want to stay here tonight, baby?" she asked.

"Yes," I said taking off my coat. The question was not unusual because we had moved around since I got back from Yemen. Our new apartment in the same building where my parents lived near the American Embassy wasn't ready yet. In the meantime we lived in four places; sometimes at my parents' old place on Stretensky Boulevard. Everything there remained as it had been some years ago, because when my parents bought a new cooperative apartment at 13 Tchaikovsky Street, they also bought all new furniture. Then there was my grandfather's place in Kaliningrad, where my grandmother died. He moved to Moscow and got a one-bedroom apartment near Moscow University on Lenin's Hills. Just like our old place on Stretensky Boulevard, the Kaliningrad apartment was the same as it had been for many years. We'd often spend a couple of days there just to get away from Moscow and our routine.

I wanted to pay for our new flat myself and figured it would take us a year of work abroad to do so. And then, of course, there was our family *dacha* by the Pirogovo Reservoir. Its title now was transferred to Katya, our little daughter.

Natasha preferred to stay with my parents, so that my mother could help with the baby. I didn't mind that. The apartment was quiet and comfortable and had a great view of the Moskva River and part of the American Embassy. In the next apartment, there was surveillance equipment. Once or twice a day, footsteps would sound along the corridor and then—silence. The other "neighbors" kept themselves busy quietly reading the pulse of the enemy.

That evening I didn't say anything to my parents about the KGB appointment either. My baby daughter, Katya, played in her crib. She laughed as I lifted her small white body high, and she held her breath as I let her gently down. She was nine months old, with blonde hair and blue eyes. Although relations between my parents and Natasha were still somewhat cool, they were much happier now that the baby was here.

The weather warmed a bit the next morning, rain mixing with snow as it slowly descended onto the dirty cobblestones of Neglinaya Street. Only a few people were out on the street. But as I crossed the square I could feel hundreds of eyes on me. The KGB bastion always gave one that feeling, because, it was in fact true. I felt no severe apprehension, however. I had always approached the KGB with care. I had kept my American connection so well-concealed that I hardly had a conscious thought of it. Rather, I was more self-confident. I wasn't afraid anymore.

The glass sign on the second door on the Neglinaya Street side of the building read, "Reception of the Committee for State Security." I pushed the heavy brass handle and entered a foyer and suddenly felt as though I had entered a giant tomb. A guard with a Makarov in the holster asked me my business and when I told him, called someone on the phone. "Vasily Ivanovich will be with you shortly," he said crisply.

After a few moments, a man in his early fifties entered the foyer. He wore a dark gray suit, a red-dotted tie, and black shoes with rubber heels so that he walked without a sound. He was balding, neatly groomed, and seemed energetic.

"Welcome, welcome, Comrade Sakharov!" He stretched a hand toward me. His handshake was limp and slightly moist. "Come in here. Let's talk a bit. Smoke?" He offered me a Schipka, Bulgarian cigarettes very popular in Moscow.

"Thank you." I took one.

We entered a large reception room lined with bookshelves and containing an antique desk, soft chairs, and a table facing a curtained window. He directed me to a wooden straight-backed chair that faced his desk. He took his seat behind the desk. "Sit down. May I call you Vladimir?"

"Surely." I crossed my legs and tried not to gag on the Bulgarian cigarette.

"You know the reason why we called you, Vladimir."

I nodded.

"We know you are best suited for our purposes. More than that, your Yemen record shows it."

"I am very glad and honored by your trust," I said, wondering what he was driving at. "Anytime I can do something for my homeland, I'll do it." I looked him straight in the eye.

"Very good," he said, "I know you are worthy of our trust. Here's what we'd like you to do. We'd like to put you in our special school for a year or two. You'd have to sacrifice a bit of your family life. You'd be able to see your wife only once a month or less. Your Arabic is outstanding, but we'll keep that aside for the moment. We are interested in making your English absolutely perfect, with emphasis on American slang."

I looked for an ashtray, trying to buy time to think. He pushed an ashtray over and I crushed out the Bulgarian butt. Ivchenkov's recommendation had bought me more than I'd bargained for. I could hardly believe my ears, but Vasily was saying something for which I wasn't prepared at all.

If I caught his drift, I was to be trained for work in the United States. This could mean I'd have to forget my Arabic. But then, I thought, they wouldn't be so dumb as to waste an Arabist. And, as the thoughts were rushing through my mind, I remembered my old acquaintance at the IIR, Yevgeny Negrul.

Yevgeny had graduated several years before me. He had English and Chinese, and miraculously ended up working in Chinese communities in America. Someone who speaks Chinese, lives in America, and works for the KGB could be very instrumental in establishing and maintaining a fair-size intelligence network weaved out of those particular communities' members. I knew there were Russian, Armenian, and Arab communities in America, and the KGB had to cover them all. I thought that could be one of the applications of my Arabic.

But, going to the KGB school in Belye Stolby near Moscow didn't appeal to me. Who wants two more years of studies after the five and a half which I'd just gone through? Not me. Ciphers, recruitment techniques, arms, communications, sabotage techniques, and more history of the Communist party, more world economics, more world Communist movements, more law and those stupid legal practices. I couldn't bring myself to that. Not right away.

184

I knew about the ongoing KGB reorganization precipitated by Oleg Penkovsky's case and Yuri Nosenko's defection. The party was not satisfied with KGB performance. Although Oleg Penkovsky was from the GRU, it was the KGB who failed to nail him before he passed all that "information on missile fuel" (that's what they used to say about it at that time) to the Americans. Nosenko's case in 1964 was the last straw. The KGB needed some fresh blood which would not only establish the new ruling elite inside the KGB itself, but would also help expand its international operations. I knew many heads in the KGB had rolled again, as they had after Stalin.

I continued looking at Vasily Ivanovich ingenuously.

"We'll make a true American of you," Vasily went on, and the irony of what he said was not lost on me. "Whether you'll end up working in the Arab countries against the Yankees, or in the United States for us, we'll decide later. In the meantime don't tell anyone about this."

"I won't," I assured him, "not even my wife."

"Good, now you'll have to be mentally prepared to work under diplomatic cover or without any cover. You know what that means. In that case we'll take very good care of your family."

Vasily was talking as though I'd already agreed to be dropped somewhere by parachute to work illegally, or infiltrate a Jewish immigrant group and follow them to Austria, then to Israel, and perhaps beyond.

I could live with diplomatic cover. This would be more of the usual liaison work that I'd have no choice but to be involved in no matter what MFA post I'd get abroad. But illegal work was a different story—it would cut me off. I'd be of practically no use to the CIA.

As a diplomat I'd have access to all documentation and operations of intelligence and diplomatic personnel, news agencies and the military. If I ended up as a KGB illegal, I'd be in the field with knowledge only of my specific assignment and of my undercover contact. I'd see little of the whole picture.

Vasily continued, "We'll give you one of the best apartments in Moscow, maybe a *dacha*. How about a car? We'll provide you with free clothing, shoes, whatever."

"Material things don't mean much to me," I said. "I just want to be constructive in building our new Communist society." That was the kind of answer that always kept authorities at bay. Of course, an answer like "I'm sorry, I'm not interested" was totally out of the question. One can never say no to a KGB offer. Such a no could end one's career. Therefore I stuck to engaging myself in patriotic rhetoric as the unwritten protocol dictated. Surely, Vasily didn't expect to hear anything else. *Sonofabitch probably goes to his wife at night,* I thought, *has a shot of vodka, and maybe a sardine for a chaser, watches the TV and goes to bed.* I pictured him in bed with his wife. *She probably holds a grudge against him, because he hangs his smelly socks on the chair near the bed. On top of that he probably snores like a pig. On weekends he gets together with his colleagues and they listen to "forbidden" Vysotsky or "dissident" Okudzhava recordings and giggle.* The more I thought of him that way, the more comfortable I felt. But little by little Vasily was taking ground from under me. The questions became specific.

"When can you be available for school?" he asked.

"A couple of months or so," I replied hesitantly.

"It must be much sooner," he hurried, "like . . . two weeks from now." He looked at me very seriously, as though I was already in the KGB. "Sure," I said, "sure, Vasily Ivanovich."

The conversation continued for two hours. It was clear they wanted me for the KGB's American operations. I calculated my options, but there didn't seem to be any way out. Foolishly I had begun to enjoy seeing just how much I could bait this KGB heavyweight into patronizing me with his sales effort. After all, one wasn't often in the position of having the mighty KGB supplicating for one's favor. The more I strung him out, however, the more difficult it became to back out.

"I'm glad to hear you talking this way," he said. "Shall we go ahead and set it up?"

In the end, I capitulated. It was only after I'd left that I realized I'd made one final mistake. I'd signed the documents, including a nondisclosure statement, that would commit me to the training program. I was now a member of the KGB, whether I liked it or not.

When I got back to my parents, I violated my nondisclosure statement by outlining to my father what had happened at KGB headquarters. I was very interested in his reaction.

"Look, sonny, you don't want that," he said slowly.

"Why?"

"Because you don't know anything. If you knew as much as I . . . then you wouldn't ask." He paused. "Sometimes I'm sorry for, you know, where we all are now. I mean, our family . . . If I were a plain worker, I'd be happier. But I just happened to get up there . . . You're going to be up there. You'd feel better, later, if you made it there without working for the 'neighbors.'" He looked out the window at the panoramic view of Moscow. "You'll have less dead souls on your conscience. See, what I mean?"

"Yeah, I see," I agreed, "but how would I get out of this? You never did."

"It's because I never really wanted to. I wanted the best for you, for mama. Now, it's Katya . . . you have a chance to live an honest life. Don't fuck it up. I'll see what I can do."

As we were talking, Natasha came in with Katya. She had taken her out for a stroll. "Hi, darling," she said, taking off her Italian-made overcoat and her blue fox hat. "Sorry we're late. Hello there, Papa."

My father nodded at her and returned to our conversation. "Listen, Vladimir, if you want this baby to be well, then you have to be with her more. Take care of your family first. That means forgetting about this KGB business. Don't go there, please. ·If anything goes wrong, you won't have a chance with them. Once you're out, you won't get a job, except maybe cleaning the streets. MFAs are good guys. Go there. They are more human than the KGB. You don't owe them your soul."

"But I've already promised." I told him about the documents.

"Don't worry, I'll take care of it. Now you must drag it out. You've got a medical exam tomorrow?"

I nodded.

"Okay, reschedule it for three days from now."

I managed to postpone the medical examination, but when the time came my father still didn't have an answer, so I went for the exam. They gave me a regular checkup—blood pressure, skin, heart, eyesight. I knew the KGB had a stringent requirement for eyesight. So I figured it was an easy way out. Intentionally, I mixed up some numbers on the board, but I didn't mix them up badly enough. The doctor said I just made it. Disappointed, I went home.

My father was waiting with a bottle of Courvoisier on the table. "You are out! Sonofabitch, you ain't gonna worry no more." We finished the bottle and listened to a recording of Nat King Cole, "Just One of Those Things."

A week later I was again summoned by the deputy director of personnel of the IIR. He instructed me to go to the Ministry of Foreign Affairs for my assignment.

My red MFA I.D. said *Sotrudnik Ministerstva Inostranykh Dyel* (Employee of the Ministry of Foreign Affairs). The deputy director of the Middle East department greeted me. We talked for five minutes. "Oh, Arabist, we need you, welcome," and so on, and told me to go to the consular department to get acquainted with procedures. It was decided I'd be assigned to the consulate general in Alexandria, Egypt. The exact position would be determined in a month when I was finished learning about the current situation in Egypt.

The IIR graduation ceremony was on January 26. The hall in the Rossiya Hotel was large and very cold. The tables stretched from one end of the room to the other, each festooned with flowers and set with champagne, Georgian wines, and cognacs. The attending graduates, directors, professors, and their spouses and dates were allowed to sit according to their preferences. Natasha and I were joined by Victor Kudryavtsev, who was assigned to the Soviet Embassy in Algeria. He had been assigned to do KGB work there as well. Also at our table was my best man at the wedding, Nikolai Kryuchkov, whom I was to meet again three years later during a brief stopover in Iraq. Also with us were Igor Melichov, a *stukach* in good standing who now was assigned to Aden, Zdravko Velev, a Bulgarian who was assigned to Libya, and the ever-present Anatoly.

After numerous toasts, three of us—Victor, Nikolai Kryuchkov, and I—found ourselves heading for the restroom at the same time. As we entered, there was a young black man, probably one of the 20,000 Third World students then studying—and being recruited by the KGB—at Patrice Lumumba University in Moscow.

Victor nodded towards him. "Hey, let's get the sonofabitch." Victor hated blacks and became violent about it when drunk.

Nikolai smiled. "The motherfucker deserves some enlightenment."

The black student saw Nikolai's face and tried to sidestep out of the room, but Nikolai blocked his way and kicked him hard in the groin. The black doubled up as Victor chopped down on his neck with both hands clenched together, then delivered one more blow to his face as the student went down. Blood from his nose and mouth spread on the floor where he lay motionless. Silently and quickly the two of them relieved themselves and walked out of the bathroom.

Again, as with the incident in Hodeida, I shamefully did nothing but watch. Victor's father was high up in both MFA and KGB circles, so any heroics on my part wouldn't have been understood. And after all, beating up blacks in Moscow was a favorite Russian pastime. I couldn't stop that, just as I couldn't stop anything else that was happening. With this in mind I locked the door to the restroom and waited until everyone left. Then I made my way back to our group.

Back at the table, I found Natasha's chair empty. She was dancing with someone, as usual. Anatoly pointed at a vacant chair next to him. I went over. "Listen, Vladimir, I've got some news. I'm joining you in Alexandria as the consul general's translator. Isn't that great?"

"Oh, sure, great. We'll be working close." I bit my lip.

Natasha returned, radiant from her dancing.

"Look who's going to be around in Alexandria," I told her.

"Are you really," she said, smiling at Anatoly. "That's wonderful. Why don't you come over for dinner tomorrow at our place. Six o'clock."

Things are going to get cozy in Egypt, I could see—just Natasha, me, and the KGB.

13: Soviet Sphinx

A train ride from Moscow to the Black Sea and a cruise on the Soviet luxury liner *Latvia* brought Natasha, eleven-month-old Katya, and me into Alexandria in style. It was April 1968. We went ashore at all three stops in Varna, Istanbul, and Athens. My father had given me a German camera as a farewell present and I took dozens of pictures of Natasha and Katya at each stop.

The *Latvia* approached Alexandria early one Wednesday morning. From the upper deck I could see King Farouk's winter palace just left of the port entrance. The port was crowded with merchant ships, mostly Soviet. To the right, I noticed four or five Soviet destroyers and a cruiser. Behind them was a dry dock. The missile boats were hidden deeply inside the harbor, near warehouses and what looked like a customs building. Far to my right I could see where the city was giving way to desert. That's where Al-Alamein should be, I thought.

The *Latvia* was heading towards the passenger pier, which I noticed had been recently built. The modern design of the passenger customs building didn't fit in with the overall spirit of the port, the king's castle and the old cargo boats.

A crowd of peddlers was pushed back by two uniformed Egyptian customs officers, who were exchanging what sounded like pleasant talk with three other men. I concluded those men, dressed in elegant suits, must be Soviets.

And, surely enough, one of them was waiting for us. As we walked down the gangway we were met by Victor Sbirunov, an energetic man in his late thirties, dark-haired, who stood about five-feet eleven-inches. He wore a British-made steel gray suit and a dark blue tie. I noticed he was trying to keep his slightly bulging stomach in. His pleasant round face with heavy, slightly protruding lower jaw and deep-set eyes expressed genuine gladness when he introduced himself as Vice-Consul of the Soviet Consulate General in Alexandria.[1] We didn't have to go through customs, so Sbirunov picked up Katya's portable crib in one hand and a suitcase in the other and walked briskly to his car. I noticed he was all aggressive self-confidence as he walked to his Opel. I knew in advance what Sbirunov's position really was and watched him closely, trying to foresee what was in store for me.

The drive to the consulate general took about fifteen minutes. I've never seen such wild driving, but Sbirunov was obviously accustomed to cars crossing and stopping and turning and changing lanes and directions without signal or warning.

"You'll get used to it," Sbirunov smiled at me as he broke into the seaside drive and had to swerve sharply to avoid a donkey cart. *"Ya, himar!"* he shouted in Arabic. Turning his head back to Natasha, he said, "I don't speak Arabic. It's just about the only word everyone uses on the road. *Ya himar* means 'Hey, you jackass.'"

"Here is the consulate," he pointed out as the car turned onto a cross street. I saw a huge Mediterranean-style mansion that towered over the street from the depth of a garden protected by a high stone wall. The trees inside the spacious garden were much taller than the mansion itself. Sbirunov made another turn and slowly drove up a steep street. "That's your house." he pointed to a villa on the right

---

[1] I found the difference between consulates and consulates general in the Soviet diplomatic system to be quite striking. While consulates perform intelligence and some consular duties, consulates general are structured more like embassies. Their functions are of a more political character, and the consul general himself occupies second rank to the ambassador within a host country. There is no exception to the rule that consular officers are "neighbors."

and stopped the car at a wooden gate. The gate opened into a large yard and we walked through the passageway toward the villa.

"All these properties belonged to one of King Farouk's generals. They were expropriated and the general now lives somewhere in Greece." Sbirunov showed us into a dark marble hallway.

"The first floor is mostly for recreation," he continued as we went up some redwood stairs. "We have a library here and our doctor's medical office. The second floor," he pointed into a long corridor, "is occupied by *dezhurny commandant* (the guard) of the consulate and another consulate employee—Anatoly Kuznetsov, you know him. Also, there is a lounge over there." He stopped so we could catch our breath. "I keep it locked most of the time. There are some great antiques there. Italian, Spanish . . . also a piano." I thought, *thank God for the piano*. "And here's where you'll live, Vladimir. I'll show you the consulate later." He opened a door on the third floor and gave Natasha the key. "Get settled and come over for a bite to eat. I'm across the hallway."

Sbirunov left us alone. The apartment had two furnished rooms on one side of the hallway, a lounge with two sofas and a stereo, a kitchen and a huge bathroom with a bidet on the other side. One side of the apartment overlooked the luscious grounds of the consulate general and the other side had a door leading to a sun deck overlooking the Mediterranean.

We all decided it was a splendid place, rather like a resort, only I'd get paid for living in it. As far as I was concerned, the setting was heaven compared to Yemen. When Natasha came close and said, "You know, we can start here anew," I agreed without any hesitation.

After a light lunch in Sbirunov's quarters, Natasha retired to unpack while Sbirunov's wife, Lyuda, began to clean up. Sbirunov invited me on a drive to see the city. As we passed through the clean, ancient streets in Sbirunov's Opel Kapitan sedan, the setting sun tinted the white buildings a rosy hue. Modern hotels along the seashore blended with the more ornate Arabian architecture. I caught the smell of kebab and falafel wafting from restaurants as we passed, and caught sight of colorful displays of jewelry and other goods in the shops. Warm breezes blew in from the Mediterranean.

We crossed Mustapha Pasha Square and drove down Saad Zaglul Street. Hundreds of small businesses on both sides of the street were shadowed by large signs in Arabic and in English: "National Egyptian Bank," "Bank Mysr," "Amon Maritime Company," "Menatours Travel." We slowly moved along a dark street with gold and jewelry shops. I thought Natasha would love it. Here and there I could see flocks of frolicking Soviet specialists in white shirts and gray pants going in and out of stores.

In contrast to what I saw in Yemen, Egyptians on the street struck me as well-dressed, elegant-looking people who moved with that special Middle Eastern pride and respect. Out of the corner of my eye I caught a glimpse of a store filled with traditional Egyptian artifacts and samples of Arab craftsmanship. My respect and admiration for Arabian and Egyptian culture which I studied at the IIR was reaffirmed during that first tour given to me by Sbirunov.

"Wait till you see Al-Montaza and Al-Maamura," he said turning back.

"What's that?"

"Oh, used to be the summer palace of the king. Now it's a resort. I usually drive up there on Sundays. Only ten kilometers east," he said while we were waiting for a stop light.

"Well, what do you think?" Sbirunov finally asked as we passed a man-bull statue and pulled up at Nadi Al-Seid, the hunting club, which stretched across the narrow peninsula named As-Silsila (The Chain).

"It's breathtaking. I really like it."

"I'm glad. You've got to like the place where you work; otherwise, you're miserable. Just think about how many people would like to have what we have."

"I can tell even in this short time that this will be a place I'll never forget," I said. "Once you've been here, you'll always want to come back, but you won't be able to."

"That's right," he said. "There is no such thing as coming back, not in our trade, my friend." Here at least was a man with sophistication and sensitivity, I thought, not your run-of-the-mill field man. But he was more dangerous in the long run too, I thought. This was no Ivchenkov.

"How is Lev Skryabin doing?" Sbirunov suddenly asked.

"Fine. He's just back from Indonesia. Do you know him?" I didn't expect the question.

"Oh," Sbirunov smiled, "we worked in India together for three years . . . became close friends . . . that was in the early sixties . . . he's a great guy."

"You mean, he's a 'neighbor' too?" I smiled back.

"No, straight MFA, but you know . . . we always find things in common. Right?"

"Right," I agreed. Skryabin, Molotov's nephew and my father's good friend, was good enough reference for me.

Sbirunov told me more about himself. He came from Southern Russia and started his career as a militia officer in the city of Ordzhonikidze. Then he went to the law institute in Moscow and a two-year intelligence school in Belye Stolby. "I was just lucky," Sbirunov said. He was immediately sent to England for a year's training in KGB operations under the embassy's cover. His next assignment was India, where he spent four years under a vice-consul cover in the Soviet diplomatic missions in Bombay and Calcutta. Upon his return from India, Sbirunov had another year of the KGB's "qualifications-improving" courses and finally was assigned to the consulate general as the KGB resident in Alexandria.

The hunting club, where we had stopped for a drink out on the terrace, had a thirty-five year history of ownership. Originally it belonged to the chief of King Farouk's palace guard. So I was told by the manager of the club, an Armenian, who came up to shake hands with Sbirunov. After the revolution the club was taken over by the local police, then by the Alexandrian governor and finally by the central government. The manager proudly mentioned that Khrushchev himself ate and drank at the club, Marshall Grechko, commander of the Soviet Armed Forces, visited the club on two occasions, and that those were just some of the dignitaries.

The club's atmosphere expressed subtle wealth. There were no flashy colors in the lobby, nor in the dancing room. Restaurant tables were set far apart from one another and surrounded by velvet chairs. The huge deck where we sat was enlivened by brightly colored sun umbrellas. Sbirunov was drinking a Cinzano. I ordered Stella, a local beer. Sbirunov continued, "Remember Ivchenkov? Wasn't he the one with you in Yemen?"

I nodded, sipping on that terrific beer.

"I met him in Moscow five months ago. He's been transferred back to the Center. Poor guy has terrible ulcers. He'll probably be

194

grounded for a couple years. In any case, we talked. Did you like him?"

I lied. "Yes, fine fellow, stalwart patriot."

"Now," he paused to sip his Cinzano, "we'll be working together, me and you. Just remember one thing, if anybody—the navy, the GRU, the consul—asks you to do anything for them, come to me before you agree to it. I'll be your guiding light." He smiled and raised his glass toward me. I toasted back.

I hardly needed reminding.

On the way back we toured the consulate general. The guard opened the door and we walked along an alley covered with red sand toward the marble steps of the entrance. I noticed about fifty yards into the garden that there was a sunken tennis court which seemed to be in excellent shape.

"See we've got everything here—tennis, volleyball—you name it," said Sbirunov as he showed me through a heavy glass door.

The luxury inside was stunning. The consulate more closely resembled a royal palace than a think tank and operational control center. Pale pink, white, and blue marble covered the floor and the spiral staircase leading upstairs. Stained glass windows projected a rainbow of colors on the marble floor and onto a giant crystal chandelier in the hall. There were gold ornaments on the ceiling and, in the corners above, four huge doors which looked like the ones I saw a long time ago in the old Morozov mansion in Moscow, now the headquarters for the Soviet Committee of Friendship with Foreign Countries, a KGB front organization.

"The door to the left is Shumilov's—that is, our consul general's." Sbirunov pointed to the corner.

"This is mine to the right, straight ahead in the office of our consul from the Central Committee—he's got the biggest office," he laughed. "And that is yours, there, in the corner."

I walked into my office and estimated it to be about seven hundred square feet. A large fireplace with a mirror reaching the twenty foot ceiling was on one side. A wide door on the other side opened into a beautiful garden. Then I noticed there were two desks in the room and looked at Sbirunov: "Whose is that?"

"Oh, it's Anatoly's . . . Kuznetsov's. Hope you don't mind . . . just a year. Then surely you'll get promoted . . . Look, even Nikolai Lipilin, the embassy's attaché, and he is a navy commander, has to share his room in the basement with an interpreter. Don't worry. You wanna take a vice-consul's room? We have one . . . belongs to Guselnikov."

Later I found that Vasily Guselnikov was the only MFA diplomat among the staff of seven. The rest were from the KGB, GRU, Central Committee, and State Committee for Economic Relations with Foreign Countries (GKES).

"It's okay. I don't mind. It's not the first time," I said, and added, "By the way where is he?"

"I sent him to Cairo. I wanted a little quiet time with you."

The thought of Kuznetsov watching me, especially considering his KGB internal security duties, made me feel less enthusiastic about my new assignment. Once could be a coincidence—but this was the second time around.

The Egypt I entered in 1968, less than a year after the Six-Day War with Israel, was a nation still dazed by the beating it had taken. President Gamal Abdel Nasser's armed forces had been humiliated and had lost much of their Soviet-made aircraft, tanks, and other arms. The revenue-producing Suez Canal and Sinai oil fields were gone. Already deeply in debt, Nasser again had turned to the Soviet Union which offered unlimited aid in rearming and rebuilding. But that meant Egypt was going more into debt. Not that the Soviets were that interested in pressing for payment; Moscow didn't need yet another of poor Egypt's cotton crops, her only source of foreign exchange. The Kremlin was after bigger game. While keeping the Egyptians dazzled in the glow of its bountiful generosity, the Soviet Union was busy exacting its own secret and pernicious price. The Israelis were just the nominal victors in the Middle East. It was the Soviets who had Egypt just where they wanted. Egypt was ripe for Sovietization.

There were two levels to the Soviet Union's involvement with Egypt at the time, one above board, the other covert.

At the above-board level was the rhetoric of revolutionary brother-hood—of common goals toward the liquidation of Zionism and imperialism, the statements of undying solidarity with our Arab

196

socialist brethren—backed by the continuous flow of Soviet ship-ments into Alexandria, the daily delivery of arms, advisors, and more specialists. The Soviet civilian colony alone numbered 6,000 on my arrival and it was growing rapidly.

At the covert level, the orders from Moscow were to penetrate and subvert the country at every stratum. This meant quickly establish-ing a base in Egypt for the expanding Soviet operations in the Middle East. To accomplish this, propaganda efforts were coordinated. The goal was not only to bolster the partnership of the two countries but to encourage the Egyptians to pattern their newly reorganized armed forces and Nasser's ruling Arab Socialist Union party on the Soviet model. In this area the Soviets were meeting almost total success.

To complete the process of Sovietization, the massive Soviet military-diplomatic-political-intelligence community was in the midst of a well-organized effort to recruit and develop likely Soviet agents in every military, political, and government organization in Egypt.

Our specific orders—as I found out in extensive briefings and policy reviews during my first months in Alexandria—were to look for promising recruits among those who either held power or had the potential to do so. This meant officers and officer trainees in the armed forces, customs officers, bureaucrats, ASU officials, national and local police, technicians, labor leaders and managers, journalists, students, and businessmen. One group pointedly excluded were local Egyptian Communists. They were regarded by the KGB as untrust-worthy idealists who would compromise the all-important marriage with Nasser's party and government.

As I settled into my new job, I found that in my position as Secretary of the Consulate General, I would be involved at both open and covert levels. All my training at the Institute came into play. My fluency in Arabic, especially, put me in a position of great demand by all Soviet intelligence services in Alexandria.

My rank of a secretary was third from the bottom of the diplomatic ladder. Most IIR graduates were sent abroad on their first assign-ment, as *stazher* or "probationer." The next step was an interpreter at the embassy or consulate. Each stage took two years. The next rank was secretary of the consulate, or *referent* of the embassy, depending on where the former graduate worked. Up the ladder were attachés, secretaries and counselors. It was very seldom that a career MFA diplomat would make ambassador's rank. One either had to be KGB or directly connected with the Central Committee.

I skipped the two lower ranks mainly due to my weird luck in Yemen and an excellent reference from Ivchenkov. Now I had to work my way up from there.

At the above-board level, my job included, first of all, the usual consular duties—arranging for visas and passports, rescuing Soviet citizens who got into scrapes with the law, and settling the never-ending squabbles among the members of the Soviet colony. This brought me into very close contact with Egyptian police, *mukhabarat* and *amn* (intelligence and counterintelligence), and immigration police. I also handled shipping and customs arrangements for Soviet shipments—military and otherwise—which came through the port of Alexandria; I attended diplomatic receptions, wrote reports and took notes of conversations with most foreigners if the discussed subject deserved attention.

Because of my Arabic, I was called upon to make numerous public relations speeches. One duty I liked was to visit about twice a week Soviet military and cargo ships to read lectures on local culture, customs, and rules of behavior. Every other Saturday I monitored security and passenger movements when Soviet passenger ships made scheduled stops in Alexandria. Thus, I got to know most of Soviet navy brass and many of the passenger and merchant captains.

At the covert level, I found that Sbirunov and his colleagues would be using me as a recruitment front-man. Since my consular duties put me in constant contact with Egyptian officials, I was to scout each of them for qualities that would make them candidates for recruitment—sympathies with the Soviet Union, overwhelming ambition, job dissatisfaction, and exploitable weaknesses for drugs, alcohol, or women. I was to cultivate these persons as friends, soften them up, and convince them to go to Moscow for training or finesse them into doing the Soviets some favor that might turn out to be embarrassing later. When the candidate was sufficiently wooed, I was supposed to turn him over to Sbirunov, who would direct other operatives to complete the job.

This further development would peg the recruit as a full-time agent, or as one used through blackmail, or as a sympathizer called upon for favors, or as someone the KGB would pay off or help climb in ranks—in return for loyalty, inside information, and assistance in further recruitment.

The other part of my duties turned out to be more chaotic and, also, more dangerous at times. Sbirunov would lend me to GRU or navy intelligence, or just to someone from Cairo who happened to be in Alexandria on emergency. I would end up illegally popping into security areas, off limits even to the Soviets, to find what was going on there or occasionally to lift a document. Those were always rush orders and I was asked to go because I could bullshit my way in Arabic out of almost any situation. Or I would be asked to try to get files on foreigners from the immigration police. I managed, somehow.

All in all, the KGB couldn't have been happier anywhere—even in the Soviet Union itself. Nasser's Egypt in 1968 was a lamb waiting to be devoured.

It wasn't easy to understand the structure of the Soviet colony and its agencies in Alexandria, but I did the best I could. A month after my arrival, Sbirunov took me to Cairo for meetings at the embassy. I was introduced to Valentin Polyakov. Vice-consul of the embassy's consulate section. He was an old friend of Sbirunov, and like him a KGB major, but with much less responsibility. Polyakov mainly handled the intelligence network, recruitment, and control of Soviet citizens married to foreigners.

"You'll work quite a lot in this area with Polyakov," Sbirunov stated during our meeting, "since you had a lot of this type of experience in Yemen . . . Do you agree, Valentin?" He turned to Polyakov.

We were sitting in one of the embassy's offices, painted all in white and scarcely finished. Polyakov, a man of very common appearance, nodded and looked at me, sizing me up. "Sure, we'll work together. This will take a load off your shoulders, Victor. Good help is hard to come by these days," he smiled at Sbirunov.

"Well, Vladimir, all I want from you is to keep track of movements of these people. Here's the list. Get to know them. Meet with each personally. Their greatest asset is their travel to Emirates and places where we can't go. All legit, since they're married to Arab citizens, who, in turn, hold down good posts. So, take care of our women. Okay? And, report to Victor or to me directly. You know we try to avoid meeting them face to face, but you can do it."

There was no official reason why Victor and Valentin couldn't have met with the women agents themselves; it was part of their undercover duties for the KGB. I realized that they were pulling rank on me in order to unload a rather risky and dirty little job. If in the process I were caught by Egyptian counterintelligence it would be my neck, not theirs, and I'd be shipped home, not them. In any case, I couldn't refuse their orders.

I learned from the list that nine Soviet Mata Haris operated out of Cairo and Alexandria. I had become familiar with this portion of KGB operations through my two weeks of briefings at the MFA. The operation worked simply and efficiently. Some Arab students who studied in the Soviet Union would be approached by pretty Russian blondes. The girls would be KGB employees. If a marriage developed, so much the better. The wife would travel with her Arab husband to the Middle East. Then there was always a possibility that the husband would be employed on a sensitive project or do business in a country inaccessible to the Soviets, like Saudi Arabia, Qatar, or Oman. The benefits for the KGB would be immense. The wife would provide information, act as a scout to screen further candidates for recruitment, or just find Soviet sympathizers. We had four agents of this kind. Another four were married to Egyptian military officers.

But one of the nine women on the list was an exception. She married an Egyptian, either for love or to get away from the Soviet Union. She got into trouble; her husband didn't treat her well and she wanted to go home. Later, she came crying to me, asking for a ticket home. I referred her to Sbirunov, who convinced her to stay and work for him in exchange for getting her out of the country in the future.

While in Cairo, Sbirunov took me to two other officers after the meeting with Polyakov. One was in his late forties, slim and agile with sharp, dark features.

"Vladimir Grusha, counselor of the embassy," Sbirunov introduced us.

"Very glad to meet you, Vladimir. I think I met your father in New York back in the fifties."

"Oh, you might have. He goes there quite often."

"That's it. Nikolai Sakharov. I remember."

Both Grusha and Sbirunov smiled broadly and approvingly shook their heads.

"Welcome, welcome, Vladimir," and he turned to Sbirunov, "Victor, take good care of him. When I am in Alexandria, I'll stay over in your place and invite myself to have dinner with both of you."

For Sbirunov, such sudden casual intimacy from his direct superior couldn't help but be favorable and promising. "Well, Vladimir," he said when we left Grusha's plush office, "see how nice it is to be recognized."

Colonel Grusha was the KGB second in command. Actually, he didn't report to anyone except Moscow Center since Grusha was entrusted with the highly secret duty of handling all the illegal agents in Egypt, including President Nasser's security advisor, Sami Sharaf, nicknamed Asad. Grusha was once expelled from New York in 1957 while attached to the United Nations. After Egypt, Grusha continued his work in the United States showing up as an attaché to the Soviet Embassy in Washington in the 1970s.

Our last meeting of the day was held in the large office of the top KGB resident in Egypt, Pavel Nedosekin. Even Sbirunov spoke of him with fearful respect. No wonder: Nedosekin was charged with powers far greater than the ambassador, Sergei Vinogradov. His word could dispose of any Soviet diplomat, specialist, general, or doctor who worked in Egypt.

Nedosekin didn't get involved in external work; he ruled the internal affairs of the Soviet colony. All incidents involving Soviet citizens were reported via KGB residents and KGB internal security officers in Cairo, Alexandria, and Aswan. SK, or KGB officers in charge of the Soviet colony, usually were inserted into every Soviet group, including delegations and tourists. There were about forty-five such officers, just to spy on Soviet citizens in Egypt.

General Nedosekin's background earned him a high position within Soviet intelligence and counterintelligence. He started his KGB career in the early forties as a young NKVD Smersh officer who was sent into German-occupied territories of the Soviet Union and Poland to organize and interface with the partisan movements. In the woods of Bryansk he underwent his firsthand training in blowing up depots and trains, in mass annihilation of local citizens, and in killing traitors.

He married a partisan radio operator and they made one of the most fearsome couples in the Soviet intelligence community. They worked hand-in-hand abroad and at home, drunk on their power, until Nedosekin became the Soviet arch-spy in Egypt. One of Nedosekin's major achievements in the past was efficient handling of the Hungarian revolt in 1956. When I met him in Egypt, it was rumored that he was being considered for the post of Deputy Director of Counterintelligence Service of the First (Foreign) Chief Directorate of the KGB, the most powerful and secretive service within the KGB.

Nedosekin pointed to a conference table and we sat down. I was going to offer a friendly greeting, but I squelched the impulse when I noticed Sbirunov's expression had changed drastically. His easy smile was gone and his back stooped a bit. He seemed poised to jump at any time and carry out whatever Nedosekin told him to do. Nedosekin was a man who presented great danger, but I decided to look as natural as I could. I lit a cigarette, crossed my legs, and moved the chair to face Nedosekin halfway.

"Welcome, Comrade Sakharov," Nedosekin said in a gray voice. He wore a dark blue suit. I recognized it as made in England. An expensive Christian Dior tie matched the suit's color and punctuated the whiteness of his shirt. I noticed a pair of glasses on the table and a file. Nedosekin's fine features, his rather oblong face and bland expression, could have prompted an outsider to think of him as an English businessman or a Hollywood producer.

"I am glad to meet you and hope to serve the interests of the Soviet government as well as I can," I started.

"Yeah, I know," interrupted Nedosekin. "I know all about you. Tell me now, why didn't you report on Ivchenkov's actions in Yemen? You drank with him? You know his behavior was stupid, sometimes. I also heard that all of you got together on the plane back home, even the pilots, and drank all the way to Moscow," he continued without raising or lowering his voice. "I also heard you used to be quite a taxi rider way back in Moscow. Is that true?"

I didn't know what to say. There was no way for anything to go unnoticed. I said, "I thought Ivchenkov was the top of the line, plus I thought he had orders. Secondly, on the plane everybody was glad to get out of Yemen and celebrate. As far as taxi business is concerned, that was a long time ago."

"Don't justify your acts. We all have shortcomings, Comrade Sakharov, just work well and listen to him." Nedosekin pointed to Sbirunov.

I knew that Nedosekin was playing a typical game. First, he'd come on strong to show how powerful he was. Then, he'd slow down and let me think I was part of the train.

"And," he continued, "be alert. Watch out for those who drink too much, who go to nightclubs, who fool around with women, and who engage in speculation. Immediately report those to Sbirunov or to me. Understand?"

No matter how outraged and disgusted I was, I nodded and assured Nedosekin that it was precisely what I was going to do.

As we left Nedosekin's office, I asked Sbirunov, still silent, "How do you think I can carry on with all those things?"

"Don't worry. Do what you can. More important, don't screw up. See, if you can't handle your job, you can always justify it by blaming others for non-cooperation. But, if you go and fuck a belly dancer and Nedosekin finds out about it you're through."

Sbirunov was still somewhat tense.

"Let's get some dinner." he said.

"Fine."

We went down the stairs by the ambassador's office on the second floor. The security guard sat at the desk to the left. Some Arabs waited on a couch against a tall glass wall overlooking Al-Giza Street.

As we passed through the entrance, I heard a loud voice behind me, "Vladimir! Wait." I turned and saw my former classmate, Aleksander Kalugin. We stood and chatted a minute or so while Aleksander told me that he just married the daughter of the minister of civil aviation and was assigned as a consular clerk to the embassy. I congratulated him, but didn't say much about myself. Sbirunov was impatiently waiting outside.

We decided to spend the night in Cairo. Sbirunov dropped me off at the hotel. "I gotta go," he said as I got out of the car, "some business in Zamalek . . . Enjoy yourself . . . and get a room for me." He handed me five five pound bills. "I'll be late."

I didn't remind him about dinner. It was a good chance to spend some time alone. The street was crowded with cars and people. Store windows threw bright lights on the sidewalk. I entered the hotel lobby and walked up to the check-in counter. The stand on the counter was covered with postcards and, as I paid eight pounds for each room to the clerk, I remembered I had to do something very important. I picked up my key and instead of taking the elevator up to my room on the seventh floor, I walked out of the hotel.

Just around the corner, there was a souvenir store that sold postcards. I walked in and picked one out. It had to have a picture of Alexandria. Then I went back up to my hotel room. I made sure the door was locked and wrote on the card, "Greetings from beautiful Alexandria. Respectfully yours." I addressed the card to a post office box in Amsterdam and put it in a mailbox four blocks away from the hotel.

14: Quiet Flows the Nile

"What do I do now?" I asked Sbirunov after we'd led our guest into the consulate general reception room. "There isn't anything in our instruction book to cover this, except perhaps under special provisions for attached visas, and even there it says we must have authorization from Moscow to issue such a visa."

Sbirunov scratched his temple. "Well, I'm sure you know it also says that in exceptional cases, the issuance of visas without higher authorization could be decided upon by the head of the mission, or his deputy. So you see in this case I *can* decide."

"Oh," I nodded, "fine, but the guy doesn't have a photograph with him."

"It's okay . . . sometimes . . . Moscow knows . . . plus, we'll confirm his arrival by wire, or they'll do it out of Europe . . . Don't worry. Just do the paperwork." Sbirunov paused. "There'll be more."

The paperwork took me a couple of minutes. I went upstairs to the *referentura* (restricted area where classified documents and communications were kept) and photocopied the man's passport. I took five more minutes to fill out the standard forms that I had to complete on anyone who requested to travel in the U.S.S.R. The forms called for as much detailed information on the person as I could possibly gather. Personal history, political leanings, connections, habits, associates, and financial status were very much desired by Moscow. Three copies were sent to Moscow, coded OVIR 1, OVIR 2, and OVIR 3. The initials OVIR stand for *Odtel Viz i Registratsii,* or Department of Visas and Registration. In actuality, however, the forms are routed to the First (Foreign) Directorate of the KGB (OVIR 1), the KGB's second (Internal) Directorate (OVIR 2), and to the Consulate Department of the Ministry of Foreign Affairs (OVIR 3), operated jointly by the KGB and the MFA.

The First (Foreign) Directorate would use the information to assess whether a tourist, visiting businessman, or student were a likely candidate for recruitment while in the USSR or abroad. The Second (Internal) Directorate would be in charge of following him during the stay. The Consulate Department, meanwhile, would file the information for reference of any other department that might want information on the visitor—for example, trade or cultural affairs officers who might be in contact with him. This was standard operating procedure for every visitor to the U.S.S.R.

Attached visas, *privesnye*—one of the formalities I was trying to expedite that day—were new to me. I knew it meant the visa was attached to, instead of stamped on, the visitor's passport. That was all. So after I'd finished and Sbirunov and I escorted our Arab guest out the consulate door, I turned back to Sbirunov and asked him to come back up to the *referentura* and check my work to be sure I hadn't made any mistakes.

"Are you crazy!" Sbirunov shouted. "You don't fill out anything when an attached visa is issued! Why do you think we don't stamp anything on his passport?"

It sank in. "So no one knows that person has ever been in the Soviet Union," I replied.

"See?" Sbirunov tore up the forms. "No one, means *no one!*" He paused. "*I* will inform those who *are* supposed to know. And you just make a note that one attached visa was issued, for the record. But no names! Understand?"

"Yes, sure. It's my first time," I apologized, and lit a match to burn the torn-up forms."

"It's all right," Sbirunov said, "you'll learn."

I learned that attached visas were used primarily for citizens of countries with which the Soviet Union didn't have relations and/or who would not want anyone back home to know they'd visited the Soviet Union.

Once I learned the routines, I handled many of these cases. Most of them were students from the Persian Gulf Emirates and Saudi Arabia. They wanted it to look as though they were going to Europe for study, but once in Alexandria, they secretly rerouted themselves to the U.S.S.R. and would stay for any length of time. Since they were going to a lot of trouble to go to the U.S.S.R., they must have been sympathetic to the Soviet cause and therefore prime prospects for the KGB to recruit as agents when they returned to their oil-rich homelands. The high volume of traffic indicated there must have been a strong KGB recruitment network on the Arabian peninsula and the Arabian Gulf.

The attached visa device was also used for Communist party members from countries where those parties are prohibited. But these visitors, while tolerated for public relations purposes, didn't interest the KGB as much as a third group that also used the attached visa device—terrorists. Members of the Palestinian guerilla organizations made regular trips to Moscow for briefings, training, and financing. Top guerilla leaders, for example, Palestine Liberation Organization leader Yasir Arafat, traveled more openly and didn't use this pipeline. He was a regular visitor to Cairo during that period and would talk with the Soviets as well as Nasser while there. Occasionally he would continue to Moscow for another visit.

Anatoly Kuznetsov was busy performing his KGB *stukach* duties, just as he had done at the IIR. But to my relief, he was active far from my sphere of operation. Sbirunov had him working in the Soviet specialists' colony.

Natasha and I continued to see him socially, however, because he had married one of Natasha's best friends, a brunette named Nadya. Natasha had introduced Anatoly to Nadya in Moscow and the two became close and finally married during those first five months in 1968 after graduation and the move to Alexandria.

At first they would come for dinner fairly often, but then Nadya started coming alone and she would spend long hours talking to Natasha. The marriage wasn't going well. After a honeymoon glow that lasted about two months, he had lost interest in her, she complained. She had attempted several times to rekindle the romantic flame, but each time with little success, and the last time, she ended up pregnant. She wasn't sure if she wanted to have the baby, but finally she decided to go ahead. She would go back to Moscow to give birth, and when Anatoly finished his two-year tour of duty in 1970, he'd join her. Maybe then they could work things out.

Natasha and I went down to the docks to see Nadya off. She was traveling to Odessa on the *Latvia,* the same ship we'd sailed to Alexandria. Anatoly was there, but I didn't say much to him. A noisy farewell party ensued in their cabin. Natasha had a box of presents she asked Nadya to take to my parents in Moscow. Her indiscretion with the five-thousand-nik lingered in their memories and I doubted presents would have much effect, but I kept my opinions to myself and decided to get away from the party and take a stroll on the deck.

I ran into Sbirunov and thought it would be good to check in with him. He was going over the passenger list with the first mate—a KGB political officer, or *pompolit.*

"See what we've got there?" he was exclaiming. "Two Americans from Beirut. You know them?"

"Yes," the tall, uniformed *pompolit* answered. "They are rich tourists going through Odessa to Moscow. An old couple."

I tapped Sbirunov on the shoulder. "You need me?" I asked.

"Go ahead, do whatever . . ." he answered distractedly, "but don't forget tomorrow morning."

I couldn't forget tomorrow morning. I was looking forward to it, although the assignment was one of those baffling ones doubtlessly created by some overzealous bigshot at Moscow Center. Sbirunov and I were going to Al-Alamein, four hours drive from Alexandria, and I was excited about seeing it. I knew the countryside along the way—golden sand dunes, green, purple, and blue sea. I had heard the tanks and military equipment could still be found there from the famous World War II battle in which the British broke Rommel's Afrika Korps. While in Al-Alamein, I had to fulfill a strange request from Moscow. There were three or four huge cemeteries there where thousands of allied and German soldiers were buried. Moscow wanted an independent count of how many soldiers from each country were interred in those sandy graves.

Thinking this over, I walked along the deck of the *Latvia.* I looked up and saw a man coming towards me. He looked like Omar Sharif, so much so that for a second I was taken aback. He came right up to me and stopped. He was very well dressed, and was probably one of the Egyptian military intelligence men who always hung around the docks.

He smiled. "You are Mister Sakharov, aren't you?" He stretched out his hand.

"Yes, I am. How did you know?"

"Your predecessor, Robert—I don't remember his last name— well, he worked for the consulate general. He told me your name before he left. Anyway, he used to work with me in many different ways. By the way, my name is Sallah Al-Badawi. I thought you'd like to continue the relationship."

At that moment the announcement for all visitors to go ashore came over the ship's public address system. We went down the gangway together.

Natasha and Katya were nowhere to be seen and I got a little worried. Sallah stayed right with me as I looked around and then walked away from the crowd and over to my car which was parked nearby. Finally, they appeared. Natasha, ever flirtatious, brightened when she saw the handsome Sallah. I took Katya in my arms and made introductions. Sallah gallantly kissed Natasha's hand.

Natasha pointed at Katya. "Volodya, we are getting hungry. Maybe we'd better stop at a restaurant on the way back home."

I looked at Sallah. "Would you like to join us?"

Sallah looked at Natasha. "By all means, please come with us," she said.

"I am honored." Sallah smiled and the four of us got into the car. Our dinner marked the beginning of a remarkable friendship. Breaking with the Soviet mission's rule of never letting foreigners pick up the tab, I let Sallah pay.

Sallah proved to be aware of many things which were happening in the Soviet colony and he understood the difficulties I had coping with the complaints of the Soviets about their comrades, or by Soviets about Egyptians, or by the Egyptians about the Soviets.

I asked him if he was connected with the government in any way. "Sometimes," he said.

Intrigued, I dined with him several times in the next weeks at Al-Montaza, Al-Maamura, and Abukir restaurant. Not taking any chances, I kept Sbirunov informed of our get-togethers, telling my

209

KGB boss that Sallah seemed like a recruitment prospect. But the more I got to know Sallah, the more my first impressions were confirmed. He was no sucker for recruitment. First of all he was too smart, secondly he didn't have exploitable weaknesses. He had a seemingly limitless supply of money, lady friends, and free time, but he always conducted himself prudently. He drank, but not too much; he enjoyed himself, but discreetly. He liked some Russians personally, but would never fall for the Soviet-Arab brotherhood routine. He respected Nasser, but never praised him for bringing Soviet influence into Egypt. He had a certain disdain for Egyptian *fellaheen* (peasants) but not a royalist arrogance; he admired Western culture, but was not eager for it to displace Arab values. He seemed a man of personal integrity—a rare quality—and this inspired my respect. He could be a useful ally if cultivated properly. I didn't entirely trust him, but I did like him.

I knew better than to approach him with any propaganda pitches. He was too valuable an ally for my own purposes. I would run into him often as I made my usual rounds and I noticed quickly that, in day-to-day dealings with police and other officials, doors always would open smoothly if Sallah accompanied me.

Sallah's job, ostensibly, was as a partner in a local freight forwarding company and I began to use that company to transport incoming Soviet supplies. But Sallah asked questions that a freight forwarder never asked.

"Who is Sbirunov?" he asked me once when we were sitting in the cocktail lounge of the Fuji Club—an "in" night club with the rich, Westernized Arab youths and non-Soviet foreigners.

"Why?" I responded, sipping a Cinzano.

"Nothing, it just seems like he has a lot of clout with your people and some of our people too."

"Well, you know the type . . ." I hesitated. "Some people just project a sense of power. . . ." I tried to turn it into a joke. "Just look at me, for example."

"No, that's not it." Sallah switched from Arabic to English and said flatly, "He must be your security man."

I steered away from that one. "You know Sallah, speaking of security, I can't get your Egyptian system straight. You have police, that is understandable. But then there is *Mudiriya* or *Idarat Al-Amn*, which is security too. Then there is *Mubahith*, which either is an intelligence or investigations department." I paused. "Then on top of it all you have *Mukhabarat*, which, due to the ambiguity of its meaning in Arabic, could be either 'intelligence' or 'counterintelligence.' Can you explain it to me?"

Sallah launched into a rambling explanation that clarified nothing for me. Maybe the East Germans have it straight, I mused; they'd been in charge of advising those organizations. But I doubted the real Egyptian professionals had been so foolish as to follow East German directions either. They'd humor the Soviet allies as Nasser's guests, but do things their own way.

Sallah and I looked at each other. I knew he was the best of Egyptian counterintelligence that the KGB and its recruited flunkies worked to push aside. I decided not to tell Sbirunov any more about Sallah than was absolutely necessary.

But Sbirunov was no fool either. "Vladimir, I think you must drop it," he told me in his office one day. "The man definitely works for the government and is not recruitable. He might even be trying to recruit you." Sbirunov laughed.

I told him that I'd be careful, but dropping Sallah was a mistake. With Sbirunov's permission, I said, I'd like to continue the contact informally because I felt Sallah could be useful with Egyptian authorities. Sbirunov agreed reluctantly. "But watch it . . ." he warned.

Fortunately, my position was soon vindicated. Several weeks later, my telephone rang at two in the morning. I heard Natasha say "Not again" as I rolled out of bed to answer.

It was Sallah. "Come over to Ras et-Teen police station quickly," he spoke rapidly. "They've got two of your men from the Cairo embassy here, I'll wait for you."

I immediately woke up Sbirunov.

"You go to the police," he said after catching on to what I told him, "and I'll wait in my office."

The Ras et-Teen police station was in the direction of the port, five or so miles from the consulate general. As soon as I walked in I saw Sallah talking to a uniformed police major. They were standing on a wooden bench on which two young men were sitting. Both men were handcuffed and looked very angry. To my great surprise I recognized one of them as Victor Degtyar, son of the Soviet Ambassador to Pakistan. His sister, Tatyana Degtyar, had been an old friend of mine, first introduced to me by Victor Kudryavtsev six years ago. Natasha also knew her and had just received a letter from her. Tatyana was getting married to another friend of mine from the IIR, Igor Bondarev, whose father was attaché of the Soviet embassy in Washington, D.C.

Victor saw me and the expression on his face changed. He knew that I knew about his approaching graduation from KGB Intelligence School with an American specialization. His assignment to the embassy in Cairo was a three-month internship. It became apparent that the KGB was cultivating an elite handful of agents who would have both a U.S. specialization and a good working knowledge of the Middle East, and thus was assigning a few of its spy school graduates to Middle East internships before they would be transferred permanently to the United States. This made sense in light of the Soviet grand strategy of driving a wedge between the oil-rich Arab countries and the United States. A U.S.-based KGB operative, who might be an information officer or other Soviet embassy official, or might be operating undercover—for example, posing as a U.S. businessman, or working as one of U.S. foreign policy decision-making advisors—would do well to have an intimate knowledge of the Arab world in order to help disrupt U.S.-Arab relations. In the light of this, it became clear to me now why the KGB bigshot Vasily Ivanovich had made that offer to me in Moscow which I had so narrowly avoided.

"What happened?" I asked the police major and nodded hello towards Sallah.

"They got drunk and began harassing some girls at the Al-Maamura Club. They complained . . . Al-Maamura police came and arrested them; they resisted. . . ." He shrugged his shoulders. "But, you see, Mister Consul, they close the jail for the night there, so we had to take them in here."

"I'll be responsible. You can let them go now," I told the officer. He didn't reply, but instead invited me to follow him into an adjacent room.

"Look, Mister Consul," he said after he shut the door, "I'm going to let them go . . . this time. But not because of you—because of him." He gestured toward Sallah. "I can't interfere with our counterintelligence."

He stepped back into the room and unlocked the handcuffs. Sallah didn't make a move.

I shook his hand. "Thank you. I didn't know you were so . . . uh . . . influential."

"I don't think I would have done it for anyone else." He smiled. "Those guys," he pointed toward the bench, "should have spent a day or so in our magnificent jail."

"I understand," I said. "Sallah, it doesn't matter anymore. Why don't you show me your I.D."

"It really doesn't matter . . . here." He opened his wallet and handed me his I.D. It said *Muwazzif al-Mukhabarat*. It's difficult to translate *Muwazzif* into English. Just like *sotrudnik* it means "an employee entrusted with authority, a loyal, reliable and trustworthy member of a government organization."

"Now, I must accompany you to the consulate," Sallah said.

"Why?"

"Procedures."

The three of us got into my Volga and Sallah followed us in his Fiat.

At the Consulate General, Sbirunov was waiting with coffee. "If you tell about what happened to anyone," he hissed at me, "I'll wipe you out."

I assured him I wouldn't say anything. Victor Degtyar, son of the ambassador, a KGB general and deputy minister of foreign affairs all in one, was too powerful a young man even for Sbirunov to let get into trouble.

Having left the young KGB agents to Sbirunov to sober up, I went outside. Sallah's Fiat was parked near the consulate's back exit. I walked to the car intending to look inside.

Suddenly Sallah's voice from behind stopped me. "Vladimir! Wait!" I almost jumped.

"No, no, it's okay." Sallah came out of the darkness. "I just want to tell you something now that you know me better."

"What's that?" I caught my breath.

"It has to do with that guy at your office, Anatoly Kuznetsov."

"What about him?" I asked, taking a British cigarette which he offered to me.

"I saw him follow you a couple of times. There's something

snakelike about him, if I dare say so—do watch out." He paused. "You are my friend."

We shook hands and I thanked him for everything. He got into his car and started the engine. "Oh, by the way," he added, "if you need anything, let me know."

I laughed, "Likewise, my friend, *arrivederci.*"

As I made my way back home, I knew there was no reason for me to be angry at Anatoly. So he was at it again. *They won't hesitate to step on you, betray you—even your friends—pick your brains, go behind your back. This is the way the world is set up.* It was no surprise. But I had to be careful, doubly so in light of what I had to protect. Anatoly was probably after small game, an indiscretion or two that he could hang around my neck in order to earn himself a few points. That would be bad enough, but if he were to catch me as a spy, he would be a Soviet hero. He didn't even deserve it. I must dispose of him. *This is the way the world is set up. . . .*

Although they didn't resemble each other, the quiet, toughmindedness of the nationalistic counterintelligence man Sallah reminded me of Anwar Sadat, a man far more important than he. At the time, Sadat was Vice President, but his importance was underestimated by the Soviets.

I never got to know Sadat. I would see him at official receptions from time to time. But he was overshadowed by Nasser and Egyptian VIPs. However, one of my jobs was to arrange vacation trips for his two daughters and see to their security on the *Latvia*. The ship would take them to the Soviet Black Sea resort, Artek. Sadat's children were accompanied from Cairo to Alexandria by Sergei Arakelyan, the Soviet ambassador's personal secretary and interpreter. Arakelyan, a tall handsome Soviet Armenian, was an old friend of Vladimir Segal, my IIR Arabic teacher. Thus we had something in common and shared it over a drink at the Abukir restaurant.

The Soviets didn't think much of Sadat. They assumed he was just another yes man. Their darling was Ali Sabry, chairman of Nasser's Arab Socialist Union party and the man they figured to succeed Nasser—not that they thought Nasser was in any imminent danger of passing on.

By 1970 the Soviets reached one of their goals—putting the Arab Socialist Union under the control of the Central Committee of the

CPSU. Ali Sabry, ostensibly the top political leader under Nasser, had become a conductor of the CC will, like the heads of socialist and Communist parties in Eastern Europe, Mongolia, and North Vietnam.

Sabry's meetings with the leaders of the Communist Party of the Soviet Union (CPSU) in Moscow became more frequent and less open. On several occasions he'd take off in the middle of the night, I was told by Arakelyan, on board a special plane to Moscow. Sometimes he would accompany Nasser at secret negotiations in the Kremlin, but sometimes Sabry went alone. Only the Soviet ambassador and the counselor of the embassy in charge of the ASU were aware of those trips.

Thus Sabry became a natural successor of Nasser, and the ASU turned, by the Kremlin's calculation, into an extension of the will of the Egyptian people. Soviet political support for Sabry brought him exposure in the press, radio, and TV second only to Nasser, while Sadat was considered by the Soviets as not strong and popular enough among the Arab leaders to effectively implement the policy of Soviet-sponsored Arab socialism.

Such overconfidence and insensitivity to Egyptian nationalism and Pan-Islamism was to give them a costly lesson. While they continued to flood the ASU with propaganda, Soviets failed to understand that the ASU was no substitute for Islamic and Egyptian nationalism.

Two days after the Degtyar incident, Sbirunov called me to his office as if nothing happened. He told me to dial 60000 and get an appointment with Ahmed Hilal, director of Al-Montaza Park and its hotel.

"We want him," Sbirunov said firmly. I wondered why the KGB would need an old man like Hilal, who had been in his position for thirty years. "We want him," Sbirunov said firmly. "We suspect him of being a member of Nasser's opposition."

Now the picture was clear to me. It had been a long standing KGB policy to develop its network within the government opposition, either to bring down an existing government or, in Nasser's case, to maintain "sleepers" in the opposition, in case something unforeseeable happens to the government.

Several days before, I had talked about this with Boris Turbanov, the chauffeur who was transferred to Egypt from Iran, where he had driven for the Soviet ambassador. Although the Shah was on friendly terms with the Soviets, the ambassador and the KGB officers were regularly meeting with opposition leaders in Iran and in neighboring Iraq, where they felt at home to keep their hopes alive until the day when the Soviets could help install a more pro-Soviet regime.

Hilal's recruitment didn't work out very well. I set up a meeting, took him two bottles of Scotch, and arrived to be confronted by an arrogant anti-Soviet who gave the liquor back to me, saying he didn't drink. I invented several more reasons to meet him so I could at least write a personality profile and get some background data for Sbirunov. I didn't get anywhere. Finally, I thought, it was enough. My trying to get to Hilal was becoming too obvious.

"Here," I said as I walked into Sbirunov's office four weeks later and put the report on the desk, "You try it now."

"All right." To my surprise, he didn't mind. "It's too important. The Al-Montaza Hotel is the place for high level meetings. . . . Then we gotta put that fucking rocket base somewhere."

"It's not my fault, Victor," I said, "I really tried."

"I know, you helped a lot."

As I left his office, I figured out the real reasons for the necessity of Hilal's recruitment. In this case, his being a member of the opposition was not so important. The Soviets didn't expect any problems in Egypt. What was needed was Hilal's agreement to give the park grounds for a Soviet SAM-3 base and to let the KGB install surveillance equipment at the Al-Montaza Hotel. If nothing else, this could be useful for blackmail. In the end, the KGB got its way.

It took a while for my postcard to Amsterdam to be answered. But that was the plan, since I'd needed some time to see the sights. I was ready when the message arrived.

The Greek passenger liner *Esperia* called regularly at the port of Alexandria, and it was no problem for me to pay a visit on board, since in my consular capacity I developed many acquaintances with foreign captains. *Esperia* carried foreign tourists around the Mediterranean and resembled the Soviet liners *Latvia* and *Litva*. One of my duties, established by Sbirunov, was to casually talk to foreign captains to see if I could pick up any bits of information on movements of foreign military supplies, electronic equipment, and other goods outside Alexandria.

I had visited the *Esperia* several times before, alone or with Sallah, to have a drink at the bar and talk about those beautiful girls in Athens. My friend Sallah seemed to be interested in the same type of information as I was. In fact, he was very helpful in introducing me to some of his contacts on foreign ships.

I made my way down a corridor leading aft from the bridge. I cautiously opened the second cabin door and peeked inside. I froze, then smiled. A young, pleasant-looking Arab, clean-shaven and dressed in what looked to be an expensive Western business suit, sat on a bunk bed smoking a cigarette.

"Oh, excuse me," I said quickly, "must have the wrong room." I started to close the door.

A familiar voice said in English from inside the cabin, "That's okay. Why don't you join us?"

I stepped inside and closed the door behind me. "Hello, George."

The Arab's name was Yussef, at least that was his name to me. He was not Egyptian—by his dialect I gathered that he was Lebanese or perhaps Syrian—but he could move freely in Egypt and he would be my contact for the rest of my stay. Periodic future meetings were arranged in Cairo, where the size of the capital city and my regular forays there on Soviet business gave the best cover. I didn't say anything about it, but George sensed my disappointment that we'd not be working directly together.

"Do you want out?" he asked. "We could get you out if you're ready."

"That might be difficult. This place is getting to be a regular Soviet Union. It's risky."

"Still . . . it is possible."

"Yes, I know . . . but not now. I'm doing all right; as long as I know I'm doing something against them. Now let's get down to business. As you well know, *Die Zeit ist knapp.*" *The time is short*—the expression had more meaning now than my wisecrack so long ago in the Moscow subway.

217

15: The Soviet Treatment

Unfortunately, the resistance of Sallah Al-Badawi and old Ahmed Hilal were exceptions. The KGB's efforts to recruit Egyptians—and Armenians, Syrians, Lebanese, Copts, and other minorities living in Egypt—were a smashing success for the most part.

Typical was the incident that began with a reception celebrating the fifty-first anniversary of Russia's October Revolution. The gathering took place at the consulate general in Alexandria, and was attended by the Soviet diplomatic corps, Egyptian VIPs, army commanders, navy officers, and prominent Egyptians and foreigners, including Greek and Russian Orthodox and Coptic priests. Over three hundred people filled the sumptuous reception hall and adjacent offices from which all the furniture, safes, and cabinets had been removed for the occasion.

As the Soviet and Egyptian poobahs arrived, I made my way to the entrance to position myself for official greetings. I left Natasha talking to an East German trade representative. My father had been right about one thing—Natasha could handle herself beautifully in these kinds of social situations.

As I made for the door, I was surprised to spot an old acquaintance coming up the wide marble staircase. It was the Egyptian navy commander Gallal, whom I'd met in Hodeida and gotten to know well at our farewell party there. He still looked like an Italian film actor. He recognized me and rushed over.

As we gave each other a traditional Arab embrace, I noticed one of my Soviet bosses give us an attentive look. This was Chinquiz Rasulov, whose official title was Vice-Consul of the Soviet Consulate General in Alexandria, but who was also the GRU resident there. Rasulov, a dark-skinned, round-faced, pot-bellied man with a regal demeanor, looked Arabic, a characteristic which served him well in his extensive cultivation of the Egyptian military.

I dragged Gallal over to the bar and we spent almost an hour swapping reminiscences of Hodeida. Since he'd left Yemen, he told me, things had gone very well. He'd been promoted from commander in charge of a missile boat squadron to vice-admiral in charge of a destroyer flotilla. I congratulated him on his success.

I brought Natasha over and introduced her, leaving them to talk so that I could attend to other guests. As I walked away, the pudgy Rasulov grabbed me by the sleeve and pulled me into the rear garden.

"How do you know that man?" He asked forcefully. "Do you realize how high up he is?"

Rasulov's professional pride had been wounded by my getting in tight with this Egyptian officer. So I explained the circumstances of my acquaintanceship with Gallal. Rasulov calmed down when he heard the story.

"You think we can, uh, get him on our side?" He carefully selected the words.

"I suppose I could get him for you," I said condescendingly, more out of a desire to deflate Rasulov than anything else. More conversation ensued, followed by a meeting in Rasulov's office later that week.

I told Rasulov that Gallal was a loyal Egyptian, and no flaming socialist or Soviet partisan either. He was probably no good for ideological conversion. But Gallal did have a weakness for money. He lived beyond his means trying to keep up with the older, richer officers with whom he now had to socialize. Blackmail was the ticket, Rasulov could see right away.

It happened that at the time there was an Italian engineer who had interested Rasulov in an emulsion process for cleaning ship hulls.

The process, he claimed, would obviate the need for time-consuming periodic scrubbing, or at least increase the time between each major dry-dock servicing. For a fee, the Italian would give the Soviets instructions on the process and supervise a Soviet maintenance crew to do the job on one of our warships.

After checking him out, Rasulov agreed to try it on one Soviet ship, a destroyer-class vessel, and report back to Moscow if the process looked promising. Rasulov, whose job included liaison for Soviet navy maintenance in Alexandria, cleared the arrangement through the necessary channels and the job went ahead with a modicum of success.

But it worked even better as a vehicle for setting up Gallal. Rasulov's next step was to invite his Egyptian pigeon to a night club for a few drinks. At a secluded table, with only the three of us present, an offer was made. Rasulov offered to send the Italian along with a Soviet crew to clean one of the Egyptian destroyers under Gallal's command. If Gallal liked the results, the Soviets could use the process on his other ships. Rasulov said he believed in the process so much that he would see to it that the job was paid for out of his own budget. In fact, Moscow had authorized this time-saving procedure to be used as part of its continuing effort to provide Egypt with the very best in modern military technology.

Shortly thereafter, a Soviet crew and the Italian were sent over to do the work on the Egyptian, Soviet-built destroyer. Meanwhile, Rasulov, Gallal, and myself got together again at the officers' club. Rasulov handed Gallal an envelope containing the 3,000 pound fee so that Gallal could pay the Italian.

Unbeknown to Gallal, who was not directly involved with the project down at the docks, the Italian contractor had already been paid in advance by Rasulov. When the job was done, the Italian quietly left for the Red Sea, to help clean corroding and crust-ridden Soviet ships.

Gallal, as expected, came to Rasulov's office. He hinted around about the Italian. Rasulov feigned embarrassment. There had been a bureaucratic foulup, he said. It seemed that, through Raslov's error, a double payment had been made to the Italian. If Moscow found out there'd be hell to pay. Rasulov never asked Gallal directly if he'd paid the Italian too; he only apologized for the inconvenience. That crooked Italian must have pocketed both fees, Rasulov ranted. Gallal didn't volunteer anything. Rasulov looked over and gave me a smug smile when Gallal left. He knew he had him now.

I was sent out to put the icing on the cake. I caught up with Gallal as he was getting into his car. "Friend," I said. "Money is not important. Rasulov is a good man so I suggest we forget the whole thing. Plus, they've got their hands full with more important matters," I assured him.

So it was that Gallal was put on the take. Rasulov took over his cultivation from there. I don't know what he did next, but the standard procedure would be to work a simpler, more direct swindle for him on the next go round, now that the GRU knew he didn't object to taking a little graft.

About three months later I ran into Rasulov again. "I'm really obligated to you for that Gallal business," he told me. "I've already informed my people that you did an outstanding job."

The recruitment of Gallal by the GRU was followed by KGB recruitment of Major Abdel Maksud Fahmi Hassan, of Egyptian security. The procedure was pretty routine. Sbirunov thought he'd be a good man to have because he handled security around several consulates, including the Spanish consulate in Alexandria. At the time, Spain represented American interests in Egypt. A small group of Americans was secluded at the Spanish Embassy in Cairo. It worried the KGB *residentura* that enemy number one couldn't be watched. "They gotta be doing something," Sbirunov once said, "they can't just sit around and wait!"

Once recruited, Abdel Maksud could tap the Spanish consulate in Alexandria. The employees there just might give away something interesting about those Yankees in Cairo. Besides that, Abdel Maksud had access to all foreigners' files in Alexandria. And that meant a great deal for the KGB.

I had heard about the KGB black market money-changing operations ever since I arrived in Alexandria, but I didn't get involved until one evening in spring 1969. That night, Victor Sbirunov—getting directly involved in some KGB dirty work himself for a change—took me to downtown Alexandria and introduced me to an Arab he identified only as Kosoruchka. I never found out his real name, but this nickname means "crooked hand" in Russian.

Kosoruchka was an old black-marketeer who could be found

almost any time of the day or night sitting on a small chair at the side of his tent-shop, from where, as cover for his currency operations, he sold chewing gum, Pepsi Cola, and cigarettes. The shop was located directly in front of the hotel where Soviet navy officers lived and in the basement of which was located the computerized center of the Soviet navy strategic command for the Mediterranean.

You'd never know from looking at Kosoruchka that he was a millionaire many times over, according to Sbirunov. He was dirty and ruddy from the sun, more like a beggar than a currency speculator. He lived in a shack near the tent, with no plumbing, but owned properties in Lebanon, where he kept most of his money.

Soviet specialists frequented him to exchange their Egyptian pounds for dollars or other hard currencies. The specialists were paid their meager salaries in Egyptian pounds, but found that Egyptian law forbade them from taking more than $11.75 worth of Egyptian currency out of the country. Neither would any bank exchange more than twenty-three dollars worth of Egyptian pounds for one person. So before boarding their Soviet ships back home for vacations or for the end of their tours of duty, specialists would visit Kosoruchka and he would take their Egyptian pounds for U.S. dollars, or Sterling or Deutschmarks—at a rate that insured him a healthy profit. The specialists would then have hard currency to eagerly spend in the shops of Athens or Istanbul where they'd stop on their way home. Kosoruchka in turn could use his now swollen purse of Egyptian currency to buy narcotics and contraband from local sources, items which he could smuggle out of the country in return for still more dollars.

His money changing for the specialists, however, was small potatoes compared to his deals with the KGB. Kosoruchka was one of many pipelines that the KGB's main financial division—the Narodny Bank ("Popular Bank" or "People's Bank")—used to accumulate slush funds of hard currencies that were almost impossible for Western intelligence agencies to trace. The Egyptian government would pay Soviet contractors for their work on numerous Soviet construction projects. These fees—always paid in Egyptian pounds—were supposed to cover Soviet labor costs and, to a lesser degree, materials. But, in fact, the Soviet workers were being paid less than half of what their work was being billed for. Furthermore, the Soviet materials were being shipped in from the U.S.S.R., but the embassy and consulate were not shipping the Egyptian currency back home to pay for them. This left the Soviet contracting organizations with large surpluses of Egyptian pounds which they turned over to the diplomatic missions. The Egyptian currency then secretly passed into the hands of KGB operatives who exchanged them with Kosoruchka and his ilk for hard currency. Then these currencies would be sent to Moscow Center via sealed diplomatic pouch. The KGB could then funnel this untraced money back out of the Soviet Union to finance worldwide undercover operations.

As Sbirunov and I drove downtown that evening, he handed me a small envelope. "Here, it's enough for your introduction. Count it."

I counted. "It's a thousand Egyptian pounds. Shall we hit the night spots with it?" I laughed.

"Yeah, that'd be great. Unfortunately the motherland needs the stuff more than Egyptian hookers do."

"You never know, Victor," I said, putting the envelope in my pocket.

"You'll give it to him," Victor continued. "Ask him for two thousand American dollars in exchange."

"Sure, no problem."

Kosoruchka saw Victor and me approaching and got up from his chair immediately. "Mister Victor, *Ahlan wa sahlan,* welcome, welcome," he said, shaking Sbirunov's hand.

"This is Mister Vladimir," Sbirunov pointed at me, "He needs help. He might need it often."

Kosoruchka smiled and nodded.

Then, as I had been instructed earlier by Sbirunov, I took the envelope from my pocket and said in Arabic, "I need some money. How much would you give me for one pound?"

"Are you kidding," he said, "my lowest is ten pounds. And that is based on a rate of one and a half American dollars for one Egyptian pound." The legal rate of exchange then was 2.3 dollars for one Egyptian pound.

Then he looked in the envelope. After some bargaining we finally agreed on two dollars per pound and I put the American money in my pocket. The bargain wasn't bad at all.

On the way back, Sbirunov was in a cheerful mood. He joked about how the poor little specialists get shortchanged by Kosoruchka. He ordered me to keep an eye out for any Soviet specialists who show up at Kosoruchka's place and to take names down if possible, "so the chiseling little sons of bitches can be severely reprimanded."

I would be seeing Kosoruchka regularly, it turned out; Sbirunov said I'd be assigned to return there at least twice a month to make transactions. "See, Vladimir," he joked, "you do this once in a while, but don't you try to change your own money, because your motherland would know about it!"

"Uh-huh," I mused, trying to do some figuring, knowing as I did that at least five other runners in Alexandria and twenty in Cairo were regularly being sent to make similar exchanges. The operation was pulling in about $120,000 a month—that was $1,440,000 a year from Egypt alone. *Multiply that by the number of other Third World countries where the U.S.S.R. has similar operations,* I thought.

One side of Sbirunov's activity always intrigued me—his work among clergy. Egypt has always been a country tolerant of many religions. The head of the Russian Orthodox Church in Alexandria, Father Anatoly Kaznovetsky, worked under Sbirunov's supervision. In addition to the KGB-ridden Moscow *Patriarkhiya* (Church Council), Kaznovestky also received orders from the State Committee on Church Affairs, which we used to jokingly refer to as "KGB Department on Church Affairs."

I had first met him in Sbirunov's office. He was a six-foot three-inch, 330-pound bear of a man in his late forties, who wore a traditional long black beard, but dressed in a business suit instead of clerical garb. Sbirunov told me to give him whatever assistance he asked. In the ensuing months this turned out to entail acting as translator for him with Arabs and making travel arrangements. I also got to know him socially. Privately he was a boisterous, cheerful man who loved good food, wine, music, and telling stories. He would sing Russian folk songs with great gusto long into the night.

On the business side, he was a lieutenant-colonel in the KGB who frequently attended church ecumenical meetings in Africa, Europe, and the Mideast, and also hosted religious leaders visiting Alexandria. All the while he was reporting to the KGB through Sbirunov. One such report reviewed the various religious groups in Alexandria in detail—Moslems, Catholics, Orthodox, Copts—with emphasis on religious leaders who were recruitable as friends of the Soviet Union and who would be earmarked for further contacts. Another time I helped Kaznovetsky—with whom I spent a great deal of time—arrange an international religious conference in Ethiopia, where he was able to develop a strong rapport with Coptic Christian leaders there who subsequently visited him in Alexandria.

Kaznovetsky's oft-repeated public relations theme to all these religious leaders was that, despite what they might have heard to the contrary, as a member of the Moscow patriarchy he could assure them that there was a separation of church and state in the U.S.S.R., but the Soviet government always supported the rights of all people, including Moslems, to their own religious practices. Meanwhile, being a cleric made an ideal cover for his other KGB errands of information gathering, agent recruitment, money exchange, and passing on instructions.[1]

I thought about Kaznovetsky as I lay in bed after I got beaten up on the way from his plush apartment on the seashore in Alexandria. I never could figure out why three big Egyptians caught me at two in the morning and beat me almost to death. Maybe it was retaliation for my protest to a local police station about my apartment having been bugged and looted some nights earlier.

Maybe some Egyptians were getting fed up with the Sovietization of their country.

---

[1] This use of religious cover by the KGB was by no means confined to Egypt. Boris Turbanov, our chauffeur, had once worked three years for the Soviet ambassador to Iran and told about similar, larger operations in that country. KGB operatives from the Soviet Middle Eastern Republics of Azerbaidzhan and Turkmenistan were working with Moslem religious opposition to the Shah.

225

16: A Day in The Life

It was ten at night when the big news came. Natasha hadn't returned yet from the Alexandria Soviet Cultural Center where she gave Russian lessons to Arabs. Katya was asleep. Before retiring, I did my usual bug check under the bed with a flashlight. The insecticide was working; I spotted none of the usual cockroaches.

The phone rang irritatingly just as I was settling down. It was Shumilov. I could tell something big was up. "Vladimir, *yeb tvoyu mat.*" ("Fuck your mother.") He always became especially foul-mouthed when he was excited. "Are you asleep?" His voice was sharp, and he rattled off another burst of *mat.* "These fuckers at the embassy think we can perform fucking miracles. *Ne khuya pizdorvantsi ne ponimayut!*" ("Those pussy-rippers don't understand no prick!")

I tried to figure out what he was attempting to tell me.

"Kunayev is coming!" he shouted finally.

"I'll be right there," I answered, hoping that I could get Sbirunov's wife to come over and babysit Katya. I hung up, called her, and was at the consulate within five minutes.

Dinmakhamed Kunayev was a very big visitor, indeed. He was recently elevated to the Politburo of the party Central Committee. He was a protégé of Leonid Brezhnev. Word was that Brezhnev had

226

brought him in from a peripheral party post in Tadzhikistan to take charge of the Central Committee's secret political activities in the Middle East. Besides Kunayev, Brezhnev's "Cosa Nostra" included Andropov, Kirichenko, Kirilenko, Suslov, and Polyansky. This group had been running affairs both inside and outside the Soviet Union with "godfather" Brezhnev's blessings.

When I arrived at Shumilov's office, he was scribbling something on a pad. A tiny table lamp on Shumilov's desk projected a narrow streak of light on his red face.

"You know Kunayev?" he rumbled as I walked in.

"Yeah, big man from the Central Committee," I answered.

"Right!" Shumilov exclaimed. "This big man is arriving here first thing in the morning."

I knew why he'd called me. The job of being tour guide to dignitaries from Moscow always fell to me.

"We're going to give him an official welcome in the consulate garden at around ten tomorrow morning," Shumilov said. "Then we'll take him around the grounds. Now, as we go around, don't talk about the boat, the billiard table, or the piano." All three were items Shumilov and Sbirunov had finessed through the Moscow supply pipeline for our personal use. "We have to make a good impression. If he asks about the tennis court, we can't ignore it. Just say it's for the Soviet colony."

I nodded understandingly. I was looking forward to meeting one of Brezhnev's most powerful yes-men.

Shumilov babbled on, "Vladimir, whatever you do, make sure Kunayev's whims are satisfied. Keep him happy at all costs! Take my chauffeur and my official car. Try to anticipate what he wants. Remember, he's not going to ask for everything directly. Look for a wiggle of the head, anything! I've heard he likes to go to stores and shop, so take him around town, all right?"

"Right, *yeb tvoyu mat*," I said, "you got it!" Shumilov seemed to relax as I got into the spirit of things.

As I departed that marble mausoleum of a hall, I noticed a light shining under Sbirunov's door. Sbirunov was on the phone. ". . . Yes, I'm certain he's no longer with us. Yes, just wait . . . regretting it would be too late . . . yes, just wait . . . through the ship . . . and Genady, tell them I'll get the stuff tomorrow . . . Yes, we'll see you in Cairo . . . Soon."

I waited a minute after he hung up, looking up and down the hallway in the faint light provided by the dimmed chandelier high above me. My heart was pounding and my palms were getting damp. I tried to keep these kinds of spying procedures to a minimum, picking up what I could in the normal way, but sometimes I found opportunities too tempting to pass up. This time I didn't like what I'd heard. Sbirunov could well have been talking about me, I thought. But no use sweating it. Only one way to find out. I burst through the door without knocking.

"Hands up!" I shouted. "Get up against the wall. Get your booze out of the safe. Kunayev is arriving!"

Sbirunov laughed and pointed his pen at me playfully, as if it were a pistol. "This thing is loaded, watch out!"

"Ah ha," I said, "loaded with falafel. It'll get you a black eye." I plopped down in a chair and lit a cigarette. I filled him in on our imminent royal visit.

"Big deal," he said, "probably Kunayev is on the get-acquainted tour. It's so difficult for someone from the backwoods—or I'd say, back deserts—to come into the Central Committee and be instantly in touch." Sbirunov sighed. "But what can you do?" In any case, all is for the better."

Immediately I agreed, but noticed that Sbirunov was slightly irritated—maybe his professional pride was slightly hurt by the party's interference with the KGB international domain. Maybe he just didn't like all those national minorities ruling his Russian homeland. I thought it might have been both.

We discussed plans for the next day. Sbirunov, it turned out, already knew about the visit. He'd be coming in the ambassador's car accompanied by Counselor Sinelhikov and young Kirichenko. (Young Kirichenko, son of the Kirichenko of the Central Committee, was skyrocketing up the diplomatic ladder in the embassy. It took him seven years to move from *referent* to counselor.) "You know the routine—shopping, sightseeing—Who knows by the time we're through . . ." Sbirunov giggled.

"And what if he's bullheaded and wants to make trouble?" I asked.

"Our high party officials are not bulls; they are extensions of the will of the people." Sbirunov smiled sardonically.

I thought, remembering other visiting officials, that the will of the people must be shopping for shoes, dresses, jewelry, and chewing gum, and taking time off to drink cognac and Coca Cola. On the way back to my apartment, I stopped off to wake Boris Turbanov, who lived on top of the consulate general's garage. Why should he sleep? I walked up the stairs to his quarters and saw Tanya Ratnikova, the consul general's attractive, young stenographer-secretary. She had a room opposite the chauffeur's and was leaving the communal bathroom down the hall. Tanya was the daughter of a KGB colonel and her goal was to marry well, just like her predecessor, Lyuda Abashina, who had landed an MFA diplomat who'd gone on to become second secretary of the Soviet Embassy in Tokyo.

Tanya had been a good source of information because she was the only typist in the consulate general with a security clearance. As such she was overloaded with typing for the KGB, GRU, and MFA. On top of that, circumstances permitted me to cultivate a friendship with her without arousing suspicions from Sbirunov. Tanya was unmarried and regulations prohibited her from leaving the consulate general grounds without an escort. Sbirunov ordered me to accompany her whenever she wanted to go out shopping or sightseeing and to keep an eye on her. I was supposed to report where she went, whom she saw, what she said, and anyone who showed an "unhealthy interest" in her.

"Hello, my lovely," I said, when I met her in the hallway that night.

"What brings you to this dump?" she asked.

"I came to see Boris Turbanov."

"Oh, wanna tell him about Kunayev?" She winked. "Don't bother, he knows about it already. Why don't you come in my room for a cognac?"

Tanya always knew everything. Maybe she knew what Sbirunov was talking about on the phone earlier. I went in with her to try to find out, at least that's what I told myself.

The top party leader, Dinmakhamed Kunayev, was a short, bulky man in his late forties, looking like many a local party secretary from the outlands, or a collective farm, or a shoe factory. He walked through the main gate of the consulate escorted by young Kirichenko, the counselor of the embassy who'd come up from Cairo for the occasion, just as Sbirunov said he would.

Kunayev strode in with the purposefulness and slightly bowlegged gait of a Genghis Khan entering the gates of Moscow, taking graceless, military-measure steps in his old-fashioned made-in-Odessa shoes and a gray Czechoslovakian suit. His round, Tartar's face was expressionless when Shumilov stepped forward to greet him. Shumilov reached out to shake hands and then raised his eyebrows as though waiting for further ceremony. But he got no more than a perfunctory handclasp from Kunayev, so Shumilov began to introduce the rest of the staff.

When my turn came to be introduced I had trouble stifling a smile. All I could picture, for some reason, was Kunayev eating pilaf with his hands, and getting grains of rice stuck under his fingernails. I looked at his outreached hand, half expecting to see the rice, and I pictured him wolfing down pilaf while he kept his arrogant posture. Trying not to laugh, I coughed as we shook hands, and smiled at him. His expression didn't change and his hand stayed fish-limp in mine.

I set up the sightseeing trip exactly as I had done for other visiting dignitaries. I knew what they all wanted. We got Shumilov's black Volga sedan and Kunayev planted himself in the back seat while I rode shotgun up front with the chauffeur.

"Drive!" Kunayev barked, as soon as we'd closed the door.

"What would you like to see?" I asked politely. "We have our naval base, rocket base, air base, army base, specialists constructing an irrigation system, our auto repair school, our shipyard—any of those?" Kunayev turned his head rigidly from side to side.

"Maybe the king's palace in Al-Montaza?" No, he didn't have time for any of those things, he groused.

"Okay," I said, "we'll just drive you towards the city center. We'll stop if you need anything." I glanced over at the chauffeur and winked. Boris winked back.

As we proceeded, Alexandria's opulent charms seemed to have no effect on Kunayev. Finally his head began to turn as we drove down Saad Zaglul Street, lined with stores and shops.

"Would you like to shop?" I turned to him, barely getting his attention as he peered out the windows. "Maybe we'll take a walk along this street."

"Yes, let's stop." Kunayev waved us over imperiously, just as we approached a row of jewelry shops off Saad Zaglul. A dozen small shops along the row displayed dazzling Italian, Swiss, and Egyptian jewelry in their windows. I knew one had to watch out for fakes, but still a careful buyer could come away with a real bargain in precious, or semi-precious, exquisitely-mounted stones. I explained the setup to Kunayev and took him to Mustapha, a jeweler I knew I could trust.

Kunayev nodded, but when I finished, he said, "No, you can *never* trust those Arabs, especially the merchants." Then he smiled and added, "but, young man, *my ne lykom shity* (literally, "we are not dressed in bark," meaning, we are no fools). I know how to deal. Take me to your man."

This disturbed me because I knew that my jeweler always offered low prices immediately to me and my guests, because I was one of his biggest customers.

The jewelry row was a narrow, darkly shaded street. As we walked toward the shop, Kunayev asked me, "Is there crime here?"

"No, not that we know of," I answered.

"Good, keep it up. Arabs need our way of life. We don't have crime at home and that's a positive influence on our friends."

I nodded, not mentioning to him the stealing, drunkenness, wife beating, fist fights, and other righteous examples being offered daily to the locals by our Soviet colony.

Ad-Dukkan, the store, was a tiny establishment with a glass facade through which could be seen artful displays of its wares. As we entered the glass door I saw Mustapha, the owner, sitting behind the counter.

"This is a friend from Moscow," I told him. "Please help him with your good merchandise."

Kunayev was all over the store, picking up and examining the goods with a kid-at-Christmas expression on his face. He selected a dozen gold rings, with topaz, alexandrite, garnet, and other stones, and another dozen each of necklaces and bracelets. "For my family," he said. He looked at Mustapha and said, "That's it."

Mustapha counted and gave him a bill, saying in Arabic, which I translated, "I am giving you a bargain because you are a friend of my friend here."

But Kunayev started to haggle. Mustapha wouldn't go down. After five minutes of arguing, Mustapha scooped up all the jewelry with both hands and held them up to Kunayev. "Look," Mustapha said heatedly, "this is a pound of gold and good stones. I am giving it to you for three hundred pounds. In America this would cost you . . ." Mustapha whistled and raised his eyes up to the ceiling.

Kunayev got out his wallet. I noticed it was bulging with money.

As we left, Mustapha said something, still in Arabic, smiling as if giving us a fond farewell, so that Kunayev wouldn't catch his drift. *"Mush kwayis,* Vladimir," he said, "I lost money on the deal and he leaves without so much as a thank you. Don't bring him here anymore."

I answered, in Arabic, smiling and waving back in farewell, "Don't worry, I won't. Anyway, he's not a Russian, he's a Genghis Khan."

The rest of the day consisted of more of the same. I dragged Kunayev from shop to shop; he haggled and bickered at each as he amassed his treasure. It wasn't the bargaining that bothered most of the other merchants, however, since that was a fairly normal routine. It was Kunayev's brusque condescension and open rudeness. He bought shoes, coats, underwear, dresses, spending hundreds more Egyptian pounds.

We loaded up the car and were driving around Ismail Pasha Square when he let me know he wasn't finished yet. "Do you know a place where I could get *gipiur?*" he asked.

Gipiur is a rare, diaphanous, silken material highly prized in the Soviet Union for making dresses, evening gowns, and blouses. I also knew that there was a highly profitable contraband trade in the material back home, because little was imported or produced in the U.S.S.R. A yard of it abroad was going for fifty to ninety American cents, while back in Moscow it would cost twelve to fifteen rubles (sixteen dollars) and twice that much in Georgia or Soviet Armenia. Many Soviets who went to Egypt stocked up on *gipiur,* a nylon gauze, even at the risk of being detained by customs. Because of his exalted position in the Kremlin, however, Kunayev didn't have to be bothered by customs checks.

I took him to a shop that I knew sold the material, a shabby establishment in the heart of the Old Souk ("Market"). As we approached, I saw a bunch of Soviet specialists hurry out. They'd seen us coming. Kunayev marched inside and promptly bought four hundred yards of *gipiur,* just about exhausting the stock. Mercifully, he didn't haggle over the price this time. He was in too much of a hurry to get his loot back to the car.

232

By five in the afternoon, he seemed to be tiring. I suggested one last shopping foray, this one out to the free zone near the port to purchase transistor radios, television sets, and a stereo. Kunayev's face lit up again. One needed U.S. dollars or other Western currency in the free zone, so we went to our usual black marketeer to exchange Egyptian pounds for about seven hundred dollars. Kunayev fondled the dollars for a long time as if they were the dearest thing to him.

The free zone was inside the port's passenger terminal. We had to go past the regular guard at the entrance to the port, and then past another guard at the terminal door which led to the duty-free shop. I had made that journey many times before with other bigshots from Moscow or for my Egyptian friends who couldn't shop there. One couldn't buy anything at the store and take it out of the zone unless he was leaving Alexandria and had a boarding pass to prove it. Otherwise it was illegal.

Kunayev wasn't interested in such nonsense as regulations and dashed into the store while I was flashing my "go-everywhere" diplomatic card to the guards and winking to the duty-free shop clerk that Kunayev was alright.

In 1969, seven hundred American dollars, spent in Alexandria's duty-free shops, was a lot of money. A Grundig Satellite multi-band radio went for $160, a Phillips electric shaver cost $14, a Telefunken stereo system and AM-FM tuner cost $300, high fashion dresses, suits, and shoes cost between $9 and $50, a carton of Winston cigarettes cost a dollar, and a fifth of Cutty Sark Scotch could be had for $1.90. Other gadgets, accessories, and vanities were extremely cheap, even by the standards of those days, and it was easy for Kunayev to load up the car.

Kunayev made purchases as fast as he could peel off the bills. Back in the car I made sure nothing was bulging out of the trunk and the windows, because I was embarrassed—not because we did something illegal, but because the guard at the entrance to the port would again shake his head from side to side and smile as we passed by him. "Russi, Russi, just look at yourself."—I knew that's what he thought. But no one would stop a car with diplomatic plates. At day's end we drove back out through the guarded checkpoint of the zone, the trunk and every available space in the car loaded with Hitachis, Grundigs, and Phillipses.

I begged off the dinner in Kunayev's honor that night, saying I had to catch up with my work.

"Good, young man," he said, "I'm proud of our young working diplomats. You have a great future ahead of you."

At home, I showered and apologized to Natasha for getting back late, but it turned out she'd come back from the cultural center only ten minutes earlier. By seven, Katya was fed and we'd sat down to dinner, when my ubiquitous KGB overlord Sbirunov knocked. He said he'd wait downstairs.

Natasha was irritated. "I wish we'd have just one evening together."

"I'm sorry, it's not my fault."

"Well try to get home early."

"It's up to him," I pointed downstairs. "Tomorrow night we'll go to the movies," I promised. "There's a Matt Helm film playing, you know with Dean Martin." She brightened a bit.

Sbirunov and I took his Opel to the busy pier where the Soviet freighter *Moskovsky Komsomolets* was berthed at the military pier. Soviet crews were unloading tanks and plane parts from her holds with quick, military efficiency. We parked and Sbirunov led the way up the ship's gangway. I was still thinking about his mysterious phone conversation that I'd overheard last night.

The *pompolit*, or captain's assistant on political matters (read KGB), awaited us. He took us to a large suite near the top of the bridge. It had two rooms, one a combined dining-work area, the other a bedroom. The dining table was covered with *zakuski* (hors d'oeuvres) and two bottles of vodka, and had four chairs around it. A desk in the corner was crowded with papers and charts. The *pompolit* invited us to sit on a couch opposite the table. "Is it all right if we talk?" he asked Sbirunov, wagging his head at me. I felt sort of out of place.

"Yes," said Sbirunov, "let's get down to business before pleasure."

The *pompolit* was in his mid-thirties, tall, with a suave, circumspect manner. I wondered why the KGB had wasted him on ship duty, but then I'd met KGB officers on ships who didn't seem to mind it. Every Soviet ship, merchant, passenger, military, or fishing trawler, has at least one KGB officer occupying the *pompolit* spot as first or second mate. Their duties are to monitor the crew, act as a liaison with shore-based KGB operatives around the world and carry out other intelligence work as ordered from Moscow Center.

This particular ship's regular ports of call were Alexandria, Latakia in Syria, and Tyre and Tripoli in Lebanon. It delivered arms from the Soviet Union to Egypt and Syria and, directly and indirectly, to Palestinian guerillas.

By their tone with each other I concluded Sbirunov and the *pompolit* were of equal KGB rank. As the conversation unfolded, it became clear that the *pompolit*'s priority assignment was to help coordinate the network of *agenturnaya razvedka,* or secret agents' network, in Egypt, Syria, and Lebanon.

While we sipped Borjomi mineral water, the *pompolit* placed a file in front of Sbirunov and looking at me again, asked, "Are you absolutely sure it's okay?"

"Yeah, he's with us," Sbirunov said, "no problem. Vladimir, take a look at this."

I looked into the folder while the *pompolit* lit my cigarette. The file contained three pages of badly photocopied documents, mostly in Arabic. They asked me to translate and both of them took notes as I complied.

The file opened with a letter from an Arab to his brother in Lebanon. He wrote that he was studying in the United States and was looking forward to graduating and returning to Beirut. The writer was homesick and doubted he could last through his remaining three years in the United States. When I came to the Arabic word *uhashak,* the *pompolit* asked me to stop. I couldn't see if there was a comma in the middle of the sentence, so the sentence could be translated "I hate it while I'm here," or "I miss you while I'm here," depending on the context. This phrase worried both the *pompolit* and Sbirunov. After musing over it, they let me finish the translation, which continued along the same seemingly innocuous lines. It was obvious to me the letter came from one of those agents recruited and trained by the KGB and sent to study in America. I'd heard about those operations, but had never seen anything firsthand until that moment.

"Well, Vladimir, what do you think about that letter?" the *pompolit* asked, when I'd finished. "I mean the general tone. We suspect he has turned against us and is working for the Americans."

His hint didn't clarify anything for me, so I parried. One could just as easily conclude that the letter was simply to let his contact in Beirut know that the agent had settled in place and didn't want to be bothered for a while. He needed time to look around.

"Now, look at this," the *pompolit* said, turning the page to another letter. This one was in shorthand. A man signed Ousama claimed that someone—the name was blacked out—has been long connected with the Americans and was seen many times at the American University in Beirut with Americans and was suspected of friendliness towards them.

"Now what do you think?" Sbirunov's turn came to ask me. Now I realized what last night's phone conversation had been about.

"I think many Arabs go to the American University, but that doesn't mean the guy turned against us."

"But he didn't even tell us about his ties to the Americans," Sbirunov interrupted.

"Well," I shrugged, "I don't know, I wasn't there. Maybe he thought that if he told, you wouldn't talk to him. You should know better."

"What are you going to tell them in Cairo?" the *pompolit* asked, turning to Sbirunov.

"I'll tell them it's a fifty-fifty chance. They'll just have to watch him. He's their job now."

The case apparently disposed of, we partook of a huge dinner and polished off the vodka, the feast lasting until midnight. Sbirunov was half drunk, but insisted on driving. After the events of that evening, nothing would have made me nervous.

17: Armies of the Night

The lights of Alexandria played off the palms surrounding the Al-Montaza Hotel, giving the streets a greenish cast, and rippled onto the sea beyond in ghostly streamers. King Farouk's Palace was closed for the night and the action had moved to the hotel. The cars of rich Egyptians and the German and Italian tourists could be seen driving through the guarded gate of the surrounding gardens. A wide road led from the gate to the shore, where I turned right and came up on the hotel.

The Al-Montaza Hotel was my favorite place in Alexandria. Intelligently designed, it blended with the surroundings—the sea and a tiny harbor where I'd fished on weekends while Natasha and Katya enjoyed the sun on the hotel's sea deck. The waiters stood at a distance always ready to jump at a move of a finger. I'd seen good service since then, but the waiters at Al-Montaza were absolutely the best.

I walked past the *bawab* (doorman) who bowed as I entered the elegant lobby. From there I could see the glittering dance hall was filled with lavishly dressed couples who seemed out of place in this Soviet-occupied city. There were no Arab Socialist Union posters on the walls and no Soviet specialists around. The combo played a mixture of pop and soft rock.

I passed through the labyrinth of dancing pairs and headed towards a darkened corner where a man I knew only as Kotsarev sat with Tolya Egorin and a young attractive brunette whom I'd never seen before.

"Sorry I'm late. Couldn't catch up with the schedule since this morning," I said greeting them.

Kotsarev raised himself from a chair and shook my hand. He was a man in his early fifties, rather bulky and roughly mannered. He was a colonel in the general staff and had been the GRU resident in Egypt for the past five years. His red face reflected the amount of liquor he had consumed in the previous hours.

"Vladimir Sakharov," he nodded towards Tolya Egorin.

Tolya didn't get up but pointed to the opposite chair, laughing. "C'mon, Kotsarev, we know each other pretty well. Didn't you know?" Tolya's manners resembled those of a rich playboy who lived for the sole purpose of enjoying life. I met him several times before. He ran the APN (Agency for Press and News) office in Cairo and never appeared to be anything but an APN correspondent—flamboyant, arrogant, and brilliantly educated. Tolya was in his midthirties. Tall, blond, handsome, and a sex symbol for many a Soviet colony woman, he seemed to go through life with a complete disregard for the KGB and CC. However, I found that disregard really stemmed from Tolya's position. He was a young lieutenant-colonel in the GRU, with a lot of clout behind him. The clout included a powerful uncle back in Moscow, a responsibility for coordinating overall military intelligence operations in the south Mediterranean and, of course, his access to independent means of communications. No KGB officer could possibly know what Tolya transmitted via his personal teletype to Moscow. The mystery was strong protection. Besides, Tolya was not involved in any internal security affairs, which claimed for him a silent respect and strict professional intelligence.

"Where's Natasha?" Turning to Kotsarev, Tolya said, "This fellow is real bad. Keeps his princess locked in. What would our Partcom say about his male chauvinism? How is she, by the way?"

"She's okay. Teaching Arabs Russian at the cultural center

tonight," I said, looking straight at that young woman, who by now had crossed her legs but still didn't say a word.

"Ah, ah," Tolya exclaimed, intercepting my look. "Not for you. She's for him," he pointed towards Kotsarev. "He's leaving tomorrow for good, so we'll let him enjoy her."

Kotsarev shrugged his shoulders, slightly embarrassed. Then, looking at me, he said, "Vladimir, Tolya is replacing me. More than that, his rank as of tomorrow is Press Attaché of the Embassy. I want you to know that and cooperate with him completely. Remember, you are still a general staff lieutenant."

"See," Tolya nodded towards Kotsarev, "the boss is displaying directorial charisma. Let's excuse ourselves and hit the strips. It's his last night out."

"Good luck, Vladimir." Kotsarev rose and shook my hand firmly. I bowed my head and immediately intercepted the look of the brunette.

As we were walking to our cars Tolya said, "You want her?"

"Sure, she's beautiful."

"I wouldn't try, I mean, she's available and even quite solicitous, but I wouldn't go near her. Not now, my friend."

"Why?" I asked as Tolya was opening the door of his brand new Opel Accord.

"Because the fucking broad is coming out of 'close neighbors.'"

"Oh, yeah?" I exclaimed. "What a marvelous setup. A 'close neighbor' spook has infiltrated the 'distant neighbor' camp. Right on! What's she doing?"[1]

"Oh, she's a secretary. Basically a lay for Kotsarev, but the old man didn't give a shit. If I were him, I'd be more careful," Tolya continued, getting into the front seat. "In any case, there are no regulations against fucking oversexed 'close neighbors'—for me, at least. You, aren't you with them?" He shook his finger at me

---

[1] In our jargon, the word "neighbor" was originally used to identify a KGB officer, because the MFA building had once been located next to the KGB building. However, "neighbor" soon became a word of reference to GRU officers. Not to mix the two, the jargon was developed further, so that KGB officers became "close neighbors" or just "neighbors" and GRU officers "distant neighbors" because the GRU headquarters in Moscow are located way out on the banks of the Moskva River.

laughing. "Don't fuck where you live and don't live where you fuck, man." We both laughed and I walked towards my Volga.

I dropped the Volga at the consulate general garage. Tolya followed me and we continued in his Opel to the port. The guard at the main gate recognized me and let us in. We drove through the darkened piers and reached the wharf, which had been converted into a naval base. To the left of us, huge workshops stood quietly, guarded by Egyptian soldiers. We drove through another gate and turned right where the floating base was banked. The floating base was used by the Soviet fleet commander as headquarters, communications center, and as a rest home.

My weekly visits to the base made me an honorary member of the crew. The first man to greet us was a young duty officer who immediately dispatched a sailor to notify the commanders of our arrival. The sailor returned in a minute and showed us to the compartment. Nikolai Zhuravlev, the commander, and Valentin Stroganov, a lieutenant commander, were having a drink. A dish with pickled tomatoes, prepared by my wife, stood in the middle of a narrow table strapped to the wall.

"Welcome, Baby," Stroganov was very happy to see me. The nickname, "Baby," actually said in English, got stuck to me after Natasha called me *Volodya, moi baby* once in the presence of the Soviet Navy top brass. Strangely, it didn't sound out of place then, for everyone was drunk. But Stroganov picked it up and so did the rest of navy intelligence. So that became my code name and everytime I was needed they asked for "Baby." I didn't mind that—"Baby won't you please come home. . . ."

I introduced Tolya, hinting that he was a bigshot from the "distant neighbors"—just in case he didn't know. "What's new?" I asked after we all sat down and large glasses of "submarine liquor" (pure alcohol mixed with Pepsi Cola) were put in front of us.

"Not much!" Stroganov said.

"I heard you had some troubles on the Red Sea," I said, referring to an incident which took place a week ago. One of the crew members on a destroyer had gone berserk and got hold of a submachine gun and killed six other crew members. I wasn't surprised; after a two-year stay aboard a ship without home leaves, stuck somewhere between the Persian Gulf and the Antarctic. . . .

"Unfortunate, very unfortunate," Stroganov said, putting a whole pickled tomato in his mouth. "The sailor went crazy. Thought Jews were attacking him."

"How did you transport him back home? I mean, it had to be too much trouble," Tolya interrupted.

"We didn't have to. As soon as we rounded him in a cabin, he continued shooting inside the cabin. One of the bullets ricocheted and killed him." Stroganov smiled, and smiled, and everybody understandingly smiled with him. "So we didn't have any problem in transporting him. The only thing, you know Vladimir, was the problem of talking Aeroflot pilots into taking the casket aboard the plane."

I nodded. More than once I was confronted with the Soviet pilots' superstition of not allowing corpses on regular passenger flights. Once I even had to argue with a captain of a Mogadishu-Moscow flight who flatly refused to accept two caskets which I delivered. The only way I could talk him into it was mentioning that they were combat pilots killed in action. In that particular instance those were not pilots, but agricultural specialists from Kazakhstan. They had drunk methyl alcohol.

To the great satisfaction of both commanders, the rest of the evening was spent in a dirty nightclub in Al-Azareta. When we took them back to the base, Stroganov, getting out of the car, told us to wait a minute. He returned from the house carrying a box.

"Here, that's for you."

I looked inside the box and there was a model of a Soviet atomic submarine. "Tell Sbirunov to wipe his nose when he sees it," Stroganov laughed.

The model was much better than the one that Sbirunov had. He was very proud of it, since it indicated his high spot with the navy staff. Now I had an even fancier one. The model was made of ebonite with stainless steel details and was mounted on a desk stand.

"Hey, man," exclaimed Tolya as we drove back to the consulate, "how come you deserve so much respect? What did you do for them?"

"Enough," I answered. "You know, they're the 'close neighbors.'"

"Yeah, I know," he sighed. "Look. Why don't you think of coming to us. I'll be here for a very long time. We'd make a good team. Think

241

about it. Think about a full time career with us." I said I'd think about it, but I knew my answer already.

The GRU was heavily involved with Soviet military advisors who were collaborating with the Egyptian high command in planning the rearmament of Nasser's armed forces and setting a timetable for another go at the Israelis. (There never was any question of a negotiated settlement in the Soviet calculations, of course.) As the rearmament plan took shape, the GRU was able to report back to Moscow that the Egyptians would be ready for another full-scale offensive in 1973, and it would be advisable to have a test combat with Israel about then. In other words, their projections turned out to be accurate.

To help buy time until the build-up could be completed, the Soviet forces were bolstering Egyptian defenses, which now had fallen back west of Suez. This included the Soviet-manned SAM-II and SAM-III anti-aircraft missile sites along the Nile, and Soviet-piloted MIGs patrolling out of Egyptian air bases, and a large Soviet naval presence in the area.

The latter, in reality, was to fulfill Soviet needs. Moscow was increasing naval might worldwide and locally. They used Alexandria as a base to challenge waning American naval strength in the Mediterranean. This was the start of a ten-year accelerated Soviet naval buildup that was aimed at making the U.S.S.R. number one on the high seas.

The rearming of the Egyptians, despite all the sound and fury over it, had secondary significance. The more advanced weapons were kept out of Egyptian hands. Even those systems that were there were operated entirely by Soviet troops; the Egyptians were not allowed near them. Meanwhile, obsolescent MIG-17s and MIG-21s were gradually being delivered and turned over to Egyptian pilots, but only as the Egyptians became trained enough to handle them. In the meantime, Egyptian navy crews were being trained to take over older destroyers that Moscow was turning over to Nasser's fleet.

Having put the Mediterranean in their pocket, Brezhnev's "capos" were now concentrating military and naval presence in the Red Sea, Aden, the Arabian Gulf and Oman, the waters surrounding Saudi Arabia and the Indian Ocean. The buildup in Syria was rapidly increasing. Even my friends, the captains of Soviet merchant vessels, were puzzled, telling me that by 1970 they were delivering twice as much equipment and armaments to Syria as to Egypt. "Isn't Egypt enough?" I was once asked. No, Syria was simply next in line in the scheme of Soviet penetration. Next would be Afghanistan, then Iran, then Bahrein, the Emirates and, finally, Saudi Arabia, the last American ally in the area. The circle was getting tighter and smaller.

The play was developing smoothly according to the script which had been read to me by my old Professor Milogradov at the IIR in Moscow.

Soviet pilots and sailors who had to work with the Egyptians during this 1968–70 transition were none too happy about it. Since my duties included lots of contact with them—I was responsible for supply delivery paperwork—I heard a lot of grousing. It was actually Soviets looking down at their less-skilled, culturally different hosts. "Those Egyptians stop work three times a day to pray to Allah," Soviet naval officers from a destroyer would gripe. "It wouldn't matter if we were being chased by an Israeli gunboat. We damn near bought it last time out."

The Soviet pilots, meantime, complained about leading a squadron of MIGs on patrol into Israeli-held territory. The squadrons usually would consist of one Soviet leader with two or three Egyptians flying low to try to evade Israeli radar. Every time Israeli jets came out to intercept, the Egyptians would hightail it, leaving the Russians to face the interceptors alone.

It was such a regular occurrence that Russian pilots even had jokes about it. An oft-heard one concerned a Russian pilot over the Israel-occupied Sinai desert. Suddenly he hears Israeli ground control crackling over his radio: "Incoming flight, identify yourself. . . ."

The Russian pilot answers: *"Yeb tvoyu mat!"*

Israeli ground control responds: "Oh, Boris, it's you. So how are things going today? Any mail from Odessa?"

On my runs to Cairo, I used to get together socially with my IIR classmate Aleksander Kalugin. One of his duties was to handle arrangements for Soviet personnel who died in the Egyptian theater. Once I accompanied him to the airport where he supervised the transport to Russia of three Soviet airmen who had been killed by Israelis over the Suez Canal.

I also got to know some of the Soviet flyers quite well back in Alexandria. One of them, Fedor Kosarev, lived in Moscow not far from where I lived and traveled on the same ship with me when I went home at the end of my Egyptian tour of duty. He said that despite the dangers and the disrespect for the Egyptians, most of the Russian pilots liked being assigned there. It was better, he said, than duty along the Chinese border, where he had flown similar and even more risky reconnaissance missions into China. The money was better in Egypt too, because, it being overseas duty, they got bonus pay and could buy foreign goods to take home with them as well.

The inter-agency rivalry in the Soviet intelligence community that was intimated by Tolya never reached the proportions one finds among the United States services or in other Western countries. Moscow held the reins too tightly to allow that. But this was a time of some looseness by Soviet standards. The new organization of Soviet world strategy was being completed; the last piece fell into place in 1971 when Yuri Andropov, head of the KGB, was elevated to the Politburo. This put the KGB under direct party control. Only the GRU remained relatively independent, but its importance was minimal.

A new order was emerging and even I could not make out all of its components. In Moscow, the order had seemed clear. The party—or rather the Central Committee—ran everything, and the KGB enforced its will. In Egypt, however, there seemed to be another force working on the KGB, GRU, the military, and the diplomatic corps. And, following the direction toward which Sbirunov and other KGB operatives appeared to bow, the trail led to the sumptuous Cairo offices of Vadim Sinelnikov, counselor of the embassy, and his retinue of five tight-lipped diplomats. They did not seem beholden to anyone. Their offices were like a heavily guarded battlefield command post where few of us went.

Sinelnikov had a journalistic background and experience in work among foreign media, politicians, lawyers, and other public-opinion–influencing institutions. He had done his apprenticeship in London, under a diplomatic cover. He was also a veteran party official. He was polished and elegant in appearance. He wore expensive, British-tailored suits well on his six-foot-one frame. Sinelnikov was in his mid-forties, had fine features and a rather aristocratic appearance. He enjoyed his reputation as an aggressive *bon vivant* by partying with high-level Egyptians in expensive night-

244

clubs and restaurants in Cairo and Beirut, where he went without having to obtain permission from a superior like any other Soviet diplomat.

He addressed everyone on the embassy staff, including KGB men, with an air of authority and no one interfered with his activities. He seemed to have a direct line to Moscow, but still, he was not part of the KGB chain of command.

Aside from Sbirunov's occasional references to him, I knew little about him and had no contact with him until June 1969. His daughter was arriving from Moscow on the *Latvia* to spend her school holiday with her father in Cairo, and it presented an opportunity to curry his favor.

She was due in on Wednesday morning. Her father was busy in Aswan, so it fell to me to meet her and drive her back to Cairo. I took the opportunity to make it into a two-day vacation for Natasha, Katya, and myself.

After a quick breakfast of red caviar sandwiches and Earl Grey tea for Natasha and me and Kellogg's cornflakes for Katya, we descended the redwood stairs of our quarters and went to the consulate garage, where Boris had left the car, as usual in perfect running order. Boris and I were partners in the consulate's volleyball team, in dominoes and billiards, and he always took good care of me. Natasha and Katya wore matching dresses and giggled with anticipation as they ran toward the Volga sedan.

I drove down Al-Corniche, the seashore drive, past the restaurants and night clubs, past the Man Bull monument, past the Soviet SAM missile installations, where my old hangout the hunting club used to be, past Saad Zaghlul.

As-Silsilla Hunting Club was now a Soviet camp where no Egyptians were allowed. Russian troops manned missiles and lived there, most of them not allowed to leave the compound. Just before the changeover late in 1968, I remembered the Armenian who had owned the club coming to me and complaining about being evicted. The club had long been a favorite playground for the Egyptian elite and for tourists. He said the Egyptians wouldn't be happy about the turnover to the Soviets. I told him there was nothing to be done. It was the spot the Soviets had chosen and that was it.

The city sparkled at this hour as we drove, and a warm, salty breeze brought a timeless sense of well-being with each breath. Every turn of Al-Corniche opened to sights of new and old buildings, trees and grass blending into the Mediterranean backdrop. Aromas of falafel from a corner cafe, of perfume from a shop, of salt surf sprinkled on warm asphalt, of kebab from another cafe, mixed with the sea breeze.

The port, as usual, was all businesslike activity. I hailed an acquaintance from the Egyptian immigration police who rushed over for a friendly embrace. The Egyptian picked up Katya and carried her toward a group of other Egyptians, among whom I recognized another friend, Mahmoud from the Amon Shipping Agency, through which I put some of the customs brokerage for Soviet imports. Through Mahmoud I also had access to all lists of passengers traveling by ship through Alexandria, thus keeping track of the movements of the citizens of the U.S., England, West Germany, and other capitalist countries. Two other Egyptian police whom I knew were also there.

"Where's the *Latvia?*" I asked Mahmoud.

"Coming, Mr. Vladimir, we have already sent the pilot."

"Papa, Papa," Katya pulled my sleeve, "can I go away on the ship with you."

"I'm not going, Katya, we are just meeting someone. Then we are going to Cairo."

I turned back to Mahmoud. Handing him my Soviet passenger manifest from the embassy, I asked him, "Could you see to these people? I've got to meet the daughter of a hotshot diplomat and deliver her to Cairo." It was against regulations, but Mahmoud was trustworthy, and besides, I was a good customer.

"Sure, Mr. Vladimir. You know, anything I can do for you is my pleasure."

Sinelnikov's daughter was a regular Soviet princess—willful, pretty, and spoiled. She was about sixteen, with a slim figure and the dark, serious eyes of her father. I was glad Natasha was going along as a mediator.

Right away I noticed she was accustomed to being chauffeured in Chaikas back in Moscow, as I watched her elegantly-dressed figure sink into the back seat as though my Volga was a luxury limo. Her suitcases were very light. I concluded Daddy would shower her with everything she wanted, and that would require room.

We loaded her luggage into the trunk and took off fast, with her in the back seat with my wife and Katya up front with me. I pulled through customs gates fast to avoid any delays with immigration. We took the desert road to Cairo; it was less crowded and faster. When I'd go to Cairo alone, I occasionally took another, agricultural road. It was more colorful and besides, I could scout airfields and other military installations along the way and count the missile sites camouflaged as silos and other farm structures.

We passed some lakes outside of Alexandria and I floored the Volga, still getting only eighty miles an hour. I pictured myself in the United States on one of its great freeways where I "knew" one could drive a sports car at 125 an hour or faster. The Volga began to vibrate and Natasha asked me to slow down.

When we got to Cairo, I stopped at the embassy to pick up the keys to Sinelnikov's apartment, trying to be unobtrusive so as to avoid being drafted for some vacation-spoiling task. I ran into Tolya Egorin. "Hey look who's here! How long will you be staying?"

"Couple of days."

"Come on over to my office if you have a chance, I want to show you my new teletype—especially my new teletype operator," he said, giving me a Groucho Marx leer.

Sinelnikov's apartment was a sumptuous, three-bedroom, two-bath affair with maid quarters to boot. I opened the refrigerator and found it generously packed with VO *(Vneshposyltorg—*Soviet Supply Organization of High Quality Consumer Goods Abroad) products from Moscow. We put Katya down for a nap, while Natasha, our visiting princess, and I sat around the coffee table drinking Sinelnikov's Stella beer and eating eggplant, caviar, and black bread. Natasha caught up on all the gossip in Moscow—what was playing at the theaters, how good was the new Arbat Restaurant.

Sinelnikov was due back that evening and I didn't particularly want to get involved with him, plus I thought it would be better to let him greet his daughter alone. So after a polite interval that insured a good impression would be conveyed to *père,* we bid our goodbyes and left a note apologizing for leaving and saying that, since his daughter needed a rest after such a long journey, I'd check back with him the next evening after work. I expressed gratitude to him for entrusting his daughter's care to me and our delight at having met her. That ought to do it, I thought.

We checked into the Scorobeus Hotel near Talaat Harb Street, where I usually stayed. It was not deluxe, but was clean and had a good restaurant. The next morning we went to see the pyramids at Giza.

As anticipated, I got in the front door with Sinelnikov after that, and through the duties with which he eventually entrusted me, I got to know more about the veiled but powerful force he represented.

The Soviet strategy to destroy the Western capitalist nations and put the Soviet Union in a position of global domination through economic-ideological warfare called for something more than the usual intelligence and subversion activities. As skilled as the KGB was in these arts, therefore, that job was not left entirely in its hands. What was needed was a highly sophisticated cadre to direct and coordinate all the levels of actions—overt and covert—that were called for by the emerging strategy.

To handle this, a new and highly secret branch of the Soviet high command was created—the Central Committee's International Department. Beginning in 1967, this elite group stationed key men in embassies in all important countries. They reported directly to the Central Committee and saw to it that the diplomatic missions and the KGB, GRU, military, and economic advisors efficiently worked together toward carrying out the master plan. The CC men were not beholden to any agency—if there is an analogy for it in the United States system, it could be compared to White House advisors who report directly to the President rather than working for the cabinet members (with the big exception, however, that the CC International Department operates sub rosa).

The CC International Department came into being in the period following Brezhnev's ascension to power. Its preeminence in Soviet overseas operations represented a turn away from traditional diplomatic and espionage activities. Traditional diplomacy—the information gathering, the negotiations, agreements, receptions, and other courtesies—was still handled by the regular Ministry of Foreign Affairs personnel. Intelligence information gathering was greatly downplayed and put into the hands of the GRU and a few KGB illegals. The Kremlin didn't feel a great need for ferreting out technological information or military secrets from the West because most of this was so easy to get above board. Both sides had spy satellites as well, to keep track of missile sites and military movements. Besides, the Soviets were not as much interested in hardware as they were in people. The strategy called for bringing the developing nations into Moscow's political and economic orbit.

It fell to the CC's elite political *apparatchiks* to oversee this new course at each important embassy. This stewardship included coordinating the regular KGB recruitment and subversion operations. But more importantly, the CC department's job encompassed directing more open efforts toward propaganda and political and economic manipulation. This included liaison with political leaders, minority groups, recruitment of politicians, elected and appointed government leaders, "disinformation" operations—for example, spreading false rumors denigrating the loyalty of anti-Soviet political and religious leaders—and doing a Soviet public relations job in the local media—for example, planting newspaper stories, making pro-Soviet radio broadcasts, arranging for television coverage of events in the Soviet Union, or running pro-Soviet documentaries.

The CC International Department also provided a closer link between the KGB and the party leadership. It directed the KGB in delicate economic sabotage operations that were beyond the scope of the KGB alone. These operations included economic destabilization—setting up dummy companies to take out loans from local banks and defaulting on them, buying into the banks and local companies themselves, recruiting local businessmen and contractors by throwing business their way or by bribery, buying interest in technology-oriented Western companies through a third country as middleman, and buying real estate in a similar way.

The top CC political man in Cairo was Vadim Sinelnikov, as I found out when I became involved in the CC's top priority project for Egypt. The project was to get all of Egypt caught up in celebration with the Soviet Union of the one hundredth anniversary of Lenin's birth, which was to fall on April 20, 1970.

This was more than a ceremonial assignment. Its purpose was to provide cover for a Soviet propaganda blitz in the Middle East and to enshrine Lenin as a hero to the Egyptian people. The preparations started a year before the event. I became involved in the autumn of 1969. Sinelnikov, remembering my summer chauffeuring service for his daughter, called on me to write a report on what could be planned in Alexandria for the Lenin anniversary. (Of course, my knowledge of the area and fluency in Arabic were factors, too.) He wanted the report to include radio and television programs that could be aired and articles that could be printed. He wanted to know which journalists and broadcasters were pro- or anti-Soviet, which ones had rejected Soviet articles in the past, and how these editors could be neutralized or circumvented.

I wrote the paper; and Sinelnikov approved and called me to Cairo for a meeting, saying that from this point on I'd be involved in the propaganda drive in a major way. I'd make speeches, write articles, and go on the radio. I'd have to get more involved with the Soviet Cultural Center. The Alexandria Soviet Cultural Center where Natasha worked as a Russian language teacher, like any Soviet cultural center abroad, was headed by a KGB officer. In Alexandria it was Adil Kurbanov, originally from Soviet Azerbaidzhan. The center's prime task was to screen potential KGB candidates from those who visited the center.

As Sinelnikov outlined all this to me in his Cairo office, I began to worry about how I'd find the time, what with Sbirunov constantly on my back to run his KGB errands. I mentioned these commitments to Sinelnikov.

"Don't worry about your consular duties and don't worry about Sbirunov."

"But I'm under orders not to make any commitments without checking with Sbirunov first. You know that; it's the 'neighbors,'" I said, giving him a meaningful stare.

"Fuck the 'neighbors.' They do what I say, not the other way around. This order comes directly from Central Committee." He returned my stare, in spades. I kept quiet, not daring to ask anymore questions.

"Look," he said in a more friendly way, "I know Sbirunov thinks you are the best Arabist around here. Now *we* need you. With your excellent Arabic you will communicate more quickly and clearly." He paused and lit his Phillip Morris. "Imagine thousands of Arabs and you getting them excited about how we are going to continue our support in their noble fight against the Zionist enemy and American imperialism!"

I nodded, "Yes, Comrade Sinelnikov, I can see the picture."

I left him believing that he just got himself another qualified cadre man. The conversation further proved to me what I heard and read during my work in Egypt. The Soviet Union was not the least interested in the settlement of the Arab-Israeli conflict. The Soviet goal is to keep the conflict boiling on low fire and to drag the Palestinians along. If everything was settled, how would the Soviets manipulate the Arabs? And how would they get to the Saudis? They would, I decided, only it would take longer.

I could have told Sinelnikov that pushing this big Soviet birthday party on Egypt was a mistake. Vladimir Ilyich Lenin was no Arab and would never be installed in the Middle Eastern pantheon. But even if he would listen to me, which was highly improbable, why should I help the bastards any more than I am compelled to already?

Outside, the Cairo traffic was at its chaotic norm, reflecting the nature of the city itself—cars moving in all directions with rules improvised by each driver. There was a car pulling into the middle of a street, jamming cars for blocks, a jumble of ancient and modern machines—1928 Fiat Topolinos, pre-war Opels, American Hudsons and Valiants, Soviet Volgas and Moskviches. Arab music blended with American country-western blasting from radios as I walked slowly down Talaat Harb Street. The aroma of freshly baked bread, spices, and kebab wafted from a sidewalk restaurant. Arabs, most of them well-dressed in Western-style attire, strolled leisurely. Some sat and drank tea in outdoor cafes. Young people, mostly men, were standing near the Rialto movie theater. Stylishly dressed young women walked in groups. Then I saw the wife of a Soviet specialist, garishly dressed, one hand on hip, the other chopping the air, as she shouted at an Arab shopkeeper trying to bargain him down. She was talking in Russian and apparently thought that if she could just yell loudly enough, the shopkeeper would understand her. From the look on his face, I saw that he understood only too well.

I remember those sullen looks from another time when I tried to ramrod our billiard table—which had come in from the Soviet Union—through customs to get it diverted from Cairo and sent to our Alexandria consulate. Sallah, who usually helped me in emergencies, was away that day. Figuring they all knew me, I went to the customs warehouse and started giving orders. Suddenly I felt very self-conscious. This was not the Soviet Union. I was a foreign guest, but I'd been going along with the Soviet routine so long I forgot this, just like Sbirunov and Sinelnikov and their crews.

I began to sense that the Soviets were overplaying their hand with their Sovietization drive, reaching ostentatious proportions with the

Lenin birthday propaganda drive of 1970. If there is a point at which things began to go wrong for Moscow in Egypt, this was it. But at the time the Soviets were oblivious to it.

Leaving Sinelnikov, I looked at my watch. I had one hour to kill before meeting Yussef. Our meeting was to take place around Ramses Square near the Cairo railroad station across the Nile from the embassy. From there I'd follow Yussef to a safe place which he'd preselected.

I drove around Ramses Square until I noticed Yussef's white Nasr, an Egyptian twin of a small Fiat. He nodded and I followed him at a distance, heading north on Ash-Shubra. Several miles down Ash-Shubra he stopped and parked his car behind an old shabby roadside *dukkan* (store).

I parked my car in front of the store, thinking if there were surveillance I had a legitimate excuse to stop by.

Yussef was waiting at one of the two wooden dinner tables. He greeted me in his usual businesslike manner, with only a slight smile on his face.

"Where's the owner?" I asked sitting down on a fragile chair.

"I am the owner," Yussef put his right hand to his chest. "I bought this several months ago. Al'Walad, the boy who tends to it, had to go home, so we can talk."

I noticed the store was almost empty and looked at Yussef. "Oh, I really don't care about business," he said, catching my glimpse, "it's just for one purpose."

"I understand," I said, thinking the setup was very convenient. Who'd ever suspect anything? Two men on the way out of the city happened to meet and drink a cup of coffee. Even if someone would see us there would be no problem.

We talked for half an hour and I briefed Yussef on the events which I thought would be of interest to my friends.

I also told him I was recently promoted to a position of attaché, and Ambassador Vinogradov wanted to transfer me to Cairo. However, I didn't want to work in Cairo. What I wanted was to be transferred to a country where there was an American embassy.

Our meeting came to an end and I left for Alexandria, where my new responsibilities were to take up all my time and energy.

Back at the consulate general I found Vice-Consul Chingiz Rasulov, the GRU man, waiting for me. The consulate guard told me to go immediately to Rasulov's office. I called Natasha from the consulate and told her I got back just fine and would be home shortly. She didn't sound as if she cared one way or the other. Lately, I was spending less and less time with my family. Lenin's birthday was the thing which occupied all my time.

Rasulov was not alone.

"Vladimir," he said, introducing me to a man in his thirties, short, with a baby face and feminine hands, "this is Vice-Consul Denisov. He is replacing me, since I'm leaving next week." I said I was glad to meet him and shook hands with the new GRU resident in Alexandria.

"You'll be working together," Rasulov said. I thought, *the hell I will. I've had enough of this working together shit. When was I supposed to sleep?* But, instead, I replied, "Sure, however, first you must ask Tolya Egorin in Cairo."

Both GRU officers turned to me and I continued, "Yes . . . I am not authorized to do anything unless Egorin orders."

I had made a smart move. Egorin was the top man. I knew Tolya would always back me up.

"Well," Rasulov hesitated, his face taking on a subservient expression. "I suppose then you wouldn't want to go with Comrade Denisov on our submarine for a day."

"It's not that I wouldn't go," I said, puffing my Cleopatra. "I'm about to get very busy . . . You know, this birthday."

Neither Rasulov nor Denisov bothered me, at least for a while.

The time preceding the big event of the century ran very fast. I had to speak before Arabs in the Soviet Cultural Center, at the University of Alexandria, at the Youth Club, at the ASU Club, and at the Alexandria shipyard. The speech sounded more or less the same at all those meetings. "Soviets and Arabs have common roots—fighting against Tsarist and imperialist oppression, then fighting against capitalist aggression and building a society for the people where there is no exploitation of man by man. . . . Lenin was the first to implement the will of the people to do away with capitalists . . . the Soviet Union will always be brother to the Arabs and help them fight Zionism which is headed by the United States."

A crowd of three thousand Egyptian dock workers cheered and shouted when I roared the accusations against Zionists, Americans, British. *Like Fidel Castro,* I thought, *delivering one of his four-hour speeches before his revolutionary troops.*

On the day of Lenin's birthday, I had to go with Consul General Oleg Shumilov to do a show on the radio.

The night before, Shumilov invited me to his office for a rehearsal. It was his first time on the radio. I had two years of broadcasting experience when I was moonlighting in my IIR days in Moscow as a controller and assistant editor at the Middle East Department of the State Committee for Television and Broadcasting. Every time I made public speeches I imitated the style of my old friend Taleb Mushtak, Moscow Radio's Arab newscaster. He, in turn, reminded me of Willis Conover, on Voice of America.

Anatoly Kuznetsov found out that I was going on the radio and appeared very angry with me. I didn't want that to happen at any cost—better a confrontation with the consul general than a report to the KGB from a *stukach*. Upon my insistence, Shumilov explained to Kuznetsov that the reason why he was taking me and not him (Anatoly officially was still interpreter) was because I had previous broadcasting experience. The rehearsal satisfied Shumilov and, next morning, I did my Taleb Mushtak number on the radio.

The reception at the consulate general on Lenin's anniversary was a spectacular celebration. Three or four hundred Soviet, Egyptian, and foreign guests filled its spacious rooms and garden. Tables were overflowing with booze and food, most of which was prepared by Soviet wives. A large number of Soviet navy admirals and commanders who came ashore for the occasion added to the reception the flavor of a Moscow military parade. The only things missing were the tanks, rockets, and ICBMs in front of the mausoleum on the Red Square. However, there was no lack of these in the port of Alexandria, where the Soviet fleet stood on alert to begin worldwide *Okean* maneuvers.

The *Okean* maneuvers were the first of their kind for the Soviet Union. They involved coordinated actions by fleets of warships in the Mediterranean and in the Atlantic, Pacific, and Indian oceans, and showed off the might of the new Soviet navy, which had been greatly built up in the 1960s with the aim of challenging U.S. naval superiority. The new Soviet naval forces now could flex their muscles in seas hitherto dominated by the Americans and British. For example, sixty-five Soviet warships were taking part in *okean* maneuvers in the Mediterranean alone. The Soviets, however, were not holding the *okean* maneuvers only to improve military preparedness. There was an overriding political aim, which was pointed out in the public relations statements we were ordered to make in Alexandria, along with other Soviet missions in the Third World. This was to demonstrate to the developing nations of Asia, Africa, and Latin America that the Soviet Union was ready and able to stand by them—right off their shores—against the imperialists.

One night I finally freed myself from the routine and took Natasha out to the movies. We went to the Rialto to see *Dracula Has Risen From the Grave* with Christopher Lee. Horror movies were never shown in the Soviet Union and Natasha was very excited to experience this forbidden fruit. Her excitement and nightmares lasted for two or three nights. By some crazy coincidence I was called upon by Sbirunov to perform a ghoulish task on the very next night.

"Vladimir, we've got an emergency," he said as soon as I closed the door behind me. "One of our people was drowned near Paradise Beach."

Paradise Beach was where the ambassador, Sinelnikov, and Nedosekin had villas. The beach was also very popular with the Egyptian aristocracy.

Sure enough, I thought, *the dead body will fall on my lap,* as per my consular responsibilities of arranging the transport for anyone, dead or alive, especially the KGB.

"You go there and take care of the body," Sbirunov ordered. I decided that there was no way I would go alone. So, without telling Sbirunov, I called Sallah. In half an hour we were on our way. The corpse was lying in the lobby of the Paradise Beach Hotel on top of two pushed-together dinner tables. No one was in the room except the hotel manager.

"Take a look," he said, lifting a white blanket off the corpse. I looked at what used to be a middle-aged man, rather tall and strong. The bluish white face was fixed in a terrible grimace of pain and anger. One eye was open and gave me a stare. I stepped back, trying not to look.

Sallah explained the formalities to the manager in Arabic and told me not to worry. He'd take care of everything.

On the way back we dropped into the Fuji Club and, after a few drinks, I was accompanying the club's Greek singer, Alke Petropoliadis, while he sang "Those were the days, my friend. . . ."

We never found out why that KGB officer drowned. Stuffing the casket into the consulate general's old VW bus, Sbirunov sighed. "It must have been locals. They must have done something to him . . . Such a healthy guy."

Then Sbirunov and I got into the bus and drove to Cairo to send the body on the next Aeroflot flight to Moscow. As we were following the turns on the desert road Sbirunov teased me: "Look back! He's getting up—his hand! It's gonna grab you—Now!"

I almost felt a chilling breath down my neck. Who knows, maybe the KGB had developed a network of the Undead.

PART FIVE

For Only the Lonely

18: Try Not to Be Like Them

If I'd known that deluxe compartment six was such a dump, I wouldn't have had two other returning officials bumped in order to secure it. I'd done a little politicking with the first mate of the *Ukrayina,* reminding him that two passengers he had billeted for the liner's twelve deluxe cabins weren't high enough in the pecking order to rate deluxe accommodations.

I wasn't enough of a VIP either, but the first mate knew me, not them, so I got the cabin. Unlike deluxe cabin one, which I'd once seen, number six was smaller, had tawdry furnishings, and had no view of the sea.

The lumbering old *Ukrayina,* a World War II trophy with ancient German engines, temporarily substituted for the *Latvia* on two or three Odessa-Alexandria trips because the captain of the *Latvia* and some senior members of the crew were arrested for smuggling gold. The gold was sold in Odessa to dentists. The crew was up for trial and a long sentence and the KGB was taking time to select and check out a new crew.

I had hoped to enjoy my journey back home in the company of my old friends, the sailors, but the faces on board were new to me. I was making the Alexandria-Athens-Varna-Istanbul-Odessa passage alone as well; Natasha and Katya had gone home two months ago. Just about then Moscow notified me that I was being transferred to Kuwait as an attaché of the Soviet Embassy, and would start there after a two-month vacation at home.

I had been in Egypt for two years. Normally Soviet diplomats serve abroad three years at a time, then are given home assignments for a year or two before being sent abroad again. My transfer meant that I would not have to spend another year in Egypt, and once I got to my new post there would be a good chance of extending my foreign service another year, as was allowed sometimes. I was particularly happy about being sent to Kuwait for three other reasons. First of all, I'd be able to work more closely with the Americans, because unlike Egypt at the time, Kuwait had diplomatic relations with Washington. Secondly, Kuwait, as the Arab oil producer second only to its neighbor Saudi Arabia, fit in better with my IIR specializations in economics, oil, and the Arabian peninsula. Thirdly, I thought that at last I'd be rid of my *stukach* shadow Anatoly Kuznetsov, who would be finishing out his third year in Alexandria.

As soon as I got the news of my impending transfer, I found a pretext for making a quick trip to Cairo where I met with my CIA contact Yussef at our regular *dukkan* on the outskirts of town.

"What's the urgency?" Yussef asked nervously as we sat down at the table, inquiring about my unscheduled appearance.

"I'm being transferred."

"Where? I hope not Moscow. I thought you'd get another year here."

"Kuwait," I said, "the Soviet Embassy."

"Ua-llahi! Tamam, taman!!" he exclaimed. ("Oh my God! Good, good!")

"Tell George that I'll be there sometime in November and to make contact with me after I arrive."

"I'll pass it on. But what if he can't get to you there? How should I say that you want to be contacted in that case?"

"He must make it. That's all," I said. "We made a deal that I am not to be contacted in Moscow and that the circle of people who know about me must be limited strictly. I don't want this going through any regular channels on your side or someone I don't know coming into the picture now. I can't chance being passed around from one contact to another."

Yussef shook his head. "I have no say in such things, but I'll relay your message, you can count on that. Good luck, my friend."

"And to you. I don't suppose you'll have a chance to come and see me in Kuwait one of these days," I inquired politely.

"Not likely. I'm just a middleman and I'll stay right where I am. *Salam Alaykum.*"

"Goodbye," I said, and drove back to Alexandria to get ready for my departure, not quite at ease for the first time since I'd received notice of my transfer.

My uneasiness didn't dissipate even then, aboard the *Ukrayina*. I was also feeling a little sorry for myself and in something of a churlish mood as a group of well-wishers from the consulate general were giving me the usual boozy sendoff in the cabin. My peevishness quickly was dispelled, however, when one of them gave me a more substantial cause for alarm.

I'd been driven to the ship by the new KGB resident in Alexandria, Valentin Ovinnikov, who had replaced Sbirunov when he had been rotated back to Moscow a month ago. Ovinnikov was a lightweight compared to Sbirunov, and was a lot less demanding. But sadly I didn't get to know him very well. So I was taken aback by some valuable information he gave me upon our parting. Some of what he had to say concerned Sbirunov, and I'm sure Ovinnikov considered him a valuable ally to cultivate. As for the warning he was to give me, he figured I had connections and that being in with me might help him.

As the farewell party babbled on, I spotted Ovinnikov gesturing me to come out the cabin door. I followed him down the passageway until he stopped, looked to see no one was around, and said, "Vladimir, could you do me a favor?"

"Sure. You name it."

"All right. When you see Sbirunov in Moscow, tell him to be very careful with Ustinov and Seliverstov. Advise him to keep his mouth shut, I mean socially and so forth. Those guys can fuck him up."

Ovinnikov's voice lowered almost to a whisper. "Also, you, Vladimir, be very careful with Anatoly Kuznetsov."

He didn't have to tell me about my old *stukach* nemesis, but Ovinnikov went on. "He's been saying bad things about you."

"What things?"

"You know. He found out that you got Victor Degtyar and

261

Gennady Enikeyev out of jail when they were drunk and you didn't report it through proper channels. He also has followed you on some of your meetings with Sallah Al-Badawi. Just a few times, but enough to cause you some trouble."

It was no surprise that Kuznetsov was snooping around again, but it put me a little on edge. Just how much had he seen? And what was worse, I hadn't seen him. The little bastard was doing a good job of tailing me.

The warning I was supposed to pass to Sbirunov, I figured, had to do with the activities which Sbirunov hid from the likes of me. I occasionally caught glimpses of these while fronting errands. In this dark business, Sbirunov like everyone else involved, reported to Vladimir Grusha, the much-feared KGB resident in Cairo whom I'd met a couple of years ago.

I knew that Seliverstov, one of the two mentioned in the warning, worked directly for Grusha and that the other, Ustinov, worked for the KGB in Beirut, acting as some sort of liaison with the most militant of Palestinian terrorists. Furthermore, I knew Ustinov, Seliverstov, and Grusha had all worked together from an incident several months earlier, when I had met Ustinov as he arrived in Alexandria aboard the *Latvia*.

Ustinov had just come from his Beirut post and was carrying a secret diplomatic pouch with him. When I greeted him, Ustinov was hopping mad because Seliverstov was not there to meet him, as per orders. Ustinov ordered me to take the pouch to Cairo and deliver it to Seliverstov or to Grusha himself, and to convey to both of them his irritation over the missed connection.

How Sbirunov was tied into the Grusha-Ustinov-Seliverstov-Palestinian connection was unclear. Sbirunov, being the Alexandria KGB resident, was concerned with subverting Egyptians and I couldn't figure his Palestinian angle.

The other more likely possibility was that the Ustinov-Seliverstov team had another job besides their Palestinian interface. That job would be to snoop on their fellow KGB operatives and report back to the top KGB resident for Egypt, Nedosekin, whom Sbirunov had seemed to fear most when he'd taken me to meet him that time in Cairo.

Normally, the KGB's Second (internal) Directorate was responsible for internal politics, both inside the Soviet Union and abroad.

Meanwhile, the KGB's First (foreign) Directorate was responsible for intelligence and subversion worldwide—outside the Soviet Union. There was an overlap, however, in that the First Directorate had a small counterintelligence system to keep track of its own men in the field. I had heard that Nedosekin was in line for a top First Directorate post in Moscow after he finished in Egypt. In that post he would be in charge of that First Directorate self-policing cadre. So he most likely was already using the Ustinov-Seliverstov team in that capacity, as sort of super *stukachi* undercover men in the field. As such, the duo was extremely dangerous, since, like any other *stukachi*, they always would be on the prowl for fresh meat—must keep those fat dossiers filled. Sbirunov, a man whose style it was to cut corners, would make a perfect victim for them.

I decided that I would pass the warning on to Sbirunov, though not out of any special love for him. I had another idea and I figured Sbirunov could be instrumental in it. Besides, if I didn't pass the message, Ovinikov most likely would get it to him another way and I'd have made enemies of both, something I didn't care to do.

The journey back to Moscow was tedious. The *Ukrayina* wallowed even more slowly than usual, due to continual foulups by its inexperienced crew. I didn't go ashore at Athens, Varna, or Istanbul because I'd given Natasha all my money so *she* could shop on her trip home. When we got to Odessa, the city was quarantined because of a cholera outbreak and the airport and rail station were closed. I marched five friends I'd made aboard ship to the railroad station. Flashing my diplomatic passport, I told the station master that I was escorting a top-secret VIP delegation to Moscow and pointed at the five. The nervous station master arranged for some private rail cars and a special engine, and we were whisked off to Moscow.

When I arrived, I heard that my grandfather had died in June of that year, 1970. "We didn't want to tell you until you got home," Natasha explained. My grandfather, who was 70, had taken Natasha and little Katya to the *dacha* by the reservoir, just as he so often had done for me when I was a boy. Early one morning Katya came running to wake up her mother. Grandfather wouldn't get out of bed, she complained. Natasha went to check; she saw that he already had the bluish pallor of death and pulled Katya back out of the room. As soon as Natasha finished telling me the bad news I left for the *dacha* without saying a word to her. There I took off in my boat and didn't come back for two days.

Moscow, always at its best in summer, looked better than when I had left it. The people strolling in the warm July sunshine were better dressed and seemed more assertive and cheerful. They stood in line to pack new restaurants and theaters, or window shopped along the wide sidewalks of Prospect Kalinina, looking into its new stores and in the huge glass windows of the new Arbat Restaurant, the Comecon Building, and the new high-rises. Natasha wore the new dresses she'd bought in Athens and Istanbul and I enjoyed the stares she got almost as much as she did. We saw all the new films in town and made the usual rounds of theater and social gatherings.

Just after I arrived home, a two-bedroom cooperative apartment became available to us in the building where my parents lived at 13 Tchaikovsky Street. We'd been on a waiting list two years to be eligible for a co-op and felt fortunate to be able to get one right in the building. I immediately paid the $950 down payment to secure it. That amounted to sixty percent of the total price, the rest to be paid off in small monthly payments. That was all we would be able to do on this trip, however, since the place needed painting and furnishing and we decided to enjoy the rest of my vacation and decorate the place the next time we returned to Moscow from my new post in Kuwait. For the time being we'd stay at my parents' apartment.

After a couple of weeks we left for our vacation. My mother took Katya to the *dacha* and I secured two twenty-day passes to a new, and very swank *dom otdykha* (resort) I'd been told had been built just for upper echelon MFA, KGB, and Central Committee employees. It was situated in picturesque forest country along the winding river about forty miles north of Moscow.

Since it still was new, I thought that it probably wouldn't be spoiled yet by the intrigues, graft, and demoralization of the staff by red tape—the results of *stukachi* meddling. I was right. The help was cheerful and polite and the crowd of mostly young "resortniks" was open, informal, and unself-consciously having a good time. It was a good mix of the international elite, with a few others to leaven it. There were none of the local party bosses or the old party cadre from Moscow. The old guard hadn't moved in yet.

Our suite—a sitting room, bedroom, and bath—was spacious and plush, with a polished wood dinner table lit by a crystal chandelier, a velvet couch, a mirrored coffee table, a king-size bed, and modern, German-made bathroom fixtures. Natasha and I took an afternoon walk along an old dirt path in the forest; it was an old carriage road for what had once been a Tsarist estate. For dinner, she changed into one of her Trevira dresses and I wore a white turtleneck sweater, slacks, and sports jacket.

The main dining hall was large with a simple wood-paneled interior and two large glass walls that offered a sweeping view of the forest.

I noticed a number of familiar faces from my IIR days: MFA people, family acquaintances—this was definitely our crowd. We exchanged nods and smiles as Natasha and I walked to our table, where a young couple were already seated.

"Good evening, I am Galya and this is Mikhail," a tall, slim brunette greeted us as we sat down. "It looks like we'll be eating together for the next three weeks."

Mikhail, an almost too pretty lad of seventeen, self-consciously helped Natasha with her chair while she gave him a thinly disguised concupiscent look that he returned. His face turned red when I said, "I am Vladimir and this is my *wife*, Natasha."

The dinner was delicious; the quality of the ingredients and preparation bore the imprint of the party's elite catering service. It turned out that Galya and Mikhail were strangers to each other and to the crowd. Both of them had secured passes through friends who worked in the MFA.

Mikhail was the son of a Moscow University physics professor and had recently been admitted there to study physics. Galya was a technician at the Scientific Research Institute in Moscow. Their science connections were two good reasons they were out of place. While the Soviet Union would be nowhere without its scientists, the scientists themselves aren't let in on that little secret. The best of special privileges—like access to the resort we now enjoyed—always go to the party establishment. The scientific crowd gets second helpings.

After dinner we were joined by Alek Shelenkov, an acquaintance from the Ministry of Foreign Affairs. I'd encountered him at various social functions back in my IIR days. Alek was currently assigned to the U.N. secretariat and was due back there after a sojourn in Moscow—despite his recent divorce. Under normal circumstances the divorce would have grounded him; the fact that it didn't seem to affect his career puzzled everyone in our circle. He had to have had a lot of pull, they said.

There was another key factor. Shelenkov's wife had been complaining to friends that she had become estranged from her husband because she couldn't stand his becoming "so Americanized." All he was interested in, she complained, was prowling around New York, going to bars, strip joints, and buying American gadgets. He talked only about money, she said, and played rock and roll records all the time. He even insisted she go shopping and replace all his underwear with nothing but Fruit of the Loom products.

Certainly such a blatant display of American tastes should have raised eyebrows in Moscow too, unless he had good reason for it. One likely reason was that Shelenkov was involved in intelligence operations under the secretariat's cover. Besides being a second secretary in the MFA, Shelenkov was a KGB captain, and his father was a high-ranking officer in the KGB Partcom. Whether Shelenkov's Americanization was a smoke screen or for real, he was much too valuable a man in his U.N. post—and had family connections too high up—for the authorities to quibble over such things as a divorce and Fruit of the Loom underwear.

Alek was in his usual expansive mood that evening and invited all of us down to the bar. We went to a large cocktail lounge that was softly illuminated with multicolored, indirect lighting. To my pleasant surprise, a powerful stereo system—a Phillips, I later found out—filled the room with Frank Sinatra singing "The World We Knew" and "Strangers in the Night" and the large dance floor was crowded.

The place was still too new for the *stukachi* to have filed their reports and clamp down, I surmised. The bar was well-stocked with Teacher's, Ron Rico, Beefeaters, Courvoisier, and Schweppe's tonic.

We ordered drinks; Natasha got to taste her first gin fizz. She wanted to dance in such glamorous surroundings, she said, and invited Mikhail out onto the dance floor. Alek danced with Galya and I nursed my double Scotch and thought about this unreal hideaway. I knew that by next summer this place would be squeezed dry and made to fit the deadening socialist norm; patriotic songs by Tamara Miansarova and Edita Piekha would ooze out of the speakers; and a KGB *stukach* would be sitting in the corner sipping his Borjomi, just like the one whom I saw there right now, taking in the scene for his

266

report tomorrow morning. And Natasha would still dance with someone else and be as ravishing as ever.

I finished my drink, Sinatra started "You Go to My Head," and I felt a tap on my shoulder. I turned. "You can't sit here like this all night. C'mon." Galya smiled and stretched out her hand.

As we danced, I looked over at Natasha who was on the other side of the dance floor, her head on Mikhail's shoulder.

"Vladimir, I know," Galya said into my ear, "I know everything." I looked at her.

"You don't belong here. You feel pain but you're not the type to accept anybody's help, right?"

I stiffened. "Where's Alek?" I asked her. "I thought he was dancing with you."

"He went up to his room to get some of his own tapes. He said he was tired of all this mellow-yellow stuff." Galya's hand caressed my shoulder firmly. We both laughed. Wouldn't it be nice, I flashed. What a lovely, forthright and kind young woman she seemed to be; I could see myself coming home from my construction job to our little apartment, eating dinner, making love, watching the football games on the weekend.

As we danced, Alek returned and got the bartender to play his tapes on full volume so that Jimi Hendrix could perform a miracle and instantly transform Soviet resortniks into writhing rockers. I saw the *stukach* at the corner table sit forward.

After another dance Galya and I went back to the table. Natasha took center stage among the rockers. "Would you like to go for a walk?" Galya asked.

We went through the glass doors out into the cool, quiet night.

"Is that the North Star?" she asked, as we sat down in a grassy clearing.

"I suppose." We were quiet for a while. She looked up at the sky again. "You can see it from any place in the northern hemisphere, even from America."

I wondered what she was driving at. She moved closer.

"Really? What's the difference?" I said coldly. "Tell me: why did you think I'm in 'pain,' as you said. Does it show?"

"Then you admit it."

"I don't admit anything; I'm just trying to figure you out."

"Vladimir, I don't know you and I don't know what you do. I'm

267

not even sure I want to know. Obviously, you're one of those big men."

I was relieved. It didn't sound like a trap.

She went on. "The reason I said that is when I saw you, I sensed a wall between you and everyone else, even your wife. I thought to myself that there must be a reason you'd build that wall. Am I wrong?"

"You might be right. But that wouldn't necessarily mean I'm so unhappy. I might be trying to protect my immense wealth," I said sarcastically.

"C'mon, I know you're not poor. Anyway, so why didn't you want to stay and dance?"

"You appeal to me; you're cool and enchanting."

"Thank you, but not more than your wife."

"Galya, let's leave that alone. She and I have been through a lot. Besides, how do you know I'm any good?"

"I know you're a good man and I'd like to be by your side."

We went back to the bar, but agreed to meet the next day.

Natasha and I didn't see much of each other for the rest of the holiday and we both liked that arrangement. Every day she went mushroom hunting in the woods with Mikhail and every night she danced with Alek and mingled with the crowd. And Galya and I spent all our time together, away from everyone whenever possible.

"Galya, do you like it here?" I asked her as we walked along the river the last day of the vacation.

"Oh, very much!"

"No, I don't mean here, now. I mean *here*—your life, your work, things like that."

"Why are you asking? It would make no difference if I said one way or the other."

"It could," I said. "I like you and you like me, right?"

"Right." She put her hand around my back as we strolled.

"So, there has to be a difference. Galya, what are we going to do?"

"I'd do anything."

"It's impossible."

"Don't say that. We'll think of something. There's always a way, remember that, and no matter what happens, I'll stick. Tomorrow, when we each go home, let me know if you care to try. I'd like to make you happy, the way I've seen you here."

268

It had been a long time since I'd felt that kind of youthful anticipation for life's possibilities. For the moment, reality could wait.

Three days after returning to Moscow, I took the number Galya had given me out of my wallet and called her. She was waiting at the corner of Gorki Street and Sadovoye Koltso when I pulled up in my new export-model Volga. It was a bright, sunny afternoon, the air mellow with the first hint of Indian summer.

We took Sadovoye Koltso towards Prospect Mira, where I turned left along a way I knew so well. I turned the corner of Stretensky Street, and passed my old high school, Number 139 for Working Youth, then drove on past the Industrial Exhibition and the massive sculpture of Working Man and Woman, their hammer and sickle crossed on high. Galya said nothing as we threaded through the traffic and finally reached the super highway that circles the city.

"You want to go this way?" I asked, turning onto the highway. It was almost empty, with forests on the outer side and open fields and construction sites on the inner side.

"No difference."

"But you know how long it's going to take us," I said. "Possibly a day to go all the way around. There are twelve million people in there." I stepped down hard on the gas.

"C'mon. What do I care. I just work there. I'm a technician. Let's talk about us."

We talked. But there was no getting around Moscow for us.

"They'll be sending me back to the Middle East again soon, this time to Kuwait."

"Can I write you there?"

"Yes but you'll have to sign your letters 'Nikolai.' From now on that will be your code name. How about that? But don't write about love or how you miss me or anything; they wouldn't understand," I said, nodding my head towards Moscow.

"Good. Every word will mean I love you and miss you. I'll wait for you. No matter what happens."

A week later Sbirunov came for dinner, bringing with him memories of Alexandria and a reminder for me to get on with what had to be done. He brought a bottle of vodka and a tape by the ever-daring darling of the elite, the singer Vysotsky, that he'd promised to Natasha. The three of us ate a simple meal—appetizers of pickles and marinated mushrooms, fried potatoes, and meatballs. His round face was as jovial as ever, as if he were a choirmaster instead of a KGB henchman.

Afterwards, we listened to the tape, sipped Napoleon brandy, and talked lazily of Egypt and the future, which looked bright for both of us. He was currently in training at the KGB Higher School, learning new tricks of the trade—the same training I'd luckily slipped out of before my Egypt assignment. He was only allowed occasional weekend leaves and, after a six month course, was due to be assigned to the Soviet Embassy in Ankara. It was considered quite a privilege to go to Turkey, a big center of KGB clandestine activity, and I congratulated him.

We rambled a while more on the "neighborly" gossip. A KGB *stukach*, Ivan Maltsev, who'd been at the IIR when I was there was being made a TASS correspondent in Ankara, Sbirunov told me.

"It's a joke," I said. "He doesn't know how to write mother and father." I laughed and Sbirunov laughed too. It wouldn't take much journalistic ability to act as a liaison with Iranian, Turkish, and Arab guerillas, who were being trained by the KGB in Turkey.

From there I eased into more relevant matters. I told Sbirunov all about the warning his successor, Ovinnikov, had asked me to convey when I'd left Alexandria. Sbirunov nodded as I went over the tale of Cairo illegals chief Grusha and his twin vampires, Ustinov and Seliverstov.

When I finished, Sbirunov laughed and said, "I know, I know, but thank you anyway, my friend. It's part of the reason I've gotten myself assigned to Ankara, out of reach of those three."

I didn't pry. Now that I'd proven myself such a loyal ally of this KGB man I thought I'd hand over a little time bomb that he could deliver much more effectively than me. I steered the conversation back to gossip. Finally the Vysotsky tape I'd suffered through ended and I switched to Peggy Lee. We talked more. Then I played George Shearing.

Finally the moment came. Sbirunov had started talking about the navy officers we'd met in Alexandria.

"Remember that young, pretty boy who used to be the boss of the Communist Youth Organization for the Mediterranean fleet?" I asked.

"Yes, I do," Sbirunov answered. "Martinov! The little blond."

270

"That's the one," I nodded, and thought, *here it comes you little snitch, right up yours.* "Well, you also remember, of course, Anatoly Kuznetsov who worked with us at the consulate general."

"Of course!"

"Well, remember when you told Kuznetsov he had no business hanging around navy personnel because his work was supposed to be with the specialists."

"That's right."

I noticed Natasha staring intently at me and wagging her head surreptitiously from side to side. I went on. "Well, Kuznetsov and Martinov were pretty good friends by then, so Anatoly was quite brokenhearted about your order."

"Oh, really?"

"Yes, and after you left for Moscow their friendship grew into something even bigger, something warmer." I grinned broadly.

"Yeah? Sonofabitch!"

"They spent weekends together. Anatoly's wife, Nadya, had come back here to Moscow. So Kuznetsov needed company—*his* kind of company, if you know what I mean. They spent whole weekends together in his apartment, with the door locked. Other weekends, they'd go off to the navy resort area. Now I'm just wondering which one of them is going to have the baby."

"Vladimir, how can you say . . ." Natasha started to speak but Sbirunov cut her off.

"That's okay, I suspected something funny about him anyway. I'm glad you've confirmed my suspicions. Now it will be my great pleasure to put the sonofabitch through the grinder." He sat back, smiled, and downed another Napoleon.

After Sbirunov left, Natasha and I were silent for a long while. I looked out the window at the lights of Moscow, trying to clear my head, breathing in the warm autumn air. Natasha walked up very close to me. I turned and looked at her and she stared straight into my eyes.

She spoke very quietly and deliberately. "I thought you were different, not like all of them. But you are just a plain, lousy *stukach*, who'd sell his soul for nothing. I hate you."

The night before Natasha and I were due to depart for Kuwait a cold north wind swept down from the Arctic and broke the autumn's

271

warm spell. It was raining and gusty as my father and I went to the free currency store to stock up on some special items I might need for the journey. On our way, both of us soaked, we stopped at a ramshackle *pivnaya* (bar) behind the American Embassy.

A couple of drunks, who looked as if they had reached their final goal of embalming themselves, slouched over a table drinking vodka-beer boilermakers. My father bought two bottles of watery Soviet Zhiguli beer from the red-faced counter maid. We sat at a grimy table and poured the beer into two grayish glasses.

"See, Volodya?" he said making a sweeping motion. "This is a place you must never forget. You go about your life, you do what you have to do, but don't let your problems make you end up here."

"Why do you say this?"

"Because there'll come a time when you'll be alone. I mean *alone*. It won't last forever. And you know what I think about Natasha."

I nodded, sipping my beer.

"Among us, I mean 'neighbors' and the rest, there's no loyalty. No man-to-man loyalty."

"I know. That's the way everybody lives." I looked at the drunks.

"So you gotta realize that most of the time there are only two ways. One is to be a sonofabitch and fuck 'em at every opportunity. The other, to be honest and firm."

I shrugged. "So what?"

"To be honest and firm doesn't fit where you are right now. But I don't want my son to be one of those soul-sellers. But then again, if you aren't, you might end up like those two over there."

"Well, I don't know. I think I'm reasonably honest and firm."

"Reasonably, yes. But try not to be like them. Okay?"

"Okay," I said, catching his double meaning.

"And think in terms of being alone. It will be easier later."

Our Aeroflot plane landed in Iraq for a stopover and I found myself again in the familiar atmosphere of the Arab world. We stayed overnight to catch a flight to Kuwait, which just a few years ago had established diplomatic relations with the Soviet Union. The Atlas Hotel in Baghdad resembled others of the same class I'd frequented in Egypt—comfortable, clean, and with a continental breakfast.

My old classmate and partying friend, Kolya Kryuchkov, showed up at our room, trying to hide his inebriation. Katya was asleep and Natasha was taking a shower.

His face was jaundiced. "Liver, really bad," he said.

I didn't think he would have any complaints working in Baghdad as the personal secretary to the Soviet ambassador, with all the privileges that post entailed. Iraq was considered a choice assignment.

He was depressed. "At least you can have a drink here. Where we're going alcohol is prohibited by law." I tried to catch his drift.

"It doesn't matter," he went on, sweeping his arm erratically. I'm sick of all this. All these 'neighbors.' And the ambassador's wife. I'm stuck, not getting anywhere, and you get a promotion."

"Let's go downstairs and get a drink," I said.

We found a cafe and ordered beer.

"I'll tell you what," he said, "if you want to stay out of trouble in Kuwait, watch out for Badran Resan, he's KGB."

By now I had gathered that Kolya had something to do with this Badran Resan, who worked in the Embassy of Iraq in Kuwait. But I didn't see the connection until Nikolai filled me in. Badran Resan was the KGB contact for pro-Soviet radicals among Iraqi workers in the Kuwait oil fields. However, the trick was that Resan was handled by the KGB *residentura* out of Iraq and not by the KGB *residentura* in Kuwait.

I brought Nikolai another beer. I remembered Ivchenkov's advice in Yemen, *Get them drunk—then they talk*. It didn't apply only to Arabs. Nikolai babbled on. Our friend Badran Resan went to Moscow University, where he was recruited by the KGB. He was assigned to Kuwait but the KGB *residentura* in Kuwait didn't handle him in order to avoid rousing the suspicion of Kuwaiti security. For me Kolya's revelation was invaluable.

Nikolai got into something even more interesting before he disintegrated into dipsomanic delirium. The CC-KGB *apparatchiks* apparently were using Baghdad and Kuwait as way-stations for the Front of Liberation of Saudi Arabia that I'd first encountered in Yemen. What's more, the KGB operatives and their Central Committee coordinators weren't relying on the FLSA alone. They'd started a campaign to recruit and manipulate the sheiks and subalterns of the Saudi Arabian monarchial establishment itself. If

273

they couldn't knock over the Saudi kingdom from the outside, they'd be able to manipulate it from within, thus realizing the prime Central Committee objective—disrupting capitalist economics through oil politics. After that, there would be plenty of time to get rid of any Saudi king in the endgame.

19: To Whom It May Concern

I had been in Kuwait several weeks and was driving one of the Soviet Embassy's gray Volga sedans, when I spotted a familiar face smiling from behind the windshield of a Toyota just behind me. I nodded into the rearview mirror and cautiously slipped through traffic out of the city. The Toyota followed.

Kuwait, which is a little larger than the state of Connecticut, is bordered on the south by the Saudi Arabian-Kuwaiti neutral zone, a seventy-five–mile wide no-man's land. Al-Kuwait, the capital, is built in a series of concentric boulevards connected by spokes of streets. The desert is pushed back by the clusters of modern high-rises, bank buildings, flaming natural gas vents, oil refineries, the palaces of the Emir and rich Kuwaitis, the traditional Arab *souk* (market), the "gold row," and many other sites of Arab culture. Kuwait presents a unique blend of the best in the latest technology with the conservative tradition of the Arab civilization.

Exiting the city, I headed into open desert. It took me about half an hour to reach the neutral zone, checking every so often that the Toyota still was following discreetly and that no one else followed. Not far into the zone, I turned onto a dusty side road and drove to where it ended in the wilderness. I got out of my car and waited until the Toyota pulled up.

"*Kak dyela?*" (How is it going?) said George in his impeccable Russian.

"Good," I answered, walking up to him and shaking hands.

The heat and sand swallowed up our voices, giving our conversation an unreal quality as we traded a few jokes.

"Are you still into all that jazz?" George asked.

"Of course, George. That's what keeps me going. One can even survive Tupitsyn by listening to Astrud Gilberto . . . helps when I feel like tying the motherfucker's tongue to his belly button and stuffing jellyfish down his throat."

I was referring to Nikolai Kuzmich Tupitsyn, the new Soviet Ambassador to Kuwait who had arrived two months before me. Tupitsyn, an old party hack who was getting ready to retire, ruled the small Soviet colony in ham-handed fashion, keeping most of its members under virtual house arrest, allowing them out only in twos, setting his flunkies spying on everyone and each other. Luckily for me, as I explained to George, I'd been given errands by the KGB *residentura*—similar to the tasks I'd been assigned in Alexandria—and this allowed me much more mobility.

Still, I couldn't avoid Tupitsyn completely. I was often subjected to his stammered commands. His face was often flushed with cognac, and his reddish ears turned even a brighter hue when angered. He had a pot belly, small hands, and a disproportionately small head that seemed apropos to a derogatory meaning his name suggested—in Russian the word *tupitsa* means dummy. He was less stupid, however, than avaricious; a bumptious plenipotentiary who constantly worked at wining and dining the local aristocracy and diplomatic corps, and at wheeling and dealing for expensive furnishings, art works, and other luxuries that he could haul back to his *dacha* at the end of his term when the Ministry of Foreign Affairs was due to put him to pasture. I described the demoralizing effect this had on the staff, the continual drunkenness, the claustrophobia that I even felt.

"Just keep cool," George tried to reassure me. "You know you're doing a good thing. Every one of us appreciates your effort very much."

I went over some of my general responsibilities as an attaché to the embassy, and began to describe the operation.

"We'd better have a meeting as soon as possible, under better conditions. How about tonight?"

"I could, I suppose."

"If you go out, can you explain it to your wife?"

"No problem." I'd long since stopped explaining anything to Natasha.

At eight that evening I walked into the lobby of the Hilton Hotel. I had a perfect cover for going there. An Arab friend I'd cultivated—the son of a sheik—worked there at his bank office late at night and I'd occasionally join him and ride out to the seashore in his Oldsmobile Cutlass to drink with other important Kuwaitis (a forbidden activity) on the beach. Part of my job, as in Egypt, was to make friends among the locals and scout potential KGB recruits. But here I found I could get away with subtly sabotaging the recruitment drive by not reporting all of my contacts or by filing discouraging reports on my progress. The KGB had neither the manpower nor the freedom of action in Kuwait that it did in Egypt and it was hard for anyone to check on me.

This night I slipped through the lobby without letting my Arab friend spot me and went up to a room on the fourth floor. George and another man whom I recognized were waiting for me. They were sharing some Teacher's Scotch and poured me a glass. I'd met the other man at several diplomatic receptions given by the Kuwaitis, to which both Russian and American diplomatic corps had been invited. He was a tall, handsome, all-American football type who greeted me cheerfully and pointed to a chair in front of the coffee table.

With a U.S. embassy in Kuwait, I'd be able to work much more closely with the Americans than I was able to do in Yemen or Egypt, which had no U.S. ties at the time I'd been there. This meant more frequent meetings—as often as twice a week—more intensive briefings, and, best of all, help close at hand in case I got into trouble, a possibility that by now was beginning to prey on my mind.

We set up a system of emergency communication—a post office box under a fictitious name, an emergency phone number—and a plan was made if quick escape became necessary. Eyeing the other

American, I reminded George of our first agreement—that the circle of people on the American side who knew about me be kept strictly limited. After going over the arrangements, it was agreed that it be no more than five.

The conversation went on for three hours. There was a lot of catching up to do about my personal experiences and, in general, about Soviet military-political-economic activities. As we discussed these I felt reassured that I was in the company of two highly professional, intelligent, dedicated individuals who at the same time were genuinely concerned with my well-being and my family. Now I was able to go beyond simply passing on information and, more importantly, I began to work under the guidance and specific instructions from my more experienced team members. I felt that at last I had fully joined forces with my American friends.

Kuwait was no Egypt—the Kuwaiti government kept the Soviets strictly limited. The Soviet colony never numbered more than fifty, including clerks and dependents, while I was there. The Soviet Embassy in Kuwait was smaller than the Soviet Consulate General in Alexandria. More importantly, Kuwait's efficient and tough-minded, British-trained security police kept sharp watch on the Soviets and had a free hand to crack down on any mischief.

Moscow did not challenge this—at least not openly. Kuwait officially was regarded as one of a select group of nations—including Finland and Switzerland, for example—which followed a policy of "positive neutrality," meaning that it presented no obstacles for the Soviet Union. Furthermore, Moscow didn't want to jeopardize its clandestine long-range campaign to subvert Saudi Arabia and Arab Emirates. A premature showdown with tiny Kuwait—whose population was less than a million, but whose influential sheiks controlled twenty percent of the world's known oil reserves—would cause adverse repercussions throughout the Arabian peninsula. For now, our instructions were to gather information and recruit Kuwaitis, but very discreetly. The main thrust was to secretly make use of the Soviet Embassy in Kuwait as a relay point for the budding Saudi operation. As far as oil policy was concerned, Kuwait would go along with Saudi Arabia, and influencing, manipulating, subverting, or otherwise trying to control the Saudis in any way possible, overt or covert, to the detriment of the Western capitalist world, was the name of the game. The Emirates were already moving toward establishing closer ties with the U.S.S.R.

One of the first secret directives from Moscow that I read in the embassy's surveillance-proof *referentura* showed how far along this long-range strategy had progressed by 1970.

Since I was to be charged with making economic evaluations of the Kuwaiti and Saudi scenes, Tupitsyn instructed the *referentura* chief—a man named Gilev who acted as its files and communications clerk—to give me a file to read. In it was a single memo from Tupitsyn summarizing a Moscow Center briefing for ambassadors and their top assistants in charge of economic matters. The memo was labeled "To V. Sakharov: TOP SECRET, For Eyes Only; Destroy After Reading" and signed by the ambassador.

The memo said that our sources at the latest closed meeting of the Organization of Petroleum Exporting Countries (OPEC) have informed the center that the new policy to raise world oil prices had been approved. Within the next five years the price of oil will double and possibly triple if the members continue to act in accord, which would create certain advantages for Soviet policy abroad, especially towards the capitalist countries.

The memo also stated that confidential sources at the recent secret meeting of the Organization for Arab Petroleum Exporting Countries (OAPEC) informed Moscow that the Arabs were likely to exercise political pressure on the U.S., and have agreed to an embargo against the United States in case the latter should support Israel in a future war or military incident of considerable magnitude against any Arab state. This development presented unlimited opportunities for the fulfillment of the CPSU's foreign policy objectives in the Middle East and against the capitalist countries. The document ended, "The contents of this memo are for your information only and are not subject to discussions, nor to be mentioned in any form, nor under any circumstances brought up in your conversation with foreign diplomats or local citizens."

It was worse even than I had thought. It all fit together—the Soviet-backed plan to have Egypt ready for war against Israel by 1973, the continual Soviet exacerbation of the Arab-Israeli conflict, the recruitment of influential Arabs in the oil-rich countries, the constant propaganda against American-Zionist "imperialism" and for Soviet-Arab "brotherhood," the Sovietization of Arab countries like Syria and Iraq, putting pressure on the conservative states.

Sharply and prophetically the gunsights of the Soviet Union's ideological-political-economic artillery were trained on the United States, just as they had taught me back at the Institute for International Relations. Further briefings revealed that while an embargo was expected to be short-lived, the OPEC nations would continue to push up oil prices thenceforth. Those nations would do this independently of Soviet direction, for their own reasons, of course, but Soviet policy would be to keep the Mideast inflamed and, through pressure from Moscow's radical allies—Iraq for example— to push for OPEC to make the highest possible price hikes in order to cause economic disaster among the capitalist nations. Meanwhile the KGB would work to develop Soviet sympathizers and agents among Arab businessmen and in sensitive government positions, who in turn would wield more and more economic power as the Arabs bought into Western economies with their petrodollars.

Meanwhile the clandestine drive to complete terrorist cadres in the Emirates and in Saudi Arabia itself—among businessmen, the foreign oil-field workers (mostly Indians, Pakistanis, and Palestinians), government workers, students, and members of the armed forces—continued. Kuwait, it turned out, would become a vital relay point.

Inevitably the KGB drew me into this campaign in Kuwait, just as it had in Yemen and Egypt. This time my KGB boss was a twenty-five–year veteran KGB lieutenant-colonel, Vladislav Sergeyevich Lobanov, who was KGB resident. Lobanov was a distinguished-looking man with wavy brown hair, neatly dressed, who looked like a construction project manager. Looking ahead to retirement rather than career ambitions, he was easy-going compared to Ivchenkov and Sbirunov, both of whom he knew personally. I knew that he did a brisk trade in liquors on the side, getting himself a stockpile to take home, and that gave me a little leverage with him, but not much. He still made it clear he was in charge.

One evening he summoned me urgently, causing me to interrupt my dinner with Natasha. I had promised to take her out that evening. This time she seemed more hurt than angered at my sudden departure. She wanted to have a talk with me, a talk that I had been trying to avoid, at least for a while, until I could gather my thoughts.

A guard let me into the embassy when I arrived. I thought I

detected a hostile glance from him as I passed through the heavy entrance doors and into the dimly lit lobby, my footsteps echoing as I crossed the huge ballroom back to Lovanov's office. It was becoming harder these days to keep a fearful imagination under control. The more I knew, the more I could project possibilities. *How could I get out, if this were it?* A sliver of light shined from the slightly open door.

Inside, Lobanov sat at a bare desk with only an envelope and a file on top. He pointed to a chair in front of him.

"Comrade Sakharov!" he almost shouted as I sat down, "Who do you think you are?" He pulled a long box out from a drawer. "What's this?" He pushed the box toward me across his desk.

I opened it and found a magnificently carved golden dirk in a diamond-ornamented leather scabbard, engraved with my name. With the dirk was an ornately engraved invitation to the wedding being given by a prominent local family for yet another son of an influential sheik of my acquaintance—a relationship I had kept from Lobanov, since I wanted to try, when possible, to keep the KGB away from the many generous Kuwaitis I'd met since my arrival.

Lobanov continued sternly, "Now explain! How does an attaché like yourself get invited to such a high-level event? Never mind me, but even the ambassador doesn't get invited. Do you know you've overstepped your authority? Do you know how much we'd like to penetrate this circle? And you tell us nothing? I'm going to can you, jerk!"

"Comrade Lobanov," I said, "I am not responsible for the actions of someone else. I just met the man who sent this invitation and I was going to make a complete report on this contact first thing in the morning. It happened just a few days ago when I took my wife and daughter to the beach. We met three Kuwaitis who invited us to share some chicken with them and played with Katya. We only spent about an hour together. I gave them my card and invited them to stop by the embassy some time soon. You know how friendly these Kuwaitis can be." (I didn't tell Lobanov that we'd spent the rest of the day with the Kuwaitis and invited them back to our apartment for dinner and a party that lasted well into the night, parting with expansive words of undying friendship.)

Lobanov softened. "Okay, then, but just give the report directly to me, no one else, and by tomorrow, and don't mention it to the ambassador; this is too important a lead for him to foul up, and anyway the old man will shit his pants if he finds out you'd made friends with someone who wouldn't even consider talking to him." He paused. "And I'll keep the dirk, all right?"

What could I say? I nodded.

Lobanov wasn't finished. He pulled a bottle of Scotch and two Mickey Mouse tumblers out of his desk and poured a stiff shot into each. "Have some." He pushed one of the glasses toward me, and we drank slowly for a while, not talking.

"Vladimir, I want you to come up to the *referentura* for the whole day tomorrow. I have a special assignment for you. As you know, I've been working on relationships with influential Arabs here in Kuwait. You know our connection with Bargess al-Bargess, of course." I knew that al-Bargess, the Kuwaiti deputy minister of health, was considered one of the KGB's most valued insiders, but I feigned ignorance. Lobanov explained and added, "Now I am expanding these friendships into another sector, so to speak." He looked at me knowingly, pausing to let me read between the lines. "Of course, the old idiot shouldn't know about this." He raised his eyes to the ceiling toward Ambassador Tupitsyn's quarters. "Fortunately or unfortunately, I've only a year left here and I'll be training someone to continue to develop this new operation. Looks to me as if you have the right qualities to carry it on, and even while I'm here, your fluency in Arabic can be invaluable to me." Lobanov spoke no Arabic, but was fluent in Turkish. He'd spent three years in Turkey training guerillas, whose contingency plans, he'd once told me, included sabotaging U.S. missile sites there if Moscow deemed it necessary, and who also formed cadres for urban terrorist groups active in the 1960s who expanded operations into Syria.

Lobanov took another sip from his Mickey Mouse glass. "It will be a gradual process. You will start tomorrow by being briefed up there." He pointed towards the *referentura*. "The only thing I can tell you now is that this particular operation is new, but you will find it familiar. You have some knowledge of it through your previous work in Hodeida." He laughed. "See, I know everything. I even know that you and Sbirunov both got drunk in Al-Montaza Park and ended up in a belly-dance joint in As-Silsila in Alexandria when our atomic submarine was visiting there last year."

*   *   *

282

When I got back to the apartment, the light was on in the bedroom. We lived ten miles from the embassy in a three-story apartment building near the seashore. I managed to convince Tupitsyn that I couldn't afford decent accommodations in the city of Al-Kuwait itself. And, luckily for me, there was no available apartment for my family within the small embassy compound. However, neither Natasha nor I liked our place and thought of it as something temporary. Our three rooms overlooked a street on one side and a chicken shop on the other and was hot and noisy. Two air-conditioners which I got from the embassy made more noise than the sounds outside.

Katya was sound asleep, her cherry lips moving slightly. Natasha was lying on the bed undressed. "Come here, dear," she said when she heard me come in.

"Just a second, I'll get something to drink." It was unbelievably hot and humid, even for Kuwait. I took off my sweaty shirt, wet shoes and socks and dampened pants, and got a beer from the refrigerator. "Want some?"

"No."

Our conversation was inescapable.

"Vladimir, I'm unhappy." Natasha lit a cigarette. "I'm not blaming you, but I'm tired of spending all these years away from home. Look at me. I'm getting to look older than my age. You're never home. I'm all alone with Katya. When is this going to end? Is there any chance I could have a husband who works regular hours, comes home, makes love to me, goes to the movies with me, takes me skiing in the winter and on picnics in the summer?" She took a long drag. "I don't think there is. I'm not even angry anymore; it makes no difference. Just send us back home, please! Please?"

I put my hand on her shoulder. Only now I realized how pale, almost transparent, Natasha's skin had become. "Natasha I can't make you stay, but what about Katya? She needs us both." I had the impulse to reach out and hold her, tell her that I understood her loneliness, try to reassure her that everything would be all right, that I loved her, that I would be her friend, husband, lover, everything she wanted me to be. Maybe this was the moment, one golden but final opportunity to breach the barrier between us. But I'd been behind the walls too long, living a life that demanded sharing my feelings with no one. I watched her crush out her cigarette.

"Okay," I said, "I'll order you a ticket first thing in the morning. You'll be free to leave then." She turned over and cried soundlessly into the pillow.

I walked into the living room, poured myself a Scotch and sat there with the lights out. Maybe I could tell her, really tell her. Risky, but maybe . . . I put on an old Nat King Cole record, "To Whom It May Concern" on the stereo softly. Natasha came out after a while. "Drinking," she said, "just keep on doing it, you senseless bastard! What else is left?"

"How about sex" I said. "We haven't tried *that* in three years, you cold fish. You don't let me touch you: no one would believe it. So here's my substitute." I held up the bottle of Teacher's and rang my glass against it. "So here's to the substitute!" I toasted and took a swallow.

"Please stop it!" She put her hand on mine. "You know I can't. I don't know why."

"You could last summer, with that Mikhail, or whatever his name was."

"Nothing happened between us." Natasha lit another cigarette. She'd taken to smoking heavily lately.

I decided to make a try. "Natasha, listen. What if I had an opportunity to be permanently transferred to, say, the West. Could you come with me? We could start life afresh. I'd take better care of you and Katya. I'd change."

"What do you mean, *permanently transferred?*" She frowned. "Is this some hallucination of yours?"

"No, just a hypothetical question."

"Of course not! I won't go with you anywhere except back to Moscow to get a divorce. And as far as your cherished career is concerned and what a divorce will do to it, I don't care anymore."

She left the room and I sat there for a long while. Finally I went to sleep. Three hours later I woke up, got dressed, kissed my still-sleeping daughter and left for the embassy in the velvety dawn. It was already hot. And I felt drained.

"First take a look at this letter and translate for me," Lobanov said as we sat down in the surveillance-proof *referentura* booth. The letter was in Arabic and was addressed to Kanunnikov through a post office box in Kuwait. Kanunnikov was a blond graduate of the Institute for International Relations, class of '65, specialty in English. Presently he was the TASS correspondent in Kuwait, which allowed him to travel to Saudi Arabia and the Emirates where the Soviet Union had no diplomatic representation. This provided cover for his real job, which was to act as bagman and recruitment spotter for the KGB's nascent network in those countries. Kanunikov was a captain in the KGB. He had been concentrating of late on organizing a KGB network in the tiny island country of Bahrein off the Saudi coast which the KGB wanted as a base for a front through which infiltrators could slip in and out.

The letter came from someone named Saleh, who called himself Deputy Chief of the Front for Liberation of Saudi Arabia. He wrote that although the front was established and growing in numbers, there remained serious problems in penetrating the military and other sensitive sectors of the government. The Saudi rulers swiftly and cruelly stamped out any suspected dissidents, he wrote, and some of his "brothers" had been secretly executed. He pleaded for more financial support for the front and for the Soviet press to make the front known publicly, so that propaganda could be used to counter the Saudis' repressive measures. (Moscow, however, was not about to do this for the present. For one thing, it wanted its network widened first. For another, acknowledging the front would jeopardize its above-the-table drive to curry favor wth Arab rulers and establish an embassy in Saudi Arabia, with whom the Soviet Union had recently concluded a mutual recognition pact—but on paper only, with formal exchange of ambassadors still a long way off.)

After I'd read the letter, Lobanov opened a file. "Look, we get all these letters. People get killed getting them out. Read them all and translate. Copies have already been translated at Moscow Center, of course, but I want to review them myself. I want to know if there is any nuance from the Arabic that I can dig out." I assured him I'd get to it right away.

"Wait, first I have some important instructions for you. As you know, since we do not have an embassy in Saudi Arabia, most of our work there is through the Indian Embassy. We need a double check, though, on our Indian agents there, and since we can't do it ourselves, the best way to go is through the Pakistanis. We know the Pakistanis have excellent counterintelligence against the Indians and have an embassy there too. What I want you to do is to get to the Pakistani ambassador here in Kuwait and feel him out about the Indian Embassy's work in Saudi Arabia and report back to me. But don't do anything else. Be casual about it; just make friends with him."

I smiled to myself. Lobanov didn't know that I was friends with the Pakistani ambassador already. Natasha and I liked his pizazz and elegance and often joined him and his wife at the sports club or at his residence—another contact I hadn't bothered to report to Lobanov.

"Then," Lobanov went on, "there is another assignment. I have my sights on a member of the Saudi Embassy here in Kuwait. You'll go there tomorrow for a reception. Give him our best regards, but be cautious and polite. Just talk to him, that's all. Now read this."

He handed me a second file, which read: "To the First Secretary of the Soviet Embassy in Kuwait, Vladislav Lobanov. Classification: TOP SECRET." It was from the KGB's First Directorate. It stated that it was very important for KGB chiefs in countries adjacent to Saudi Arabia to develop a highly organized and efficient system of reliable, educated individuals capable of taking charge of the area on notice. It went on, saying that since Saudi Arabia is a relatively new area of interest for our party and government, we need all information pertinent to the economic, political, social, and religious structure of the country, its international ties, as well as individual members of the government and business circles. The document recommended that the KGB residents abroad immediately engage in the collection and preparation of information on the above. The Center will instruct the *residenturas* regularly on the desirable actions.

Enclosed with the memo were sheets of detailed background information on the government structure of the kingdom, its most influential families, leading individuals, and on Saudi official and private business dealings with the United States. There was an additional, extensive background memo on U.S.-Saudi relations, as seen from the American point of view, that most likely was prepared by the KGB *residentura* in Washington.

"Vladimir, you are being made a part of this new phase of the Saudi operation because you did so well when you were involved in it four years ago in Yemen," Lobanov said after I'd finished digesting the memos.

"Oh yes," I said, "Those flights. It was fun. Too bad we can't do anything like that out of here. We really did our reconnaissance well before Abdulla As-Sallal was replaced."

I was referring to a bloodless coup on November 3, 1967, shortly after the end of my IIR internship in the Yemen Arab Republic (North Yemen). Abdulla As-Sallal's overtures toward the Chinese had shown a failure, in Moscow's opinion, to understand that he owed the Soviet Union more gratitude for having supported his government. This prompted Moscow to instigate the coup replacing Sallal with Abdulla Al-Aryani. The new Yemeni leader quickly cooled the relationship between North Yemen and China and turned to the U.S.S.R. for more military and economic aid, which was immediately granted by the Soviets who recognized the importance of the Yemen Arab Republic as a base of operations against Saudi Arabia, Oman, Aden, and the Emirates. Moscow also used North Yemen to establish its naval presence in the Red Sea. Hodeida, where I had been stationed in Yemen, became a regular port of call for the Soviet navy in subsequent years.

"True," said Lobanov, "and now that the Chinese are in Aden, we don't have a base there." Meanwhile the Chinese had succeeded in the old Aden protectorate that had become South Yemen and had pushed the Soviet-backed guerilla leader Abdel Kawi Makkawi (who had attended that safe-house meeting with me in Hodeida) back into the hills.

Lobanov went on. "Bahrein is not set up yet," he said, referring to the Kanunnikov operation, "so you see, for now, Kuwait remains our base of operations."

I spent the rest of the day being briefed by Lobanov on details of the Saudi peninsula operation. It was planned in three stages. The first stage, already well in progress, was to gather information. The second stage, also started, was to spot and develop agents, preferably among the Saudis, but also among foreigners—including American businessmen if possible—working in Saudi Arabia. The third stage called for the Front of Liberation of Saudi Arabia to become active, starting guerilla operations, or instigating social-political turmoil, or whatever Moscow deemed appropriate. "For now," Lobanov said, "the front must keep the lowest profile. We support it with training, arms, money, but that's all. Ten years from now we'll be in a position to do what we want with those Yankees and Saudis."

Lobanov laughed. "People, Vladimir, people," he said, echoing what Sbirunov had told me so often in Alexandria. "Them and their surveillance satellites," he said pointing upwards. "Let them fly and take pictures. We'll take the people."

"I still don't get how we are going to accomplish this here," I said, probing for more information. "You'll be leaving in a year, the Kuwaitis won't let us expand our staff here and we're shorthanded as it is. I don't think the TASS man can do much more than handle runs. Who's going to do the job?"

"Okay," Lobanov said, "I'll let you in on another point. The Kuwaitis are looking for someone to build a big entertainment complex here and they'll soon be taking bids for the planning, design, and construction. We're going to see to it that our people get the contract. Plus there'll be two other building contracts coming up. Once we secure one or all of these jobs we'll have the perfect opening to bring in our people—and by that I mean not just construction specialists, but *our* people."

"Is that the negotiation I've been asked to help arrange for our commercial counselor?"

"Precisely."

I had a lot of news for my friends and I returned home exhausted, trying to keep in mind all I had learned that day. "The ticket please," said Natasha as I walked in the door.

"I didn't have the time today, sorry."

We ate dinner in silence and I left immediately to meet George. I drove to a darkened construction site and parked my Volga out of sight.

"Thanks for your message," George said. "What's up?"

We talked for a long while. Afterwards George apparently sensed my dismal spirits. "We want to be sure you are safe and sound. Do you need anything?"

"Not really."

"How are things at home?"

"Oh, fine. Family and everything, just fine."

"Look, Vladimir, I want you to be absolutely open with me, because we don't want to overwork you. You've done enough already and you have our respect. The reason I ask about your home life is that I think that family and home is where it's at. Nowhere else. No matter how successful you are, if you're not happy in your own family, you'd better do something about it. You can if you take care of yourself."

"Don't worry," I said, "all is fine." We shook hands.

"Take care of yourself; keep cool."

"See you soon." I walked back toward my car. The heavy heat and the darkness closed in on me.

20: She Looks Straight Ahead, Not at Me

One afternoon in May 1971, two American teachers who wanted to take a vacation in the Soviet Union came to the embassy for visas. They were a pleasant-looking young couple. They taught at the American school in Kuwait. I put through the usual papers, feeling a little guilty about the fact that the KGB would be running a thorough check on them. I wondered how they'd react if I'd said, "Hey, I'm not what you think I am; I'm with you."

They told me how excited they were to be off on such a big adventure. When they left, I shut my office door and turned the radio up louder. The teachers probably had wondered why a Soviet attaché had a radio on all the time, playing pop music from a local English-language station. But I was only taking orders. We were supposed to play radios to foil Kuwaiti electronic surveillance, which supposedly was aimed at the Soviet Embassy. I had an even better reason for turning it up loud, however, and that was to irritate Tupitsyn. His weaselly excellency had bugged every room in the embassy except the *referentura*, which was out of bounds even for his snooping. He was in the habit of going to a room above his apartment where the listening equipment was installed, and putting on the earphones for hours while he sipped cognac.

An old Erroll Garner number came on the radio, "Misty," and I thought about starting to practice my piano playing again, as if I had the time. The embassy had a piano, which recently had been tuned, and I was sure Tupitsyn would enjoy my takeoffs on Erroll Garner. I got that old yearning to get away, just like I used to feel when I was a kid in Moscow listening to jazz and then believing that someday I'd be a diplomat, just like my father, and be free to travel and live the good life. But here I was in Kuwait, considered one of the choicest of assignments abroad, with high pay and the chance to buy just about any prized item one wanted. We could even buy automobiles for which one had to wait two years back home, and make a killing by reselling. Kuwait was called the Golden Land among MFA staffers for this reason. But surrounded by KGB, GRU, and Tupitsyn's spying satraps to boot, I might just as well have been back in Russia. In many ways, all through Yemen, Egypt, and now Kuwait, I'd never left the Soviet Union, and in some aspects, with all the KGB intrigue, it had been worse than being in Moscow.

By September I'd have to return to Moscow again, ostensibly for a vacation, but I knew it could turn out to be longer than that. By September 1971, I'd been a year in Kuwait and with the nearly three years I'd spent in Yemen and Egypt, I'd be due for a customary desk job in Moscow for the next two years. There was a chance I'd be returned to Kuwait for another year, what with Lobanov having involved me in the Kuwait-Saudi subversion operation. But even that could result in a prolonged stay in Moscow, because Lobanov lately had said the KGB wanted to make a full-fledged agent out of me. "I think you must become one of us," he said, "you have the qualifications." This meant at least a year in the KGB special school. I knew I would have a difficult time refusing this second offer from the KGB.

Inexorably I was being pulled deeper into the KGB maw, and from what I'd heard from a couple of MFA "dips" who'd passed through Kuwait recently, it was becoming even more touchy than usual at KGB headquarters these days. There was a reorganization going on there, paralleling the power struggle inside the Politburo where Brezhnev, Kosygin, Kirichenko, Andropov, and the rest of the Brezhnev mafia were trying to force out President Nikolai V. Podgorny, something they ultimately succeeded in doing in 1977.

What's more, the latest bombshell out of Cairo could have greatly increased the dangers for me. Egyptian President Anwar Sadat, who'd taken over in September 1970 after Nasser's death, had just nipped a Soviet-sponsored coup in the bud. Moscow, realizing that Sadat was a true nationalist and not the Quisling it wanted, had mobilized its agents, including Mohammed Fawzi, Ali Sabry, and Sami Sharaf (who had been Nasser's right hand man, in charge of information and intelligence, and an avowed nationalist whom no one had suspected of being Moscow's agent).

Sadat had put the whole gang of them in jail along with scores of other Egyptians who were KGB cadre members. In one stroke Sadat had all but destroyed years of expensive, painstaking KGB work. The fiasco certainly would figure into the Moscow power struggles, since Podgorny had been close to the pro-Soviet Egyptian clique and now looked like a convenient scapegoat. Podgorny, in fact, made a hasty trip to Cairo after the coup was quashed. There he tried to smooth over badly damaged Soviet-Egyptian relations, getting at least a pro forma declaration of continued mutual cooperation from the wary Sadat, but a firm refusal to let the pro-Soviet Egyptians return to what Moscow could now pine for as the good old days.

There would surely be inquiries into the Egyptian operation back in Moscow. More heads would roll. My dossier no doubt would be among those automatically reviewed, and those *stukach* reports by Kuznetsov—though his reputation was damaged by my revelations to Sbirunov about his sexual preferences—would be in there. Although my record was exceptional and the KGB apparently regarded me as one of its fair-haired boys, there were items that an alert KGB counterintelligence investigator on a witch hunt easily could earmark as reason enough for a "reevaluation." There was my friendship with the anti-Soviet Egyptian counterintelligence man Sallah in Alexandria, for example, which Kuznetsov had tracked. The little *stukach* surely hadn't just followed me around Alexandria on his own. Someone had assigned him to the task. And I had a lot more to hide than the little that he had found out. My forthcoming trip back to Moscow could turn out to be a one-way ticket to Lubyanka Prison. There one would be cordially invited to tell all.

This anxiety-tinted scenario wasn't very likely, I reassured myself, what with everything I had going for me back home. But even under the best of circumstances, the closed world back home was the very thing I'd spent my life trying to escape. Working secretly with the

CIA to offset the system had given me new purpose, but the initial glow had begun to pale in light of the growing realization that even the Americans seemed ineffectual against the KGB cobra, at least the way it looked from the inside. At the policy-making level, Washington hadn't seemed to comprehend, let alone counteract, the Soviet strategy of global economic-political warfare. Even if there was to be some ultimate defeat for the dark forces, it would be a long way off. I could take satisfaction from having done my part, but when, if ever, would there be release? My personal fate seemed to be carrying me into deeper and deeper involvement with the very system I hated, and even my secret American commitment couldn't give me much stomach for that. All the worse should this eventually lead to my discovery and demise. I had no intention of being a martyr.

Jazz, the modern legacy of old-time slave music from the land of the free and the home of the brave, had been, without my articulating it, my metaphor of personal freedom—a condition always just out of my reach. And here were those two giggly American schoolteachers I'd just given visas, vagabonding their way around the world without giving it a second thought. And they'd go sightseeing at the Kremlin and probably never be aware of the world behind its walls.

My thoughts were interrupted by a knock at the door. It was Stanislav Yeliseev, third secretary of the embassy. Yeliseev had graduated as an Arabist from the Institute for International Relations two years before me. But he looked a lot older, with his bloated face, prematurely thinning blond hair, reddened, fishy eyes, and pale trembling hands.

Try not to be like them. I recalled my father's words whenever I'd seen him. Tupitsyn was on his case and would give him no peace. He'd definitely stayed too long.

"I need something for my hangover. Do you have a shot?"

"No, you know that sonofabitch Tupitsyn doesn't let us buy any liquor any more," I said in a low voice. I felt emboldened by the radio's blaring.

"Hey, I'm dying. I'd give anything for a shot, just a small one." He bent over my desk.

"Why don't you try the guard, he might have some," I whispered into his ear.

"Fuck you!" Yeliseev shouted, "I don't care if anyone hears me. I wanna drink and I don't give a damn. I slaved in Yemen, I slaved in

Iraq, in Moscow. I wrote all those reports for those lazy bastards and what do I get? *Tupitsa* is kicking me out, home for good, do you know what that means? I lose everything, the job, the family; I end up in Timbuktu."

I'd been following Yeliseev's career for some time. I'd met him in Taizz where he was an attaché and again in Moscow on a leave. My friendship with him had caused me a problem with Tupitsyn. The ambassador had called me on the carpet over it. "Vladimir," he said, "you know the reason I've dumped Yeliseev and three other idiots here?"

"No, Nikolai Kuzmich. Not exactly."

"Drinking and lack of our Communist consciousness," he said, closing his eyes and clasping his baby hands over his chest. "What can I do? Good guys, but that's not enough to work with me. You should never refuse to help your friend, and the best help you can give him is to tell me how he behaves, what he does, how he thinks. If he does something wrong, we'll call him and help him with his distorted views and straighten out his way of life."

I knew what he was driving at but didn't respond.

"Now tell me, Comrade Sakharov, why didn't you ever tell me about Yeliseev, about how he got drunk at your place twice, about the complaining he did to you here? Didn't you think I'd know about such things? He's through; I didn't need any advice to see to that, but the point is your uncooperativeness."

I shrugged.

"Well, what do you say to that?"

"It's not possible for someone to live five years away from home and not go astray once in a while. I didn't think I should rush into serious conclusions until I found out what really was bothering the guy. He's served a long time and I think you might want to send him home with the best recommendations."

"See," Tupitsyn leaned forward gleefully, "you young people are so simple-minded. The *point* is that if someone like Yeliseev screws up, we gotta make an example of him. And I want more examples! Understand?"

"Yes, I'll do my best."

By this time I was past caring what impression I made on the likes of Tupitsyn. I liked Yeliseev and felt a little sorry for him; he was like so many others I'd known. He was useful, too, because he had a big mouth. He'd confirmed a story I'd heard before, that the KGB had received a report on the timing and thrust of the 1967 Israeli offensive against Arab forces—he'd worked closely with the MFA Mideast department—and that Moscow Center either discounted the report or deliberately failed to pass it on to our Arab "brothers."

Besides, watching him deteriorate over the years was instructive. By now he was crying over my desk. "My tickets are being arranged and I'll be saying goodbye tomorrow," he said.

The atmosphere of the place certainly was taking on a Marxist quality—as in Groucho, Chico, and Harpo. *Duck Soup* was more like it, except the killing was real. Zimin, the GRU *resident*, stormed into my office after Yeliseev had staggered out. "All right. Working hard, hey pal? Great," he said breathlessly. He spoke with a heavy accent, being an old Ukrainian army brat, his stocky build, jet-black hair, and pudgy face projecting a solid peasant energy. He wanted some military advice. "Ah, tell me," he continued nonstop, "some underground groups in the Emirates are fighting against the rulers with Chinese arms, and the yellow bastards are sending in military advisors too. What would you do?"

I couldn't believe he'd ask me a question like that. "Well, I guess if you could send them more arms than they can get from the Chinese, then we'll knock those Maoists out of there." That sounded like a good comeback for what had to be a joke.

"All right!" Zimin shouted, slapping his hand to his head. "That's the way I like it. I'll suggest it to Center." He ran out of the office.

Zimin had been talking to the Bulgarian Ambassador to Kuwait, Raiko Nikolov, who on Soviet instruction had come back to Kuwait from his long visit in Aden, South Yemen.

By 1971, the KGB established several insurgent movements around South Yemen that were to drive out the Chinese and clear the way for the Soviet advance on the Arabian peninsula. The KGB set up a base in the Dhofar region of Oman, next door to South Yemen. There the KGB and the GRU organized, armed, and trained guerrillas of the Front of Liberation of Saudi Arabia, the Popular Front for Liberation of Oman, the Front for Liberation of Dhofar, and the anti-Chinese tribesmen who belonged to the Front for Liberation of South Yemen (FLOSY). The FLOSY insurgents and other Soviet-aided factions succeeded in pushing the Chinese out of South Yemen by 1974 and bringing that country into the Soviet camp.

The takeover of South Yemen turned out to be doubly important to Moscow, because in the meantime the Saudis, recognizing the threat, had moved to wrest neighboring North Yemen out of the Soviet grip. With Saudi financial assistance, royalist tribemen took control of that country from the pro-Soviets. The Soviets responded by strengthening South Yemen. In 1978, South Yemen, well equipped with Soviet arms, and guided by Soviet and Cuban military advisors, attacked North Yemen, setting off the border war that lingered into 1979. Regaining control over North Yemen was important to the Soviets because it would expand the base of penetration into Saudi Arabia.

The struggles of these obscure tribes in remote Yemen may seem trivial to American readers, but for the Saudis it presented a real threat. Through Yemen, Moscow established itself as a power on the Saudi doorstep; the Soviets could subtly intimidate the Saudis and make them think twice about their relations with the United States.

For the present, from what I could gather from the strategy conferences I attended in Kuwait, the Soviets saw the Chinese as a more serious threat than the Americans. The Soviets wanted to get rid of Chinese competition before it upset the applecart of its long-term economic and political strategy for the Middle East.

The Chinese were also currying favor with the Palestinians by supplying them with arms and money. Moscow had long-standing connections with the Palestinians and had the advantage. But the Soviets had to play their hand more carefully than the Chinese, who at the time were more openly supporting Palestinian terrorist groups. The Soviet Union had to consider Jordan's King Hussein, with whom it also was trying to maintain good relations—with an eye to cozying up to Hussein's ally, Saudi Arabia, later. Also, Moscow didn't want to be publicly identified with the plane hijackings and other terrorist activities of the Palestinian guerrillas.

In September 1970, when I arrived in Kuwait, Hussein's Bedouin troops ousted Palestinian guerrilla forces from Jordan in a series of battles that came to be called Black September, spawning the ultra-terrorist Palestinian group of the same name. Moscow gave no overt support to the Palestinians and in fact even signalled to Hussein its continuing friendship. Meantime, however, it continued to provide assistance and direction for the Palestinians in more discreet ways. Kuwait was one of the prime contact points. Following the Black September conflict, I was interpreter at a series of meetings in Kuwait between Lobanov, his assistants, and Sheik Ahmed Khatib, a prominent businessman, member of a very influential Middle Eastern family, and an ardent Palestinian supporter. Khatib was a go-between carrying sub rosa messages of support and promises of more arms from the KGB to the various Palestinian guerrilla groups. Khatib, through his influence with the Kuwaiti government and Palestinians working in Kuwait, was also instrumental in getting the Kuwaitis to temporarily suspend their economic aid to Hussein's government after the Black September conflict. Afterwards, Lobanov let slip to me one day that the Kuwaitis—responding to Khatib's secret pressure on their foreign ministry—quietly gave several million dollars to the Palestinians, for fear the Palestinian oil field workers in their country would cause trouble similar to what happened in Jordan.

After Zimin left pondering my sage military advice, my inter-office phone rang. It was Gilev, the *referentura* chief clerk. I was needed up there to straighten out some paper work. As I crossed the reception hall I could see the ambassador drinking with some local officials. The ambassador's translator was tittering at something one of the Arabs had said. As I took that stairs two at a time I ran into Lyuda, another of Tupitsyn's private secretaries (read mistresses) and a prime *stukach* for his excellency. "Watch where you are going," she said.

"Sorry." I threw my lit cigarette at her feet to irritate her. She wore a yellow minidress, which was a mistake. Her legs looked like broken pencils. "Why don't you put on some weight so I can see you better." *Trouble, Vladimir, you are just asking for trouble,* I thought. *She'll turn this into an "incident" to report; you just know it.* And I didn't care anymore.

The Buick Skylark with the two Arabs in it was behind me again. I speeded up the embassy Volga and barreled into a traffic circle, noticing the Buick in hot pursuit. I exited onto a divided road, executed a sharp U-turn at the first opening in the divider, just in time to cut in front of the speeding Buick which was coming out of the circle after me. The surprised Arabs ran up onto the divider curb, wiping out a front wheel as I floored it away.

George was waiting at a safe-house. "Where's your car?" he asked. "Did anyone follow?"

"Just the usual routine, but I lost them. The car is three blocks from here. Don't worry; everything's fine."

We had three hours and spent most of it covering my latest news. Although he listened to everything very carefully, he seemed, by the questions he asked, to be more interested in hard information—how much money was sent where, military data, what arrangements were being made for Soviet bids on that Kuwaiti entertainment complex—than on the Soviet ideological recruitment efforts I saw as paramount.

"Look, George," I said toward the end of our talk, "it's becoming more and more evident that the KGB, GRU, and the rest of the Soviet external organizations are becoming deeply involved in recruitment and ideological subversion operations—they see individuals as the key factor to shaping the world their way."

"Yes, I understand," said George, taking a swig of his Pepsi, "but do you think ideological warfare can work here in the Arab countries? Aren't Islam and strong national pride going to make it tough to convert these people?"

"Possibly, for the present, but this is a long-range effort and in due time, unless it is actively countered, I think there is a real danger of it working. They've already had successes. Look at Iraq or Syria. Recruitment of Arabs, propaganda, keeping conflicts stirred up— they're all aimed at you, George. What are you doing about it?"

Only now, in Kuwait, did I get to read American newspapers and magazines. They weren't sold in Moscow and very few could be obtained in Egypt. My recent exposure to the U.S. press left some questions in my mind and I wanted to relay them to George. However, I didn't quite know how to put them to him.

"We do what we're ordered to do. The policy comes from the President, from the congress, the people, from groups—unions, companies, churches, you name it—acting on the government. It's very complicated. We call it democracy, but that probably isn't exactly it either. Mainly we pass on information so the President can make decisions."

298

"Wouldn't you say that's not the best way to conduct a foreign policy?"

"It's the only way we got."

"But doesn't your President have to worry about catering to the people? He's got to be a politician. You let doctors practice medicine, and farmers grow crops, shouldn't you let experts conduct your foreign policy?"

"Sometimes the so-called experts are the ones who foul it up. Democracy, as fragile as that may sound, still is the most important thing. I think you are trying to apply Soviet standards to the way things are in the states." George looked at me coldly. "We can't be like your KGB, and we don't want it that way."

"I'm not saying that, but I am trying to be reasonable. The KGB is strong, well organized, and has the complete support of the government. It's not only Communist internationalism; it's Russian chauvinism. They want to dominate the world. How are you going to stop it?"

"Vladimir," he cut in, "you and I, we're here to do a job, right? That's *it*. That's all we can do and that's our contribution. Your work is appreciated a lot. Personally, I'm proud to be working with you. Whatever good comes out of it—provided your safety comes first— that should be enough to make both of us feel good." He got up and went over to put some jazz tapes on a recorder. "What's your pleasure?"

"Anything."

He returned and sat back on the chair opposite where I was seated.

"You'll live and learn, Vladimir. It's not as simple as you think. What's with you today—philosophy, high politics?"

"I don't know, I guess I'm tired, or maybe thinking too much. I'm thinking about what it would be like to settle in the United States. And I'm afraid. I'm not so much afraid of my own people and the stresses I'm under on this side. I've learned to cope with those. But the other side is blurred to me. I realize I don't know much about it. I read where the CIA is under attack, where congressmen can poke into it and tell some reporter something about me. One word and the KGB would be using my ashes to fertilize a collective farm."

"That's nonsense, Vladimir. That kind of thing can't happen. No one would ever jeopardize your safety. It's a matter of your personal security." He got up to leave. "By the way, how's the family?"

"Fine."

"One question." He gazed at me steadily. "If things go wrong, or it becomes necessary to prevent things from going wrong, would you come alone or with the family?"

"Alone. I've already checked that out. I'll have to be alone."

We shook hands. "Okay. Remember to keep cool at all times. Good luck."

One evening Natasha and I were invited to a party at the Pakistani Embassy. We took Katya to an Egyptian who usually sat with her. At the last minute, however, Tupitsyn called and dragooned me into taking part in a reception at the Soviet Embassy. Natasha was angry. "Screw the protocol, I'm going alone," she said, and marched off to the Pakistani party.

When I got back around midnight Natasha wasn't back yet. We'd already arranged with our babysitters to leave Katya overnight, so I went to bed. The next morning Natasha still wasn't back.

I went to pick up Katya. It was still cool enough in the morning to go to the beach. We drove toward the neutral zone where the beaches were good. High sand dunes separated the road from the beach and we had to find a passage between them. The beach was deserted. The tide was very low, exposing a wealth of seashells which Katya began gleefully picking over. She had just turned four. I sat on the sand holding her little shoes and watching her as she played along the water line, laughing and scurrying just out of reach of the frothy surf, her blonde hair catching sparkles of sunshine. No problems existed, only the sand, sea, sun, Katya, and myself.

My reverie was interrupted by a gaggle of loud voices. Three men and three women were laying out a picnic about fifty yards away. I could tell from their accents they were Americans. The men placed a large ice chest in the middle of a blanket they'd layed out. They had on a portable tape recorder playing country music. Everyone got undressed. The men wore funny-looking long trunks, surfer style. The women wore bikinis. Two of them looked to be in their late forties, the other was much younger. All three had bleached-blonde hair, with short razor cuts, and wore large sunglasses. They had thin arms and legs, and large breasts. One of the men poured cocktails for everyone. Two of the women wandered off toward the surf while the rest of the group sat down on the blanket, speaking animatedly and laughing. The two birdlike women approached Katya and started talking to her. I could see heads bobbing in conversation, but couldn't hear anything. I had taught Katya some English, with the thought of someday taking her to America with me, an unreasonable notion that still hung in the back of my mind. Katya pointed in my direction. The women nodded toward me but didn't move. After a while Katya ran back to me.

"Papa!" she exclaimed, "Those two are Americans! They told me. They asked who I was with and I told them with my papa who is a Soviet diplomat! They told me to say hello to you."

The group was getting louder and the hot sun climbed higher. I was tired. It was time to go. Katya ran off to talk to them again. "Papa, I invited them to come to us," she said, breathlessly, when she returned again, "but they said some other time. Why won't they come?"

"Katya, they probably are busy. Let's go. I'll buy you a bottle of Limonita." That was a soda pop Katya got to like in Egypt. Here she was drinking Seven-Up but still called it Limonita.

Natasha was home when we returned. "Where have you been?" I asked.

"Oh, someone is worried. I don't believe it. A rock is worried. Don't bother. I get around without you very well, thank you. At least I've learned self-reliance."

"Natasha, it bothers me. Why didn't you come home?"

"I had a good time and stayed over. I have rights, too, dear."

She was getting out one of her Italian cocktail dresses.

"Suit yourself, Natasha. You want to be that way, fine, but think about Katya. She doesn't understand."

"Oh, yes, she does. She knows that her father is the one who's unreliable around here. And don't worry, I'll take good care of her." She dropped exhausted on the bed and stuck her face into the pillow.

I went into the living room and poured myself a gin. No way, I thought. I shouldn't even think about it. All of this had been set in motion long ago and the likelihood that I would at last be going to America—that far-off dreamland of my youth—loomed larger and larger. Sooner or later it had to happen, and the way things looked, sooner. And in personal terms, the fare was going to be very steep.

Now I no longer thought of America as the shimmering utopia of my youth, but as a real place where I'd have to live someday—with

301

real people, good and bad, and real problems, and real streets and beaches and mountains I'd never seen. I realized that it was a place about which I knew a lot, in one way, and very little in another.

I remembered a visit to Kuwait earlier that year by Vice President Spiro Agnew. The Kuwaiti government had invited the Soviet diplomatic corps to join the Americans and other delegations at the airport to greet him. He made a short speech when he deplaned and shook hands all round. He seemed so sincere and energetic, and he looked me straight in the eye, giving me a big smile and a hearty greeting as we shook hands. A good man, I thought, a real American.

By the summer of 1971, I fully realized, and so did George, that my time as a CIA agent-in-place was running out. Developments were conspiring to make my balancing act more and more difficult and dangerous—the anti-Soviet counter-coup in Egypt and the inevitably resulting security investigation in Moscow of all Soviet personnel who had been involved in the Egyptian missions; the fact that my term abroad was over and I'd have to remain stationed in Moscow for at least two years; and my marital crisis. The pressure, increased by the paranoid atmosphere in the Soviet Embassy in Kuwait, was beginning to get to me. Both George and I knew that I would have to get out soon and we had discussed my escape plan carefully. The immediate incident that precipitated my having to flee, however, is something I am not at liberty to discuss. Although it was minor in nature, the details of it could compromise ongoing operations and people still in the field.

The escape plan had been worked out so that if I had to get away in a hurry no further contact with my friends or the U.S. Embassy itself would be necessary. I could activate it at my own discretion or if I got a signal from them. One hot, humid summer afternoon—July 11, 1971—I got just such a signal.

I felt detached, pulled into a vacuum. It was the same feeling of alienation I'd had a year earlier in Moscow when Natasha had told me of my grandfather's death. Then I had immediately gone up to the Pirogovo reservoir and taken off on my boat for two days to be alone.

But now I couldn't leave just yet. I drove back to our apartment first. Natasha was there having a drink with an Arab businessman of our acquaintance. Katya was napping in her room. I stormed in, barely nodding hello to the Arab, and marched into our bedroom, asking Natasha to come with me.

She followed and shut the door behind her. "I don't want anybody here when I'm not home," I hissed at her. I hadn't played the enraged jealous husband role since that night long ago in Moscow with the five-thousand-nik, but this opportunity suited my purposes. I had planned to pick a fight anyway. It would be easier that way. "I don't care what you do," I said, "but don't pull any of your stuff in my house. So get him out of here. I want to talk to you."

"What do you mean?" she yelled. "Who are you to tell me anything, you motherfucker. Who do you think you are? I have my own life. When I get back to Moscow, I'm getting a divorce and that's final. We've got nothing to talk about."

"Thanks."

"I want my airplane ticket tomorrow!" she shouted.

"I'm not going to get you any ticket," I told her. "You go to your precious sucker the ambassador and you talk to him about it. I don't care anymore. You can tell him all about me, how badly I treat you, how arrogant I was."

I heard Katya crying in the other room. We'd awakened her. I went back into the living room and told our Arab friend, "I'm sorry, but would you mind leaving? I'll call you and we'll get together another time."

"That's all right, I understand." he said. "I'll see you. Goodbye."

I went into Katya's room. She was sitting on the bed, rubbing her eyes. "Katya, would you like to go for a ride?"

"Yes, Papa, where are we going?"

"We'll just go out for an hour while Mama cooks dinner."

We drove in the direction of Mina al-Ahmadi; the bright lights of the oil installations and loading docks were already on as the sun was setting.

"Papa, can we go closer to all those lights?"

"All right." We took a turn and went along the ocean. Finally we stopped at a place where the beach was accessible, got out of the car and walked along the surf in the dusk. Katya played in the sand. I didn't say anything.

"Papa, I'm getting tired, can we go home?"

"Yes," I said, and picked her up and carried her back to the car.

Natasha was in a rage. "It took you two hours. Where did you go?

303

Dinner is cold." Katya went into the bathroom to wash up.

"You can stick your dinner up your ass," I said quietly. "I'm leaving. I'm going to eat out. All right?"

I walked out.

I went back to the embassy and rang the bell. The guard let me in and I went through the lobby to my office. There was a safe there which I locked every day. It contained the latest classified information about the embassy and other diplomatic posts. I took one last look at the papers, memorizing all I could.

I also read over a letter from my father that had arrived in the last mail. My family was disappointed in me, he wrote; I didn't seem to be working hard enough any more. I was not fulfilling their expectations. An embassy employee while on vacation in Moscow had filled them in on my recent behavior. There were complaints about my not attending weekly propaganda meetings. My father advised me strongly against this—not good politics. He also advised me against entertaining too many Kuwaitis and other foreigners and to concentrate more on what was happening inside the embassy.

Otherwise the letter was warm. Everyone was looking forward to my upcoming vacation in Moscow. My new cooperative apartment was ready. We would all go to the Black Sea. Mother was in good health. Asking about Katya and how things were going with Natasha, he closed saying we'd all have a marvelous time upon my return home.

There was a knock. It was the GRU chief, Zimin.

"What are you doing here so late, Vladimir?"

"Just checking on some papers, a report I have to do in the morning. I have to review my files."

"Very well, young man. You want to play a little pool?"

"No, thank you very much. I will join you later. Why don't you go ahead? I've got about another half hour here. I'll join you."

"Fine," he said and left.

I put the papers back into the safe. My hands were trembling as I took a small box containing gold rings and bracelets that I had purchased in Kuwait and had been keeping in the safe, meaning to bring them to Moscow on my return from Kuwait and give them to Galya. Since our romance at the Soviet resort a year ago, we had continued to correspond, she sending me letters that were master-pieces of double meaning under the code name of "Nikolai" that we'd agreed upon. I put the box in my pocket, not out of any hope of seeing her again, but thinking that in case I ran into trouble during my escape, I might be able to use the gold to buy my way out.

The embassy was dark as I walked out and up the street past a grocery store and past the innermost of Al-Kuwait circular drives, the one nearest the embassy. I kept walking faster past the second, then the third, finally the fourth circle. Then I continued into the desert. I kept walking until I reached the point where the radio receiver was supposed to be. I was wearing a green sports shirt, an old jacket, and a pair of baggy slacks made in India that I'd purchased only a few days earlier. I'd taken to wearing casual attire in Kuwait.

I had a small flask of Scotch in my jacket pocket and I stopped to take a swig. I must have looked comical in that outfit there in the desert in the middle of the night. Miraculously I found the radio. I was worried that the shifting sands would have obliterated its location.

The little transistorized receiver was wired with a directional antenna and tuned to one frequency, so that by rotating it I found the signal that would guide me. I started walking. The signal was on a very narrow band so that if I turned off course I'd lose it. One song was playing on it, over and over. It was "The Girl from Ipanema," sung by Astrud Gilberto. Was this a coincidence or a touch from George?

I kept walking across the desert. Hours went by. The dark sky and black sand seemed to turn upside down and back again, rotating slowly. I walked long into the night.

At one point I heard a helicopter. I lay down on the sand, hoping my gray slacks and jacket would camouflage me. The chopper passed nearby at low altitude, its searchlight probing the low dunes. I couldn't be sure what that chopper was looking for. I didn't think the Soviets would have detected my absence until I failed to show up at the embassy in the morning. By then I had to be out of Kuwait. As soon as the thudding of the copter faded into the darkness, I got up and kept walking.

From my instructions I knew that as soon as the escape plan was activated, a jeep filled with gasoline and equipped with a two-way radio would be left somewhere along the line of the radio frequency for me to find and drive the rest of the way. There would be dirt tracks in the desert that were far from the main Kuwaiti highway, where Soviet agents might be looking for me as soon as my absence was discovered. The Soviets likewise would immediately send men to the Kuwait airport and to the seaport, so my departure from the country had to be from the back door. All I had to do was reach the jeep before KGB and GRU security got a start on combing the desert outlands. Once I'd found the jeep I was to receive further directions on its radio.

I drank the Scotch, which only made my mouth drier and turned my stomach to fire. The song repeating on the radio took on a nightmarish quality, with no ending or beginning, the notes dissociating from themselves chaotically. Then things were very quiet. I felt relieved for a moment, then froze. I realized that I'd wandered off course and didn't know how long I'd been walking without the sound. Without any reference point in the dark I had no idea which way to turn. I tried walking in a zig-zag pattern, but was unable to pick up the signal again. I stopped to think. There was no breeze and all I could hear was the sound of my own breathing. I figured it was safe enough to use my cigarette lighter for a moment so I could get a look at my Seiko wristwatch. It was four in the morning.

I put the lighter back in my pocket and then heard a click, the unmistakeable sound of a gun being cocked.

"Stop, don't move," said a voice in Arabic.

I pulled the little radio receiver out of my upper left jacket pocket and dropped it on the ground, pushing sand over it with my foot.

Three Arabs approached me. I realized they were Bedouin when I made out the camels in the darkness behind them. When they got up close enough to have a good look at me, one, who had been pointing the rifle at me, slung it back over his shoulder. Apparently I looked harmless.

"Hello. I'm an American," I said in English, then switched to Arabic. "I'm lost, can you direct me back to the road? I know my car is up there somewhere. I got out to pick up some rock samples and lost my directions, I'm a geologist."

It was an unlikely story, but the only one I could think up at the moment. I figured that Bedouins liked to keep to themselves and didn't worry over the strange activities of the foreigners they occasionally encountered in their deserts.

"Ah, the jeep," one of them said after a moment. "We passed it a

306

couple of kilometers back." He pointed into the night behind him.

"Thank you very much, *Salam Alaykum*," I said and started walking in that direction without further conversation. I was greatly relieved and soon found the jeep. Keys were in the ignition and I started it and switched on the radio, tuned to our prearranged frequency, and said in English, "Seid Ahmed has arrived safely." That had been my code name in Kuwait. "Request directions."

"Drive straight for the next two hours and you'll be met." I switched on the jeep's headlights and started driving slowly over the dirt road.

By the next day I was very far away—on an island in the Mediterranean, talking to George, being briefed, debriefed, and processed for entrance to the United States.

The Soviet Embassy in Kuwait shut its doors for a week. Two KGB counterintelligence experts who were urgently flown in from Moscow began their investigation.

21: Route 66

Three serious-looking men in business suits met George and me at Dulles International Airport. We got into a green Plymouth and drove through a labyrinth of expressways, finally reaching a woodsy countryside where we turned off and took a smaller road.

"How do you like it so far?" asked one of the men, a short, balding fellow who had been introduced to me only as Harry.

"Oh, it's very pretty," I said, looking out the window.

So far what had captured my attention were the endless fences along the roads, and still more fences partitioning the well-manicured fields. And the signs—NO TRESPASSING, DO NOT ENTER, NO STOPPING AT ANY TIME, EMERGENCY STOPS ONLY, ONE WAY, HIGHWAY PATROL NEXT RIGHT, SPEED CHECKED BY RADAR. How, I wondered, did one get to that pretty lake I saw a while back, just to the left of the highway? Where could I go to pick mushrooms?

A gray-haired man and a younger man with a crewcut welcomed us at the entrance to a secluded, ranch-style house in suburban Virginia. Inside, they showed me to my room—a single bed, a desk, two chairs, a dresser, bare walls, beige curtains.

"Now give me your suitcase," the older man ordered. "And get everything out of your pockets."

This is it, I thought, getting a pack of cigarettes and a notebook out of the suit George had bought me in some PX store. The man opened my suitcase and went through the shirts, underwear, and socks, which likewise were of PX issue.

"Just standard procedure," he said.

"I don't mind."

"It's okay now," the man said, leaving the room.

We had a little party, a few drinks, crackers, dips. George introduced me to my new overseers, whom I figured must be security people. After a while, George walked into another room with me. "Well, Vladimir, it's time to say goodbye." He took me by the shoulder and shook hands.

"George, do you know what they did?"

"No, tell me."

"They just searched me. You tell me what that means."

"Look, if you have any problems, let me know through Harry. Okay?"

"Who are they, George?"

"Well, they're not from my section. They're our internal security guys." I didn't push it further. We went back into the living room where everyone gave George a perfunctory goodbye. I went into the kitchen to the refrigerator and found a bottle of cold gin, poured myself a stiff glassful, and drank it. I sat in a chair in the living room. Another of the men, this one in his late thirties who identified himself as Jim, stared at me through thick glasses. "Well, how do you like it here?" he asked.

"Oh, just great. Wonderful." I felt the cold gin convulsing my stomach.

"You better rest today," he said, "because you have a lot of work to do tomorrow."

"Where am I going to work?"

"Here. I'll come around nine."

He came daily for the next three weeks, sometimes with assistants. "Crazy son of a bitch," I told Harry, "asking stupid questions. 'Whom do you love more, your mother or your father?' What fucking difference does it make? Parents are parents; you love them both. Or he asks 'Did you feel inadequate among your classmates in the first grade? Did you wet the bed when you were two?' Goddamn idiot."

"C'mon don't worry," said Harry, "it's a science here, you know."

"I *don't* know. It sounds like bullshit to me."

"Yeah, but it's a lot of money," he laughed.

I thought I'd have to talk to George about Jim bugging me, watching me, following me around. But Jim disappeared just as suddenly as he had shown up.

It was right after he'd given me a battery of tests that lasted a week—IQ, Vocational Aptitude, and the like. There were puzzles, like I used to buy for Katya. "What the hell are we doing?" I asked.

"These will help us to determine where your vocational talents are," he said.

"Pretty good, did I pass?"

"It's not the sort of thing you pass or fail. The IQ test shows 161 and the aptitude test doesn't show anything in particular except that you like ballerinas, good living and abstract concepts," he laughed. "You didn't know that, did you?"

"No. I thought I liked lady bricklayers, poverty, and picking potatoes."

During the months I was at the house a succession of government interviewers—I presumed from the CIA—came almost daily and thoroughly questioned me about all I knew. When I was left alone, I worked on copious written reports that they had requested on everything from the Kaliningrad space research complex that I'd seen as a boy, to IIR admissions procedures, finishing with a complete review of Soviet intelligence activities in the Middle East.

There were always two bodyguards in the house. Every night all of us would drive to a local restaurant and order the most expensive things on the menu, washing it down with drinks and fine wines—all on the expense account they said. Then we'd go to a few strip joints. I asked if there were some sort of course I could take to help me learn to survive in this alien country. But I got no answers. "You'll pick it up," they said.

All I picked up was an extra seventy pounds of fat, as the weeks of enforced inactivity and overeating and drinking dragged on.

I felt as if I were being fattened up for slaughter.

"Jim, what's going to happen," I asked my watcher one day just before his departure. "You understand that I can't be here forever. What about my work? Don't you think I should find a place to live too?"

Jim hesitated and answered slowly, "You must forget the notion of ever working for us further."

"But why?" I lit a cigarette.

"Because there are considerations."

"What considerations?"

"Various." His eyes reminded me of a snake regarding a rabbit. "You better think of what profession you want to take up in America—that is, if you have decided to stay here."

"What do you mean, *decided to stay here?*"

"Well, there are other countries, you know."

We fell silent for a moment. "Look, Jim, I am pretty good at economics, political science, management, planning, operations, laws, organization. I know a lot about the Soviet Union, what they will be doing five, even ten years from now. I mean, as far as any area where the U.S.S.R. is concerned, don't you think this knowledge could be of value here somewhere?"

"Well, it's hard to say." He hesitated. "Let me think about it."

Weeks turned into months. I asked to apply for a driver's license so I could go for a drive, even with my bodyguards if that was the way they wanted it.

"Later, when you are settled," Harry kept promising.

One morning in February 1972, Harry came to the house, smiling and bouncy. "Guess what? There's been a decision. We are going to put you in a hotel-motel management school. All we have to do is find a good one and you'll be all set."

For a moment, I thought he was kidding, and I was going to make some sarcastic remark about a matchbook cover advertisement I'd seen. But, taking another look, I said, "I want to see George, fast!"

Harry looked up, a little startled, and seeing my face said, "Okay, I'll arrange that."

George showed up three days later. "Oh, looks like you put on some weight," he said. "How are you doing?" he asked cheerfully.

I solemnly described the situation and my frustrations—how uncomfortable I was being cooped up, about my new identity, about what they had planned for me, and especially about not being able to continue my efforts against the Soviets.

"Okay, keep cool," George said, "I'm going to do my damn best to get you out of this. But I can't promise anything. But first tell me, how far would you go? For instance, you play the piano quite professionally, right? What if I told you to grow a beard and put on an outrageous outfit and go to South America on tour as a musician, and your world would be in some crummy joint at night, while you worked for us? Or what if I told you to go back to Moscow disguised and get somebody out of the country, only your chances of getting out alive would not be very good? Would you do these things?" He looked seriously at me and I felt a surge of my old self-respect.

"I swear, George, I would. Anything you ask. I owe you my life anyway. Unless I flunk out of hotel-motel school and end up destitute."

"That's not going to happen. You'll be okay and I'll vouch for you to anybody."

"Thanks."

He looked at his watch. "Tell you what, if you have any ideas vis-à-vis your former associates, let me know."

"I will, George, that's exactly what I thought I'd be doing when I got here."

"Don't write it off, not yet. I'll fight for you."

We shook hands for the last time. I never saw him nor heard from him again. I read newspapers, magazines, watched television. America was in no mood for anti-Soviet action. There was détente, wheat deals, SALT, and Watergate was beginning to preoccupy Washington, and no one seemed concerned much about the Third World.

"Here's Nick." Harry introduced me to an older man who wore a gray suit and brown shoes. "He'll accompany you tomorrow. You're going to Los Angeles."

I was relieved to be getting out of there—to anywhere, *Yebena mat*, I thought, *Ya svoboden* (I'm free).

The bank was a tacky branch office in Virginia with plastic furniture, linoleum floors, and faceless clerks. Harry handed me a briefcase as we entered. When I opened it in front of the teller and she saw all the stacks of bills, the young woman looked surprised at seeing such a large sum in cash. "I want to open a new account," I said, just the way Harry had taught me. I counted out a thousand dollars, put them in my pocket and handed her the rest of the boodle.

I signed my new name on the card. I'd practiced it, but it still came out badly. It just didn't seem to fit me.

I drank all the way to Los Angeles and all the way to the rundown motel where I was taken. The next morning I stepped out onto the streets of Hollywood, hungover and shaky, gazing at the dirty parking lot and shabby buildings that flanked the motel.

I went to the hotel-motel school to register. On the way I felt like everyone was staring at me. I caught a glimpse of my reflection in a store window—a red, sweaty face, bloated body clothed in an ill-fitting sports jacket, baggy slacks, white shirt and a Lilly Dache tie— and tried to overcome a dizzy spell.

The hotel-motel school director cheerfully accepted my application and counted out the cash I gave her for the course, as if she were used to taking it in one lump sum. "The classes start tomorrow at eight-thirty," she said, and gave me a thick volume filled with pictures of hostelries with a text printed in large type.

On the way back, I rented an apartment, a one-bedroom, furnished, plastic-modern place upstairs in a graying stucco building centered around a small, dirty, kidney-shaped swimming pool that looked like it had bathtub ring. I didn't think I'd be swimming anyway. I wanted it because it was close to a store and I wanted to be out as little as possible. I stopped by a bank and managed to get my money transferred; then I checked out of the motel, and stopped by the stairs to my new abode. I felt abandoned and useless.

I shut the door and sat on the sagging sofa facing a picture of yellow flowers on the grimy wall. I poured myself a tall glass of gin, drank it, and lit up a Winston, pouring another glass, this one of whisky. I was absolutely nobody. I didn't even have my own name. And at that moment I felt I deserved all this. I'd never see Natasha and Katya again, never know what happened to my family. They didn't deserve to be let down, hurt, possibly destroyed. Political motivations, desire for a free life, my fight for my self-respect and individuality all dissolved and there was only one vision in my mind—the eyes of my daughter. They asked me, "Why are you crying, Papa?"

I came to at four in the morning, still half sitting on the sofa. Blood was pounding in my ears; I was shivering. Invisible death rays converged on me. I waited, shaking, through what seemed like an endless time. Finally the dawn's early light filtered through the yellow Venetian blinds.

My classmates at the hotel-motel school turned out to be three winos, a couple of cleaning maids from a nearby motel, and three more persons studying under some sort of minority program. They certainly were "real people" as my father used to say. The teacher promised that the three-month course would lead to sure positions for all in the hotel industry, even such high posts as bell captain, who, he said, made terrific tips.

The two maids approached me during a recess. "Where are you from?" one of them, a slim, attractive brunette, asked.

"Norway," I said, "Just came here. Don't know anyone."

We got to talking and after a while they let me know that they were a couple of hookers who wanted to start their own business—a motel in Palm Springs maybe.

That's how I met Diane, a pretty brunette of about twenty-five who dropped out of school. She helped me spend all that money I wanted to get rid of as fast as I could. I hoped that spending it might relieve all my guilt. I don't remember how many rounds I bought in how many bars, clubs and strip joints, how many big tips I left, how much money I gave to bums, charity solicitors, Indian causes, the U.S. Olympic Committee. I figured this way I'd be accepted.

May 3, 1972 was a hot, smoggy day. The stale air filtered into my apartment through the blackened bedroom screen and wafted lazily through the door to the living room, where I sat, feet on my spindly coffee table. I turned up my stereo to drown out the traffic sounds. I was trying to get into my yearly May spirit, and for old time's sake I played a record I'd purchased recently, with Stan Getz and Joao Gilberto doing jazz samba, just like one I had in Moscow. One of the cuts was "The Girl From Ipanema." It was less than a year since my desert escape in Kuwait, but it seemed much longer than that. I sipped a Scotch and grapefruit juice. The stuff didn't seem to be doing the job anymore, either. The record ended and another dropped on the turntable, now it was an old Dave Brubeck album. *This is going to drive me nuts,* I thought to myself. Back in Russia these records made me think of America, now they reminded me of Moscow—each number associated with some memory. I switched off the stereo and called Diane. I had to do something.

Her voice sounded sleepy on the other end of the line. She'd be over in a few minutes, she said.

After that last $1,500 weekend in Palm Springs, our relationship had reached the barter stage. I'd buy her things instead of paying cash for it. But at least there was companionship and I still felt awkward with other American women I'd met.

Diane was wearing shorts and a blouse. She poured herself a drink and sat her petite body on my lap. "What's wrong, love?"

"Nothing, just fed up."

"How come?"

"I don't know, I think I'm going to get out of here, go someplace."

"When?"

"Soon."

"Could you leave me your stereo?"

"No, I've got something better than that for you."

I went to the bedroom and got a red box from the closet, something I'd been saving. "Look here." I dumped the box on the coffee table and out clattered gold rings, bracelets, and necklaces.

These were the same gold rings and bracelets I had bought in Kuwait for Galya and had taken with me in my escape across the desert.

"Take it all, I don't need it, ever."

Diane's eyes widened and she touched one of the bracelets tentatively.

"How could I? It's so expensive," she whispered.

"Take it. Put it away." I put the jewelry back in the box, closed it, and handed it to her. "Now go. Goodbye. And take care of yourself."

I locked the door behind her when she left.

I turned out the light, closed the blinds, and put another bottle of Scotch on the coffee table. I took three big swallows out of it. I lay back and smoked another cigarette. I passed out.

I woke up in the middle of the night, sweating and shaking. I got up and peeked through the blinds to the street below. A man was standing on the sidewalk. He had been there several nights already. It didn't take them long to track me down, I thought. Now they've got me. But I didn't care.

I felt defenseless. I had no weapon. Still sweating out the booze, I put on a clean shirt. I peeked out the blinds again and saw the figure crossing the street toward the entrance to my building. I quietly stepped into the hallway and heard footsteps coming up the stairs. I only had a few seconds. I went to the end of the hallway and took a fire escape ladder to the roof. My footsteps crunched across the tar and gravel. I knew the approaching man must be on my landing by now and must have heard me above. I ran to the edge of the roof and jumped. It was about thirty feet down into the swimming pool. My right ankle hit the bottom hard, but I didn't feel pain as I climbed out and hobbled to my car, which I left in the car port facing forward, an old habit. I started the engine, but my right foot was numb. Operating the pedals with my left, I screeched away. The figure was in the driveway and I shot the car by him, making him jump aside.[1]

Down on Sunset Boulevard a few minutes later, a police car, red lights flashing, pulled me over. "Driving a little fast, aren't you?" the cop said as he took my license and wrote me a ticket.

I drove down Sunset, through Beverly Hills, Westwood, winding through the movie stars' estates to the Pacific Coast Highway. Here it was more like the kind of place I'd thought I'd be living in when I came to America. I took the winding coastal road north, past Malibu. I rolled down the window and caught the fresh salt air. The ocean was a black, heaving mass to my left.

Then it occurred to me. Why was I so hell-bent on escaping that menacing figure who had pursued me? I wanted to survive. I cared about living. I wanted to make it here. My self-pity, misery, and desperation all stemmed from an unwillingness to change old attitudes and habits.

Now, driving north on open highway, the last two thousand dollars of my stake money in my pocket, I said to myself, *You've been sitting on your big ass, dummy, scared and lonely. You've got no mama and papa or wife here to help you to get out of this shit. The old life was over the minute you marched into that sand in Kuwait. You knew what you were doing and that there'd be no way back. Everything now depends on your own ability and patience. You're going to drive on, get a rest, and pull yourself together and start living—here, now, as an American, the best you can.*

[1] I found out later, when moving out of my apartment, that the man following me wasn't from the KGB, but from a collection agency. The apartment manager gave me a business card from a collection agency man whom the manager said had come inquiring about me the night I'd driven off and several nights afterwards. I then remembered that I'd received letters from that same collection agency about a $650 loan. It wasn't even my own loan. During my rounds of the bar scene I had cosigned a note for one of my erstwhile drinking companions.

I took inventory of myself. I had a lot of knowledge and guts, the stuff to make it. I still thought like a Marxist. I'd have to change that in order to make a go in this money-oriented world. I had an inflated ego, and that would have to be set aside too. If I sat back waiting for good things to come to me—because I had always been told that growing up in Moscow—I'd end up on the scrap heap again, just as I did in Hollywood.

In the years that followed I learned a lot. I met good people and people just as venal and arrogant as my old KGB overlords. I was bitter. I had no concept of money for it had meant nothing to me. As I learned to confront the American reality, I found what I'd missed in my previous life—honesty, which is not punishable by law in the United States. It took me some years to understand that the only freedom I obtained was meant to be the freedom of honesty within myself. Only much later did it occur to me that the people on the welcome wagon in Washington might simply have tried to teach me to get up promptly on my own two feet; sort of throw in a "quicky" swimming lesson for me. Once I reached the bottom, I'd have to come up. I worked washing cars for an automobile dealer. I went back to school, this time to a university, to reestablish my credentials.

My reeducation at the university was not confined to academic subjects. I learned a lot about how to survive without money in America; my teachers included some rats who shared the room I rented in a slum neighborhood near the campus and who would scurry across my bed when I'd fallen asleep after hours of studying. I drove a cab in the ghetto—and it was more dangerous than being a CIA agent. I tried to go into business. I went broke, got on my feet again. I started another business, this time successfully. I became an American citizen. I went to jazz concerts. I drove the expressways and fought the traffic jams. I became an NFL football fan.

I went to see *Gone With the Wind*, which I missed in Moscow, and one of Clark Gable's lines summed up my new life. "'I don't think of myself as heroic or noble,' he told Scarlet O'Hara, 'and I don't fight for any causes except the causes of Rhett Butler.'"

I've been up and I've been down since then. And sometimes I've been happy, and sometimes depressed and wondering if this society ever will stop the men in Moscow I'd known, those who are out to destroy it. I still wonder.

317

But whatever happens, I've gotten at last to the business of living my own life—for better or worse—and being my own person, doing business, playing and composing jazz, and writing a book. Hail to you, Nat King Cole, for it was you who made me love America and got me into all this!

In 1975, I drove the remainder of Route 66. Alone. No one followed.